W9-DJO-062

WITHDRAWN
University of
Illinois Library
at Urbana-Champaign

I

D

COST EFFECTIVE
QUALITY FOOD SERVICE
An Institutional Guide

Judy Ford Stokes, R.D.

Aspen Systems Corporation
Germantown, Maryland
1979

Library of Congress Cataloging in Publication Data

Stokes, Judy Ford.
Cost effective quality food service:
an institutional guide.

Includes index.

1. Food service—Cost control.   I. Title.
TX911.3.C65S74   658.1'552   78-25871
ISBN: 0-89443-083-1

Copyright © 1979 by Aspen Systems Corporation

All rights reserved. This book, or parts thereof, may not be
reproduced in any form or by any means, electronic or
mechanical, including photocopy, recording, or any
information storage and retrieval system now known or
to be invented, without written permission from the
publisher, except in the case of brief quotations embodied
in critical articles or reviews. For information, address
Aspen Systems Corporation, 20010 Century Boulevard,
Germantown, Maryland 20767.

Library of Congress Catalog Card Number: 78-25871
ISBN: 0-89443-083-1

Printed in the United States of America

1 2 3 4 5

658.1552
St6c
cop. 3

Home Econ.

This book is dedicated to
administrators, dietitians, and food service directors
committed to providing cost effective quality food service.

Table of Contents

Acknowledgments

I would like to acknowledge the invaluable contribution of the many individuals, clients, and organizations who have helped me to gain an insight into the specialized field of food service management. In particular, I wish to thank Gene Gray, Harvey Ogletree, and John Brecht of Laventhol & Horwath for drafting a substantial portion of Chapter 7, Food Service Costs and Maximizing Reimbursement. I am also grateful for the assistance of Michael Tinkler and Roy Walters of Arthur Andersen for the major contribution to the section on productivity in Chapter 8, Controlling Labor Costs.

I wish to express further appreciation for assistance given by Paul Rosser and Fred Parker of Rosser, White, Hobbs, Davidson, McClellan, Kelley, Inc.; David Powell of Enco Contractors, Inc.; Don Ingram and Tom Barrow of Tom Barrow Co.; Walter Rehm, Sandra Ley of Victory Mfg. Co.; the National Restaurant Association; Jim Edwards of Arthur Young; and Edd Johnson, Administrator of Miller County Hospital and Nursing Home.

In addition, I would like to express my gratitude for the assistance of Lynn Reeves Hall, R.D., Nancy Vann, R.D., Linda Hawk, R.D., Kay Norvell, R.D., Carolyn Roper, R.D., Susan Davidson, R.D., and Janice Hylen, R.D. of Judy Ford Stokes & Associates, Inc.

Brother Herman Zaccarelli, Director of the Restaurant, Hotel and Institutional Management Institute, Purdue University, West Lafayette, Indiana, deserves special mention for serving as a constant source of inspiration. Special appreciation is also extended to Milton Cooper, National Accounts

Manager of National Institutional Food Distributors Association, for all of the encouragement he provided.

The love, support and encouragement of my family and husband, McNeill Stokes, and our children, Ford and Ashley, made the writing of this book possible. I shall always be grateful to them.

Introduction

COST CONTAINMENT — INDUSTRY OR GOVERNMENT?

The decade of the seventies may well come to be regarded as the watershed years for the United States health care system. During the previous decade access to quality health care was extended to a majority of the population, and now the health care industry is laboring under the ensuing economic and political consequences. Consumers and legislators view with alarm a total health care spending bill that reached an estimated $155 billion in 1977 (compared to only $20 billion in 1960). In addition, the health care sector has also experienced a rate of inflation that stubbornly remains three to six percentage points above the other segments of the economy.

As a result, the byword of any health care institution today *must* be cost containment. Congress has mandated that if the health care industry cannot control the rate of inflation within the next two years, it will take over cost containment. The major problem with government involvement in cost containment is that it is concerned with cost to the consumer, not to the health care facility. It is generally agreed that health care facilities have done very little to contain costs since the advent of the Medicare program in 1966. This is a direct result of the program itself since there is no incentive written into it to encourage any health care facility to cut costs. Just the opposite is true. With Medicare, it seems that the more money spent, the more reimbursement is received. This has caused many facilities to keep their charges to the consumer relatively low but to obtain funding for the services from the federal government. Realizing this,

Congress attempted to conteract this discrepancy by passing a section in Public Law 92-603 of the 1972 amendments to the Medicare Law placing restrictions on the extent of reimbursement. The facility would be reimbursed only the lowest cost or the charges to the Medicare patients. This did not produce the desired result. Instead, it raised the price of health care services to the consumer because the hospitals, not wanting to be caught by the lower cost or charges, simply raised their charges. Since the Medicare law gives the Department of Health, Education, and Welfare no control over hospitals' charges, the legislation backfired.

External Cost Factor

Hospitals and skilled nursing facilities can cut some costs internally and slow the rate of inflation for health care costs; however, health care facilities cannot control external cost factors. First, there is the economic factor. The facility purchases goods and services from suppliers. If these prices are increased to the facility, then the facility must increase the charge to the consumer to maintain its present position. The federal government failed to recognize this fact when it placed a price freeze on health care institutions. When the health care institutions could no longer continue without raising their charges, the federal government removed the freeze. Then the facilities raised charges astronomically to attempt to recoup monies lost. Since skilled nursing facilities generally have such a high Medicaid utilization and many states have flat per diem rates for these services, the states are actually setting the charges for the skilled nursing facilities.

Governmental Actions

Since the advent of the Medicare program in July 1966, enforcement actions have been one of the most costly items at any health care facility. The federal, state and local requirements that have to be met have touched every aspect of the health care industry. The governmental requirements in the fiscal, professional, and dietary areas have cost health care facilities immeasurable amounts of money. One example of the increase in record keeping and statistic gathering is the cost report required by the program at the end of each fiscal year. The first report in 1966 required four pages of information on bed size, admissions, discharges, and percent of occupancy. The ratio of total charges to Medicare charges were compared and applied to total cost to obtain allowable Medicare cost. Health care facilities now face a cost report form that is in excess of 30 pages excluding supplemental schedules. As a direct result of the expanded forms, the health care facilities are now required to gather statistics in order to allocate all overhead departments to revenue producing departments. The statistics must be maintained for audit by the fiscal intermediary whose visit to the facility for this purpose may be a year after the cost report is filed.

Even governmental actions not directly related to Medicare have adverse effects on hospital and skilled nursing facility cost. For instance, the increasing minimum wage raises health care costs, since approximately one-half of all health care facility cost is in salaries. There is also the dramatic rise in FICA taxes that must be passed along to health care consumers. Not only has the rate of increase gone up considerably, but the base for the increased rate has more than tripled in the past several years. In addition, state and local governments have initiated sales taxes that have raised the cost of health care further.

These governmental actions constitute one of the most significant factors in the dramatic rise in health care costs. Ironically, government's attempting to contain health care costs, is probably the greatest contributing factor to the rise in these costs.

Social Factor

Health care managers feel that a facility owes the community it serves the best care available. This is a noble cause, but one that is not always economically feasible. Who is to pay for this service? Can they afford it? It appears that sometimes political jealousies prohibit services coordination within counties or cities, and cause competition between facilities. When one facility installs a new service or piece of equipment, representatives of another facility in the same area also want the service or equipment to compete with the other facility. This leads to costly duplication of services that the government already has intervened to prevent. As a part of Public Law 92-603, planning board approval is required of all changes in bed size, major equipment purchases, and any new additions that require an outlay of more than $100,000.

Can the health care industry control itself? Congressman Dan Rostenkowski has challenged hospitals to develop an alternative to the government's proposed cost controls. The National Steering Committee on Voluntary Cost Containment has been established to reduce the rate of increase in health care cost. The committee is composed of representatives of the American Hospital Association, the Federation of American Hospitals, the American Medical Association, the Blue Cross/Blue Shield

Association, the Health Industry Association of America, the Health Industry Manufacturers' Association, the U.S. Chamber of Commerce, and a consumer representative. The goal is to reduce the rate of increase in community hospitals by two percent each year during 1978 and 1979, so that the difference between the rate of increase in the Gross National Product (GNP) and hospital expense is reduced. Community hospitals are defined as nonfederal, short-term hospitals. In order to sharpen the challenge, the congressman introduced legislation to impose standby hospital controls if this effort is not achieved. The standby proposal imposes an increase limit of total hospital expenses of 14 percent in 1978 and 12 percent in all subsequent years, assuming a 16 percent increase in the 1977 expense forecast. There are many questions in relation to this proposed legislation that have not been answered. Health services providers feel that the health care industry can control itself economically, but to do so some sacrifices must be made. These sacrifices, however great they may seem, would be small in comparison with those required by governmental cost containment.

This book is concerned specifically with practical ways to contain costs in health care food service and to maximize their reimbursement.

SELECTED REFERENCE

Herzlinger, Regina. "Can We Control Health Care Costs?" *Harvard Business Review* 56:102-110.

Chapter 1

Food Service Cost Management

Controlling costs in food service has always been a challenge, but never has it been so vital to the economic viability of health care institutions. Since food service costs generally represent the second highest expenditure of health care institutions, proper management in this area requires serious consideration. Only nursing service costs are higher.

However, even with the *minimum* annual seven and one-half percent inflation generally experienced in the food service field, effective food service managers can minimize this runaway cash drain by careful scrutiny and total evaluation of the food service operation. By responding to and analyzing the cost-control checklist which follows, dietitians should be able to maximize cost savings *and* reimbursement for food services in health care institutions.

Controlling Food Service Costs

	YES/NO	COMMENTS
Cost Accounting & Budgeting		
1. Are food service cost components budgeted and compared to actual costs on a monthly basis, including raw food, labor, and supplies?		
2. Are these costs examined in terms of cost per meal and/or cost per patient day?		

1

	YES/NO	COMMENTS

3. Has an inventory cost-control system been initiated, monitored, and maintained?

4. Are revenues generated by the food service reflected in the cost per patient meal or per patient day?

5. Are periodic conferences held with administration and other pertinent departments to compare the actual food service expenditures with the food service budget?

Menu Planning

1. Is there a seasonal menu cycle?

2. Is a selective menu essential to maintaining or improving current patient census?

3. Is a selective menu cycle economically feasible?

4. Are therapeutic diets coordinated specifically with the general diet menu to minimize additional preparation?

5. Are menus planned to maximize labor and time efficiency?

Purchasing and Receiving

1. Are firm price quotes obtained on all food purchases?

2. Are these prices obtained through a competitive mechanism (such as a cooperative buying service)?

3. Have monthly purchasing ceilings been established for specific food items such as milk, eggs, bread?

4. Are meat and produce weighed to compare the invoiced quantity with the ordered quantity?

5. Are invoiced prices checked for agreement with quoted prices?

	YES/NO	COMMENTS

Food Preparation and Service

1. Is portion control consistent and effective?

2. Are specific systems monitoring food quantity established? (For example, how many cans of vegetables are used for each meal?)

3. Are leftovers utilized effectively?

4. Has the actual cost of nutrition-related medical requirements (therapeutic diets, mechanically altered diets, and nutritional supplementation) been determined?

5. Are records kept of the cost of nutrition-related medical requirements?

6. Is the necessity for all therapeutic and mechanically altered diets periodically evaluated?

7. Are ancillary food services (such as, supplementary nourishments, special catering functions, and activities) specifically cost detailed?

8. Has policy been set for gross cafeteria receipts to reflect accurately the number of meals served?

9. Do records reflect the actual cost of meals served in patient food service (hospital and/or hospital-based skilled nursing facility) compared to cafeteria food service?

Labor Efficiency

1. Have the number of labor-minutes per meal for the food service been determined?

2. Has the rate of employee turnover been determined?

	YES/NO	COMMENTS

3. Is the employee turnover rate periodically determined and evaluated?

4. Are job descriptions drafted and reviewed at least annually with respective personnel?

5. Are detailed duty schedules drafted and reviewed at least quarterly with respective personnel?

6. Are records kept of duties performed for at least two weeks each quarter?

7. Is the daily work distribution periodically reviewed to maximize labor efficiency?

8. Are employee and guest meals periodically evaluated for cost effectiveness?

Energy Efficiency

1. Has an energy audit been conducted of the facility?

2. Is energy efficient equipment planned into future equipment replacement budgets?

3. Has each department been trained in methods of energy conservation?

4. Has an effective preventive maintenance program been established?

Administrative Factors

1. Are periodic conferences held with administration to review service and cost factors of the food service department?

MANAGING THE FOOD SERVICE BUDGET

Although food service costs generally represent one of the largest expenditures of health care institutions, many food service departments in the past have functioned with an incomplete budget or with none at all. An occasional administrative overview may have been given to determine if the food service expenditures approximated past costs, or if they deviated too much from the norm. However, specific funds were not earmarked for such expenses as raw food, labor, supplies, and equipment replacement. Those days are gone. Tighter governmental controls on reimbursement, spiraling inflation, and appropriate patient care demand professional management tools.

Food Service Operating Budget

Establishing a food service operating budget is the foundation for the economic viability of any food service department. Budgets enable food service managers to plan for the future by providing the means to review the total needs of the department as they relate to the whole institution. A carefully considered budget makes an equitable distribution of funds more likely. The operating budget projects expected revenue .as well as anticipated expenses. It provides the hub of the management wheel around which the operation of food service revolves. Budgets are traditionally prepared several months in advance for the next fiscal year. It can be helpful to divide the year into smaller time segments representing weeks or months of revenue expenditure. All time segments can then be compiled to yield the total budget on an annual basis. The individual budgets within time segments can provide excellent tools to monitor achievement of budgetary goals.

The sample budget form detailed in Exhibit 1-1 reflects an overview of the food service department, including not only revenue, but also raw food, labor, and supply costs as well as consideration of equipment replacement and depreciation, maintenance costs, utilities and depreciation of the facility. Previously, raw food was the highest single factor of food service costs, but with the ever-escalating minimum wage, labor costs have claimed an undisputed first place in food service expenditures. Raw food and supplies capture second and third places respectively. This sample budget form further emphasizes the importance of coordinated team efforts in promulgating effective, economic management. Communication among support departments—maintenance, administration, and accounting—must be initiated before drafting an effective food service operating budget. The increased communication of the team approach can result in the ultimate goal of cost effective yet concerned patient care. Without proper communication and support from interrelated departments, the budget can become a paper albatross, a meaningless burden.

Exhibit 1-1 Food Service Operating Budget

	Monthly	Yearly
Revenue	————	————
Raw Food Costs	————	————
Labor Costs	————	————
Employer Costs	————	————
F I C A	————	————
Benefits	————	————
Contracted Services	————	————
Supply Costs	————	————
Equipment Replacement:	————	————
Major Equipment	————	————
Minor Equipment	————	————
Equipment Depreciation:	————	————
Major Equipment	————	————
Minor Equipment	————	————
Maintenance Costs	————	————
Utilities	————	————
Facility Depreciation	————	————
TOTAL	————	————

However, establishing a carefully considered food service budget can also net other positive results. Since the budget automatically sets goals, it offers incentive and challenge to coworkers, encouraging them to join in the team effort. By communicating the management goals to food service employees through a detailed review of the food service budget, employees realize their work is important in achieving the goals. By minimizing waste—including portion control and using leftovers—by reducing breakage, and by cleaning equipment properly, considerable savings can be realized. Employees should understand that as they share the responsibility of the food service department, they can also share in the benefits. With the food service budgetary goals met, employees should be aware that positions can then be secure with potential annual wage increments possible. Budgets are not meant to strangle spending, but should be viewed as a flexible management tool, a control device.

Budget-Cost Comparison

Initiating a food service operating budget is excellent, yet is far more effective when coupled with a budget-cost comparison to maximize effectiveness. It is recommended that the budget-cost comparison be reviewed monthly and at the end of each fiscal year. The budget-cost differentials should be discussed with personnel to reflect the adherence or nonadherence to the initial budget set. Budgets enable the actual economic operation to be compared to the projected or desired results. Budget-cost comparisons provide the means for control and analysis of present performance. Although previous reports are often used in preparation of future budgets, careful analysis of past performance relating to current needs and future demands must be made unless past performance is to be perpetuated. Refer to the Budget-Cost Comparison form in Exhibit 1-2.

Drafting and maintaining budget-cost comparison data are important, but it is the interpretation of these data that is most significant. An analysis gives the employees a direct way to measure their contribution toward the established goals and should be an additional incentive by emphasizing the importance of their role in the management and economic well being of their department.

Budgets are simply indicators of projected operations. They can be invaluable tools when applied to specific areas of one department as well. Examples would be controlling labor costs by setting a maximum number of hours per day and/or evaluating labor expenditures in terms of labor minutes per meal, which is discussed in detail in the chapter on labor productivity.

Meal Census

Once economic parameters have been established through a food service operating budget, it is important for reimbursement purposes—as well as

Exhibit 1-2 Food Service Budget-Cost Comparison

Facility: _____

Accounting Period: _____

ITEM	BUDGET	ACTUAL COST	DIFFERENTIAL
Revenue	_____	_____	_____
Raw Food Costs	_____	_____	_____
Labor Costs	_____	_____	_____
Employer Costs	_____	_____	_____
F I C A	_____	_____	_____
Benefits	_____	_____	_____
Contracted Services	_____	_____	_____
Supply Costs	_____	_____	_____
Equipment Replacement:			
Major Equipment	_____	_____	_____
Minor Equipment	_____	_____	_____
Equipment Depreciation:			
Major Equipment	_____	_____	_____
Minor Equipment	_____	_____	_____
Maintenance Costs	_____	_____	_____
Utilities	_____	_____	_____
Facility Depreciation	_____	_____	_____

TOTAL

for establishing an index by which to evaluate food service costs—to maintain a meal census. A strict head count divided only among patients, employees, and guests could be maintained, but in the interest of maximizing reimbursement, a more detailed census form as indicated in Exhibit 1-3 is recommended. The cost of nutrition-related medical requirements can be determined from this form, which can be fascinating as well as frightening. Proper maintenance of this form could mean thousands of additional dollars of reimbursement to each facility. The cost of nutrition-related medical requirements will be explored more fully in Chapter 2 as well as Chapter 7. The cost per meal and/or per patient day is easily determined once the total food cost and number of meals served have been substantiated. To maximize third party reimbursement, it is advisable to determine food cost per meal in each separate food service area (that is, cafeteria, hospital patient food service, and hospital-based skilled nursing facility). This is detailed in Chapter 7, Food Service Costs and Maximizing Reimbursement.

Exhibits 1-4 and 1-5 can be helpful in monitoring expenditures more closely and for gathering data for a budget-cost comparison.

Exhibit 1-3 Monthly Meal Census

MONTH: _____ FACILITY: _____

	REGULAR	THERAPEUTIC	MECHANICALLY ALTERED	TUBE FEEDINGS	EMPLOYEES	GUESTS	TOTAL MEALS TO DATE
1							
2							
3							
4							
5							
6							
7							
8							
9							
10							
11							
12							
13							
14							
15							
16							
17							
18							
19							
20							
21							
22							
23							
24							
25							
26							
27							
28							
29							
30							
31							
TOTAL							

Exhibit 1-4 Weekly Food Cost

DATE:

VENDOR	Sun.	Mon.	Tues.	Wed.	Thurs.	Fri.	Sat.	TOTAL OF VENDOR
PMA		119.60						119.60
Rogers				255.00				255.00
Colonial			99.63				230.00	329.63
Eggs, Inc.		16.50		16.50		16.50		49.50
Dairy, Inc.		20.70	44.33	19.60	18.00	20.70	45.00	168.33
Bread, Inc.		5.50	10.90		6.00	6.50	19.90	48.80

TOTAL $970.86

WEEKLY BUDGET: $1,500.00
LESS TOTAL: 970.86
    BALANCE   529.14

Exhibit 1-5 Summary of Food Service Invoices

MONTH: May
WEEK ENDING: 5/5/
DEPARTMENT: Dietary
BUDGET FOR: Food

WEEKLY BUDGET: $1,500.00

DATE	PURVEYOR	INVOICE #	AMOUNT	BALANCE
5/2	PMA	41663	$119.60	$1,380.40
5/2	Eggs, Inc.	3041	16.50	1,363.39
5/2	Bread, Inc.	11456	5.50	1,358.40
5/3	Colonial	91634	99.63	1,258.77
5/3	Bread, Inc.	4040	10.90	1,247.87
5/2	Dairy, Inc.	1133	20.70	1,227.17
5/3	Dairy, Inc.	1148	44.33	1,181.84
5/4	Rogers	041165	255.00	927.84
5/4	Eggs, Inc.	01144	16.50	911.34
5/4	Dairy, Inc.	1202	19.60	891.74
5/5	Dairy, Inc.	1293	18.00	873.74
5/5	Bread, Inc.	5163	6.00	867.74
5/6	Eggs, Inc.	02145	16.50	851.24
5/6	Dairy, Inc.	10600	20.70	830.54
5/6	Bread, Inc.	5567	6.50	824.04
5/7	Colonial	100434	230.00	594.04
5/7	Dairy, Inc.	11634	45.00	549.04
5/7	Bread, Inc.	6003	19.90	529.14

SELECTED REFERENCES

Keiser, James R., and Kallio, Elmer. *Controlling and Analyzing Costs in Food Service Operations.* New York: John Wiley & Sons, Inc., 1974.

Levings, Pat. Profit from Food Service: *A Q and A Approach.* Boston, Mass.: Cahners Publishing Company, Inc., 1974.

Riggs, Sylvia. "Can Hospital Food Service Operations Survive?" *Institutions/Volume Feeding* 82:54, 62, 66.

Chapter 2

Making Cents out of Cycle Menus

Most health care institutions have capitalized on the advantages cycle menus can provide. Cycle menus are defined as carefully planned menus which are rotated according to a definite pattern. Cyclical menus offer numerous advantages, such as:

- Minimizing menu planning time,
- Coordinating preparation,
- Reducing repetition of menu items,
- Promoting standardization of preparation procedures,
- Increasing labor efficiency due to improved coordination and organization planned into the menus,
- Simplifying purchasing,
- Taking advantage of purchasing seasonal variation of foods,
- Improving inventory control and cost control, and
- Maximizing utilization of equipment—potentially resulting in reduction of energy expenditures.

Potential disadvantages can occur if the menu cycle is too short and seasonal variation in the availability of foods is not considered. Drafting a good seasonal menu cycle initially can be time consuming yet will save substantial time since the need for planning menus weekly would be eliminated.

Seasonal menu cycles can vary from two to several weeks. However, experience indicates that the maximum amount of variety with the minimum amount of repetition can be incorporated into a three-week seasonal menu cycle. Some institutions prefer four three-week cycles per year while two three-week cycles (fall/winter, spring/summer) are suitable for others.

Another variation on the cyclical menu is to have a specified number of days, that is, an eighteen- or a sixteen-day cycle—any number that would not be an increment of seven. This system provides an ingenious way to rotate continuous menu items so they will rarely appear on the same day of the week. However, the primary difficulty with this system occurs with Sunday menus. Most institutions prefer to serve "special" food items such as roast beef, ham, and baked chicken in lieu of meat loaf, chicken casseroles, hot dogs, or other items considered less "special." If meat loaf appears on the numbered day cycle for Sunday, food service directors and cooks, wishing to please their patients, usually will serve a more "Sunday" type of meal. Therefore, after they change the Sunday meat loaf to fried chicken, the Monday shift often meets a new challenge, when chicken appears on that day's menu as well. Once the game of checkers begins to be played with the menu, it becomes an increasingly complicated game, and the patient may end up being the loser. One change tends to require two, three, and four changes that can negate the economic and time saving advantages of cycle menus.

SELECTIVE v. NONSELECTIVE MENUS

One menu consideration that surfaces periodically is whether to provide patients with a choice of foods. While this may be an admirable goal, a realistic appraisal must be made that balances the benefits against the changes required.

The following points review the advantages inherent in the selective and nonselective menu.

Selective

- Patient satisfaction could be improved, since there is a positive psychological impact when the patient chooses specific foods.
- Menu variety could be increased, which could minimize special food orders.
- Special diet orders by physicians could be limited because special diets would be ordered only as a therapeutic measure, rather than to cater to a specific patient.
- Knowledge of favorite menu items could be improved and used in future menu planning. Patient contact would be fostered if the dieti-

tian or food service director offered written guidance in marking the daily menu selection.

- Food waste could be reduced *if* menus were carefully tallied and *if* leftovers could be used on the cafeteria line.

Nonselective

- Food and labor costs would be minimized at least 15 percent.
- Demand on skill and quantity of labor would be decreased due to the reduction in number and types of foods to be prepared.
- Time required for meal preparation and service would be reduced, which would generally enable the food to reach the patient at a more optimum temperature.
- Storage and preparation areas required would be reduced.
- Quantity and types of equipment required would be minimized.
- Quantity of supervision required would be decreased.
- Food waste would be minimized with the nonselective menu, since closer control on all aspects of food service could be maintained.

Many of the advantages inherent in the selective menu are labor-intensive and increase food service costs. However, special institutional circumstances may dictate and justify the need for such an increased expenditure if a hospital–hospital-based skilled nursing facility were interested in widening the cost differential between the two, to maximize reimbursement. Consideration may then be given to providing a selective menu for the hospital patients and a nonselective menu for the patients of the skilled nursing facility. However, careful documentation of all cost components would have to be maintained. The costs allowed could be subject to arbitration and additional costs would still be incurred due to the selective menu.

In planning a well accepted yet economically feasible seasonal set of cycle menus, several considerations must be taken into account. Exhibit 2-1, The Menu Check Sheet, provides a listing of these considerations to produce an excellent set of menus. If menu substitutions do become necessary due to lack of delivery, etc., it is important that the substitutions be nutritionally equivalent to the original menu item. Exhibit 2-2 will provide guidance in making nutritionally equivalent substitutions. Exhibit 2-3 is one example of documentation of menu substitutions.

Exhibit 2-1 Menu Check Sheet

Nutritional Factors

Include the following in menu planning to meet adequate nutritional needs:

1. One serving of a good source of Vitamin C (citrus fruits, cantaloupe, broccoli) or two servings of a fair source of Vitamin C (tangerines, raw cabbage, tomatoes, and turnip greens, collard greens, baked potato in the skin, rutabagas, spinach, sweet potato) daily.
2. One serving of a dark green or deep yellow vegetable or fruit every other day to supply a sufficient amount of Vitamin A.
3. Four or more servings of fruits and vegetables daily.
4. Two cups of milk (as a beverage, on cereal, and/or in cooking).
5. Four to six ounces cooked weight of meat, fish, poultry, and/or substitute daily. (One ounce of meat substitute may be served as one egg, ¼ cup cottage cheese, etc. as an equivalent to one ounce of meat).
6. Four eggs served a week. At least one ounce of high quality protein (one egg, cheese toast, peanut butter, sausage, etc.) should be served at breakfast and a minimum of 2 ounces of high quality protein at the noon and evening meals.
7. Four or more servings of whole-grain, enriched or restored bread, or cereal daily. Bran should be incorporated into at least one menu item per day—for example, meatloaf, biscuits, cornbread, cereals, or desserts such as cobblers, cakes, and the icing on cakes.

Factors for Greater Acceptability of Food

1. Try a new menu item at least three times so it will become familiar to the residents and not be regarded as foreign.
2. Maintain variety in foods served during the week and throughout the menu cycle.
3. Vary menu combinations of food according to color, shape, taste, texture, and temperature.
4. Avoid serving more than two starches in one meal. Noodles, potatoes, and bread should not be served at the same meal.

Factors to Increase Labor Efficiency

1. Incorporate at least one menu item that can be prepared the day before.

2. Distribute the planning of menu items according to the skill of employees scheduled.
3. Plan menu items to utilize equipment efficiently (that is, surface-prepared, oven-prepared, and refrigerated-stored menu items).

Factors to Maintain Cost Control

1. Use an extended meat, such as chicken with noodles as the entree for the evening meal if the noon meal provides a solid meat, such as roast beef.
2. Minimize the use of expensive vegetables, including broccoli, asparagus, and brussels sprouts. Depending on the budget, these items could be included a maximum of once weekly.
3. Check menus in advance to take advantage of specials, for example buying in 10 case lots as storage permits. If there is a sufficient savings, storage space in some area should be located.
4. Specify portion sizes directly on the menu, including the number scoop, etc., to be utilized (for example, 4 ounce portion, No. 8 scoop).

Exhibit 2-2 Equivalent Menu Substitutions

The following is a list of suggested substitutions for certified menu items, should the need for substitutions arise. The items within each category contain a general approximation of the equivalent food value of the category.

This list has been provided for the convenience of the food service director and is to be utilized ONLY when absolutely necessary as menus have been certified according to nutritional values and in coordination with color, taste, and texture combinations.

Protein Entrees

The average protein serving is generally 3 ounces, which is about the size of a dollar bill and a quarter of an inch thick. Therefore, a combination of any three items or a triple amount of the quantity listed should be substituted to equal the amount of food value in three ounces of protein entree.

Beef	1 ounce	Frankfurter	1 each
Poultry	1 ounce	Egg	1 each
Lamb	1 ounce	Salmon, Tuna	¼ cup
Pork	1 ounce	Cheese, Cheddar	
Liver	1 ounce	& American	1 ounce
Fish	1 ounce	Cottage Cheese	¼ cup
Cold Cuts	1 thin slice	Peanut Butter	2 tbs.

Vegetables

All calculations have been based on the standard half-cup serving.

I. Collard Greens, Mustard Greens, Spinach, Turnip Greens
II. Broccoli, Tomatoes
III. Asparagus, Green Beans, Okra
IV. Brussels Sprouts, Lettuce
V. Cabbage, Cauliflower, Sauerkraut

Fruits

I. Watermelon, Cantaloupe, Apricots
II. Peaches, Prunes, Blueberries, Strawberries, Raspberries, Blackberries
III. Bananas, Plums, Pears, Figs, Raisins
IV. Tangerines, Oranges, Grapefruit
V. Applesauce, Honeydew melon
VI. Pineapple, Cherries

Starches

I. Cereal (cooked), Cereal (dry—flaked & puffed)
II. Bread, Biscuit, Muffin, Cornbread, Graham Crackers, Saltines, Soda Crackers, Round Thin Crackers
III. Rice, Corn, Spaghetti (noodles, etc.) cooked, Baked Beans (no pork), Potatoes (Irish, Baked, Mashed, Sweet or Yams)

Coordination of Diets

As soon as the general diet seasonal menu cycle has been drafted (on a selective or nonselective basis) and approved for nutritional adequacy, patient acceptability, and economic feasibility, it must be coordinated with all therapeutic diets. It is essential to coordinate the therapeutic diet as closely to the general diet menu items as possible for economy. If many different foods are served to comply with therapeutic dietary prescriptions, ignoring those menu items included in the general diets, substantial increases in raw food and labor costs can be expected. A set of economically feasible cycle menus with therapeutic diet coordinations are reproduced in full in Appendix A.

Cost of Nutrition-Related Medical Requirements

Even when careful consideration is given to aligning therapeutic diets closely with the general diet, the cost of nutrition-related medical require-

Exhibit 2-3   X Y Z Health Care Facility: Menu Substitutions

DATE	MEAL	SAME	SUBSTITUTIONS	REASON	AUTHORIZED
	Breakfast				
	Lunch				
	Dinner				
	Breakfast				
	Lunch				
	Dinner				
	Breakfast				
	Lunch				
	Dinner				
	Breakfast				
	Lunch				
	Dinner				
	Breakfast				
	Lunch				
	Dinner				
	Breakfast				
	Lunch				
	Dinner				
	Breakfast				
	Lunch				
	Dinner				

If menu is served exactly according to the master menu, check "SAME." However, if any menu substitutions are made, they are to be nutritionally equivalent to the original menu item. The reason for the substitution should be noted and initialed by the authorizing party.

ments can be staggering. Exhibit 2-4 presents an analysis of the cost of nutrition-related medical requirements that were incurred by one nursing facility. Due to the type of patients who were admitted, this institution spent in excess of $25,000 per year more than they would have for patients who required fewer nutrition-related medical services. No additional reimbursement was provided to the facility for these inordinate expenses. Blended diets represent the most significant raw food cost factor of nutrition-related medical requirements, because approximately one-third more solid food is required to serve the same portion per volume of blended diet food. For example, a number ten scoop (3.2 ounces) of green beans will yield a number sixteen scoop (2 ounces) of blended green beans. A specific detailing of the additional raw food costs incurred due to blended diets is detailed in Exhibit 2-5. Note that additional raw food costs alone amounted to $11,840.60. Additional labor costs required by blended diets in this same facility are shown in Exhibit 2-6. The blended diets added annual labor costs in this facility of $4151.88 (based on $2.80 per hour average wage), which is projected to be $4599.00 under the anticipated minimum wage of $3.10 per hour. Exhibit 2-7 graphically presents the inordinate and ever-escalating costs of this one nutrition-related medical requirement. At the facility's current average wage of $2.80 per hour, an annual cost burden of $15,994.30 is being incurred. With the projected increase in minimum wage to $3.10 per hour, the per annum expenditure increases to $16,439.60 for which the facility receives no additional remuneration. Although blended diets are expensive, they are sometimes necessary. However, establishing the cost of this nutrition-related medical requirement should encourage a reevaluation of blended diets. Some patients who receive blended diets could conceivably receive diets that are either ground, chopped, or soft in nature. The change would increase the diet's acceptability as well as reduce costs. The maxim to follow is: Don't puree the food if ground will do; don't grind the food if chopped will do; don't chop the food when whole will do, do all you can to make them chew.

Often blended foods are prescribed due to inability to chew, a choking experience, or as a direct result of a stroke. As the patient gets better, ground or chopped foods may be indicated and are relatively easily eaten with far greater enjoyment. With the exception of tube feedings—food should be liquified only as a last resort; all other means of improving the patient's nutritional status and enjoyment of meals should be exhausted first.

By comparison, other therapeutic diets do not demand as large an expenditure as blended diets. However, some additional labor is required in the preparation and serving of therapeutic diets as indicated in Exhibit 2-4. With the exception of fresh or water-packed fruits, no special dietary foods should be required for regular diet patients. Most foods can be served to diabetic patients as well, as long as the food has been prepared fat free and properly measured according to the food exchanges. The appropriate number of "fat exchanges" can be added to the diabetic patient's tray as indicated per caloric calibration. Specially prepared "dietetic" foods are not necessarily for the diabetic since many dietetic foods contain sorbitol or mannitol that produce metabolic results similar to sugar and, therefore, should not be used by the diabetic. These dietetic foods have been processed primarily for people trying to lose weight rather than for diabetic patients.

Exhibit 2-4 Cost of Nutrition-Related Medical Requirements

ITEM	ADDITIONAL RAW FOOD COST/DAY	HRS. PER DAY	ADDITIONAL LABOR COST/DAY + 25%	TOTAL COST/DAY	TOTAL COST/MONTH	TOTAL COST/YEAR
THERAPEUTIC DIETS	*	2.5	$2.80 $7.00+$1.75=$8.75	$8.75	$262.50	$3,193.75
			3.10 $7.75+$1.94=$9.69	9.69	290.70	3,536.85
BLENDED DIETS	$32.44	3.25	2.80 $9.10+$2.28=$11.38	43.82	1,314.60	15,994.30
			3.10 $10.08+$2.52=$12.60	45.04	1,351.20	16,439.60
MILKSHAKES	9.15	1.0	2.80 $2.80+$ .70=$3.50	12.65	379.50	4,617.25
			3.10 $3.10+$ .78=$3.88	13.03	390.90	4,755.95
DIABETIC SNACK	2.80	.5	2.80 $1.40+$ .35=$1.75	4.55	136.50	1,660.75
			3.10 $1.55+$ .39=$1.94	4.74	142.20	1,730.10
TOTAL COST PER ANNUM			$2.80 $25.38	$69.77	$2,093.10	$25,466.05
			$3.10 $28.11	$72.50	$2,175.00	$26,462.50

$2.80/hr. = average employee wage + estimated 25% employer costs.
$3.10/hr. = projected minimum wage + estimated 25% employer costs.

Exhibit 2-5 Additional Raw Food Costs Incurred Due to Blended Diets

DIETS/MEAL	62	Single Portions/Meal
PORTIONS OF BLENDED	24	Double Portions/Meal
(twice daily)	—	(12 portions × 2)
	86	Total Portions/Meal

*⅓ more solid food necessary for actual
total no. of servings per meal represented
by blended diet portions per meal

$$(86 \div 3 = 28.66 \text{ extra portions per meal})$$
$$+28.66 = 114.66 \text{ actual regular portions/meal}$$

ACTUAL TOTAL NUMBER OF
PORTIONS/MEAL OF ADDITIONAL
FOOD NECESSARY DUE TO
BLENDED DIETS   28.66

RAW FOOD COSTS

Total Raw Food Cost/Meal $.566

Additional Cost/Day Incurred
Due to Blended Diets   28.66 × 2 (meals/day) × $.566
                                           $32.44

Additional Raw Food Cost/Month Incurred
Due to Blended Diets $32.44 × 30 (days/month) =
                                           $973.20

Additional Raw Food Cost/Year Incurred
Due to Blended Diets $32.44 × 365 (days/year) =
                                           $11,840.60

*Breakfast items not blended.

Diabetic snacks, although necessary for some patients, can be costly. Costs should also be identified for this nutrition-related medical requirement to maximize third-party reimbursement.

Nutritional Supplements

The documentation of the monetary evaluation of milkshakes and nutritional supplements should also be made for two primary reasons:

1. to assess the actual need for milkshakes and/or nutritional supplements, and
2. to maximize third-party reimbursement.

Nutritional supplements are excellent for improving the nutritional status of some patients. However, it can be a deterrent to the patient's appetite at meal time. Careful evaluation by the health care team of each patient's

Exhibit 2-6 Additional Labor Costs Incured Due to Blended Diets*

	$2.80	$2.90/hr.	$3.00/hr.	$3.10/hr.
PREPARATION 1.0 hr./day (0.5 hr. twice daily)	$2.80	$2.90	$3.00	$3.10
SERVING 2.25/day	$6.30	$6.53	$6.75	$6.98
Total additional 3.25 hrs. labor required/day	$9.10	$9.43	$9.75	$10.08
Total additional 1,186.25 hrs. labor required/year	$3,321.50	$3,440.13	$3,558.75	$3,677.38
25% employer costs	$860.03	$860.03	$889.69	$919.35
Total additional cost/year	$4,151.88	$4,300.16	$4,448.44	$4,596.73

*Breakfast items are not blended.

Exhibit 2-7 Summary of Additional Costs Incurred Due to Blended Diets

MIN. WAGE	ADDITIONAL RAW FOOD COST/DAY	HRS. PER DAY	ADDITIONAL LABOR COST/DAY	TOTAL COST/DAY	TOTAL COST/YEAR
$2.90/hr	$32.44	3.25	$9.43 + *2.36 = 11.79	$44.23	$16,143.95
3.00/hr	32.44	3.25	9.75 + *2.44 = 12.19	44.63	16,289.95
3.10/hr	32.44	3.25	10.08 + *2.52 = 12.60	45.04	16,439.60

* 25% Employer costs

Exhibit 2-8 Daily Diet Census Record

Daily Diet Census Record

DATE: JANUARY	1	2	3	4	5	6	7	8	9	10	11	12	13	14	15	16	17	18	19	20	21	22	23	24	25	26	27	28	29	30	31
REGULAR	34	34	33	34	34	31	34	34	34	34	34	32	33	31	34	34	34	30	32	32	33	34	33	33	33	33	33	32	33	33	33
SOFT	8	7	8	8	8	7	8	8	6	8	8	8	8	8	8	7	8	8	8	8	8	8	8	8	8	8	8	8	8	8	8
BLAND	1	1	1	1	1	1	1	1	1	0	1	1	1	1	1	1	0	0	0	0	0	1	1	1	1	0	1	1	1	1	1
LOW SODIUM 1000mg	1	1	1	1	1	1	1	1	1	0	1	1	1	1	1	1	1	1	0	0	0	0	0	0	0	0	0	0	0	0	0
LOW SODIUM 2500mg	18	18	18	18	18	18	17	18	18	18	18	17	17	18	18	18	18	18	19	19	19	19	19	19	19	19	18	19	19	19	19
DIABETIC 1000 Cal.	10	10	10	10	10	10	10	10	10	10	10	10	10	9	10	10	10	10	10	10	10	10	10	10	10	10	10	10	10	10	10
DIABETIC 1500 Cal.	5	5	5	5	5	5	5	5	5	5	4	5	5	5	5	5	5	5	5	5	5	5	5	5	5	5	5	5	5	5	5
DIABETIC 2000 Cal.	1	1	1	1	1	1	1	1	1	1	1	1	1	1	1	1	1	1	1	1	1	1	1	1	1	1	1	1	1	1	1
DIABETIC other	2	2	2	2	2	2	2	2	2	2	2	2	2	2	2	3	3	2	2	2	2	2	2	2	2	2	2	2	2	2	2
LOW FAT	0	0	0	0	0	0	0	0	0	0	0	0	0	0	0	0	0	0	0	0	0	0	0	0	0	0	0	0	0	0	0
MECHANICAL SOFT	7	7	7	7	7	7	7	7	7	7	7	7	7	7	7	7	7	7	7	7	7	7	8	8	8	7	8	8	8	8	8
PUREED	10	10	10	10	10	10	10	10	10	10	10	10	10	10	10	10	10	10	10	10	10	10	10	10	10	10	10	10	10	10	10
OTHER (specify)																															
AIDES & WORKERS	8	6	9	5	10	6	8	9	7	9	9	10	10	9	9	8	7	6	5	10	10	10	9	9	8	9	9	9	9	9	9
																				5											
TOTAL – DAILY	105	102	105	102	107	99	104	106	102	105	105	104	105	102	106	104	103	98	99	104	105	107	106	106	105	105	105	105	106	106	106

Courtesy of Progressive Medical Group

needs should be made and reviewed periodically before a nutritional supplement is prescribed and maintained for any patient. In one facility, it was determined that milkshakes cost more than $8,000 annually for which the facility received no additional remuneration. Although some patients definitely needed the milkshakes, a majority of the patients would have been equally pleased with a less expensive nourishment. Therefore, nursing service and the entire health care team reevaluated the necessity for providing milkshakes and/or nutritional supplements. The costs in this area were reduced from $8,000 to $3,000 annually.

Similar costs can make a definite economic difference in the balance sheet of any health care institution. It is vital that they are identified and documented. The monthly meal census form is an effective tool for initiating the documentation of nutrition-related medical requirements. Exhibit 2-8 provides yet another way to maintain an even more accurate daily diet census record. Institutions and fiscal intermediaries are just becoming aware of the substantial influence nutrition-related medical requirements can have on food service costs. However, to obtain reimbursement, careful records must be kept.

SELECTED REFERENCES

Cabot, Elaine E. "Selective Menu Raises Satisfaction—and Costs." *Modern Hospital* 116:139-140.

Coon, Genevieve. "Selective Menu Versus Single Menu for Ward Patients." *Hospitals, JAHA* 16:61-63.

Hubbard, R. M.; Sharp, Joan L.; and Grant, Loise M. "Pros and Cons of Cycle Menus." *Journal of the American Dietetic Association* 39:339.

Santos, Lourdes; and Cutlar, Kathleen. "How Hospitals Implement Selective Menu Systems." *Hospitals, JAHA* 38:93-96.

Zolber, K. K.; and Donaldson, Beatrice. "Distribution of Work Functions in Hospital Food Systems." *Journal of the American Dietetic Association* 56:39-45.

Chapter 3

Nourishments:
A Hidden Cost

Although nourishment may be defined as a food that sustains vitality, it is not necessarily the best term for a between-meal feeding if three well balanced meals per day that comply with the Recommended Daily Dietary Allowances are provided. Between-meal feedings are often desirable, but costly. When nourishments approximate only $.15 per patient day, a 100-bed facility is incurring an additional $5,475 annual cost at 100 percent occupancy for which there is currently no specific reimbursement. Yet, many health care facilities cannot identify nourishment costs.

Nourishments can be an expensive hidden cost for the health care facility and, left unchecked, can be a significant drain on cash flow without improving nutritional status. Prudent management procedures dictate that a careful analysis of all cost factors should be made, and nourishments are no exception.

ANALYZING NOURISHMENTS

In an initial analysis the following questions should be posed.

- How much are nourishments costing the facility?
- Are nourishment requisitions used?
- Are the costs of nourishments recorded?
- Has a monitoring system of utilization been established?
- Do the nourishments provided reflect the health care needs of the patients or do they reflect staff preferences?

- Does the quantity of nourishments vary with the patient census?
- Is the nourishment order built up to a standard level?
- Does the nourishment order vary on weekends and holidays?
- Do types of nourishments ordered ever vary?
- Does the nourishment requisition change according to the staff on duty?
- Do the quantities of nourishments ordered consider inventories of the nourishment refrigerator?

Establishing effective monitoring systems of nourishments can benefit the patient nutritionally as well as add to the facility's economic well being. Listed below are items to consider in maintaining control of nourishment costs.

1. Improve interdepartmental relationships between nursing and food services; emphasize that the patient is the ultimate beneficiary and the importance of the economic viability of each department.
2. Initiate a nourishment requisition system with coordination between nursing and food services (Exhibit 3-1). The nourishment requisition should be submitted by nursing service once daily at a specific time. Each item sent to the respective patient area should appear on the nourishment requisition, then be filled and fully costed by food service.
3. Institute a system of monitoring nourishments that each wing uses, as indicated in Exhibit 3-2.
4. Evaluate the type and quantity of nourishments ordered in relation to patients' needs and requests.

Interdepartmental Relationships

Cooperation among departments is essential to economically efficient, yet quality health care. Ordering and monitoring the use of nourishments are no exception. A budgetary goal based on per patient day and/or monthly total should be established and periodically reevaluated. The goal should reflect projected therapeutic needs based on past census.

Nourishment Requisition Forms

When properly used, nourishment requisition forms coupled with a summarization of nourishment costs form can assist in directing future policy on nourishment costs and benefits.

Exhibit 3-1 Nourishment Requisition: X Y Z Health Care Facility

DATE: _____

Item	Unit	Quantity On Hand	Quantity Ordered	Amount Sent	Cost
Apple Juice	qt.				
Cranberry Juice	qt.				
Grape Juice	qt.				
Grapefruit Juice	qt.				
Mix. Citrus Juice	qt.				
Orange Juice	qt.				
Pineapple Juice	qt.				
Tomato Juice	qt.				
Whole Milk	1/2 gal.				
Skim Milk	1/2 gal.				
Buttermilk	1/2 gal.				
Tube Feeding					
Cookies	doz.				
Graham Crackers	pkg.				
Bread	loaf				
Prune Juice					
Kool-Aid					

ORDERED: FILLED:

Nursing Staff _____   Dietary Staff _____

Forms are good as long as they are used properly. In analyzing the nourishment costs of one hospital, it was determined that a nourishment requisition was being filled but not costed. After final tabulation the 75-bed facility realized that approximately $9,600 a year was being spent for nourishments. Based on 60 percent occupancy, nourishments were costing $.58 per patient day. This was inordinate for a general care institution, and once the exceptional costs were exposed, appropriate steps for reducing such waste were immediately initiated.

Summarization of Nourishment Costs

Filling in The Summarization form can prove enlightening. Why does one patient area require $11.39 of nourishments while another spends only $4.24? Therapeutics, patient requests, or an emergency could have demanded such a discrepancy. The significant factor is to be able to identify a problem so it can be evaluated.

Exhibit 3-2 Summarization of Nourishment Costs

Facility:_____   Month:_____

Day	WING A	WING B	WING C	Total
1				
2				
3				
4				
5				
6				
7				
8				
9				
10				
11				
12				
13				
14				
15				
16				
17				
18				
19				
20				
21				
22				
23				
24				
25				
26				
27				
28				
29				
30				
31				
TOTAL				

For example, one 200-bed facility reduced its monthly nourishment expenditure from $800 to $200 by evaluating the type of nourishments provided and monitoring their use.

Evaluating Results

The institution soon discovered that the evening shift of nursing personnel was double ordering the requisition submitted by the day shift to be certain that sufficient supply was available. Staff pilferage also became an identifiable factor. The institution further learned that some personnel preferred to order more expensive nourishments, such as cranberry and prune juice, as well as milkshakes.

In coordination with administration, nursing and food services, a nourishment system was established and these costs were controlled.

In anticipating future reimbursement considerations, it is recommended that costs of nourishments, special catering, and any food-related function other than three meals per day, be costed separately and documented carefully. It could mean thousands of dollars spent or reimbursed.

SELECTED REFERENCE

Barnhart, C. L. ed. *The American College Dictionary*. New York: Random House, 1963.

Chapter 4

Purchasing, Storing, Receiving Opportunities

After the essential, preliminary food service goals have been drafted through budget and menu planning, proper purchasing, receiving, and storage of food enable the professional manager to reach those goals.

PURCHASING WITH A PURPOSE

Efficient, cost-effective purchasing is a science, not luck. It begins with a realistic budget and economically feasible menus and includes proper food specifications and quantities needed to implement the menu cycle. Detailed in Exhibit 4-1 is an example of a purchasing guide for one three-week menu cycle. After the approximate quantities per cycle have been determined, a further detailing of quantities can be made in accordance with delivery schedules and storeroom capacities.

PURCHASE ORDERS

The purchase order should be the core of any purchasing system. Whether it is a classic purchase order with a number obtained before an order is given, or whether it is strictly an inhouse purchase order form is irrelevant. It is important to use a purchase order and to obtain quoted prices. Vendors have confided that there is little incentive to charge minimal prices when no price quotation or comparison is made.

The inhouse purchase order (refer to Exhibit 4-2) permits verification of the invoiced quantity, quality, and cost against the ordered quantity,

Exhibit 4-1 Three Week Fall/Winter Cycle Menu Purchasing Guide

Vegetables

Food Item	No. of Times Per Cycle	25 meals	50 meals	100 meals	150 meals	200 meals
Beets 6/#10	2	2 cans	4 cans	1 cs + 3 cans	1 cs + 4 cans	2 cs + 1 + can
Broccoli Chopped (Froz.) Spears	1	1.5 bxs	3 + bxs	6 + bxs	10 bxs	1 + cs
Brussels Sprouts (Froz.)	1	1.5 bxs	3 + bxs	6 + bxs	10 bxs	1 + cs
Carrots 6/#10 Frozen	None					
Creamed Corn 6/#10	1	1 can	2 cans	3 + cans	5 cans	1 cs + 1 can
Greens 6/#10 Frozen	5	5 cans 8 bxs	1 cs + 2 cans 1 cs + 4 bxs	2 cs + 5 cans 2 cs + 8 + bxs	4 cs + 1 can 4 cs	5 cs + 3 cans 5 cs + 4 bxs
Green Beans 6/#10 Frozen	5	5 cans 8 bxs	2 cs + 2 cans 1 cs + 4 bxs	2 cs + 5 cans 2 cs + 8 + bxs	4 cs + 1 can 4 cs	5 cs + 3 cans 5 cs + 4 bxs
Lima Beans 6/#10 Frozen	1	1 can 1.5 bxs	2 cans 3 + bxs	3 + cans 6 bxs	5 cans 10 bxs	1 cs + 1 can 1 + cs
Mixed Vegs. 6/#10 Frozen	2	2 cans 3 bxs	4 cans 6 bxs	1 cs + 1 can 1 cs	1 cs + 4 cans 1 cs + 8 bxs	2 cs + 4 cans 2 cs + 1 bx
Okra	NONE					
Blackeyed Peas 6/#10	2	2 cans	4 cans	1 cs + 1 can	1 cs + 4 cans	2 cs + 1 can
Field Peas	1	3 bxs	6 + bxs	1 + cs	1 cs + 7 bxs	2 cs + 1 bx
Green Peas 6/#10 Frozen Rutabagas 6/#10	3 2	3 cans 4.5 bxs 2 cans	1 cs 9 bxs 4 cans	1 cs + 3 cans 1 cs + 6 bxs 1 cs + 1 can	2 cs + 3 cans 2 cs + 6 bxs 1 cs + 4 cans	3 cs + 3 cans 3 cs + 1 bx 2 cs + 1 can
Squash 6/#10	2	2 cans	4 cans	1 cs + 1 can	1 cs + 4 cans	2 cs + 1 can
Succotash	NONE					
Sweet Potatoes 6/#10	1	1 can	2 cans	3 + cans	5 cans	1 cs + 1 can

quality, and cost. Attaching the invoice to the respective purchase order form facilitates this procedure. An administrative policy worth consideration is that before any invoice is paid, it must have a signature authorizing the purchase and verifying the invoice against the order. Discrepancies occur and vendors gain respect for institutions that follow these businesslike, professional policies and procedures.

Exhibit 4-2 Purchase Order

DATE ORDERED:_____   TERMS:_____

QUANTITY	ITEM	SPECIFICATIONS	COST/ UNIT	TOTAL COST
1 case	Applesauce	Fancy 6# 14 oz.	11.05	11.05
1 case	Peaches, slice	Fancy, heavy syrup	11.30	11.30
2 case	Green beans	Fancy, Blue Lake	8.60	17.20
1 case	Beets	Diced	7.35	7.35
1 case	Greens, mixed		5.70	5.70
1 case	Peas, sweet	Choice #2 sieve	8.80	8.80
1 case	Cranberry juice		11.35	11.35
1 case	Orange juice	Frozen	15.95	15.95
1 case	Tomato juice		6.75	6.75
1 case	Grape juice		9.95	9.95
1 case	Chicken noodle soup	Campbell	11.90	11.90
1 case	Dill pickles	Thin sliced	8.20	8.20
1 case	Apple jelly	Individual	3.25	3.25
1 case	Tuna fish	Solid light	34.90	34.90
1 case	Vienna sausage		25.90	25.90
1 case	Bran flakes		6.08	6.08
25#	Grits	Bulk, white	10.95	10.95
50#	Cornmeal	Plain white, enriched	3.35	3.35
5 gal.	Liquid shortening		18.02	18.02
2 cases	Cake mix	White	17.27	34.54
1 case	Graham crax		4.90	4.90
1 case	Gelatin	Assorted red	11.10	11.10
4/gal.	French dressing		11.95	11.95

BY:_____

As costs are of such primary concern in the ever-escalating spiral of the health care dollar, management must use every possible way to reduce these costs. One hospital–hospital-based skilled nursing facility has implemented a unique and effective means by which to reduce expenditures incurred. The institution exercised its right as a county-owned facility to obtain state contract prices that normally represent at least a 12 percent reduction in cost. (Any hospital that is a county, city, or county-city facility may request these contract prices. Contract prices furnished are in effect for a period of one year, and the state will furnish renewal prices on request as well.) This institution also performed a study of actual annual usage of several items ranging from medical supplies to paper goods to food items. The hospital formed a loose buying cooperative with other area facilities to order larger quantities and reduce prices further.

The vendor selected could supply quality equal to or better than the state requirements at an equal to or lower than the state contract price. The facility projected the annual volume of specific items for the vendor while retaining the right to order only the quantity needed per delivery. Each facility agreed to take delivery from respective vendors on a weekly basis and order only the amount needed or the amount to replace the quantity used during the prior week. This was done by maintaining a reserve stock over and above the amount that would actually be used in any week. The fi-fo (first in, first out) system of storage was used to prevent the products from becoming out-of-date.

By using the state contract prices as leverage and as a guideline, by being able to forecast annual consumption and by eliciting the support of other facilities in the area, this institution saved more than $70,000 a year on only 70 items!

Even though the hospital or nursing home may be relatively small, below 100 beds, and have minimal storage capacity, quantity buying is effective when integrated or coordinated with other institutions in the same general locale. Volume purchasing talks. If the storage capacity does not permit volume purchasing, cooperative purchasing with weekly drop shipments could literally save the facility thousands of dollars a year.

When a cooperative purchasing system is not initiated, a comparative pricing system should at least be considered that involves weekly or monthly prices received from several vendors on numerous items. Cost comparisons are then made by the appropriate management personnel who consider costs in relation to quality before ordering. It must be emphasized again that there is little incentive to charge minimal prices when no price quotation or comparison is made.

MONTHLY PURCHASING CEILINGS

Amazingly, several thousands of dollars in food service costs can be saved annually by evaluating food specifications as well as the quantity of food used. Exhibit 4-3 should increase the planner's awareness of current expenditures and potential savings. Do you really know how many eggs are used at breakfast? Are you positive that you are receiving the 18 to 22 slices of bacon per pound that were specified? Has it been weighed and counted? One institution was actually receiving only 12 slices per pound. It was costing almost double per portion!

Establishing realistic purchasing ceilings enables the food service directors to:

1. set tangible goals to meet the food service budget;
2. evaluate current purchasing levels;
3. assess procedures for purchasing, receiving, utilization, and security; and
4. identify problem areas.

The following maximum monthly purchasing ceiling recommendations have been drafted for a 100-bed facility.

Eggs

If eggs are served every morning to each patient, estimate 120 eggs or 4 flats (30 eggs per flat) per morning. With 12 flats per case, 1 case or 30 dozen should last 3 days for breakfast use only. Given these quantities, the monthly order can be determined.

Breakfast use *only*	10 cases/month
Cooking & miscellaneous	2 cases/month
Subtotal	12 cases/month
Scrambled egg nutritional extension recipe	—1 case/month
Total quantity to order	11 cases/month

- If nutritional extension recipe for scrambled eggs (Exhibit 4-4) were used, a savings of 15 eggs or half a flat would be realized each morning for a total savings of 15 flats or 1¼ cases of eggs per month. At an average cost of $.60 per dozen, an additional per annum savings of $270 would be realized. Only 11 cases of eggs per month would then be needed.
- Use medium eggs only, unless large eggs can be purchased at the same price as medium (which is unusual). There is only a ¼ ounce weight differential between a medium and large egg, yet there is an average $.07 per dozen cost differential. Do your cooks pull eggs by the number or by the ounce?
- There should be no cost differential between brown and white eggs.

Exhibit 4-3 Food Item Cost Evaluation

_____

Name of Facility

No. of Beds_____   Date: _____

1. EGGS

Size: Medium_____   Large _____

No. Cases Ordered/Month _____

No. of Flats Used @ Breakfast _____

Single Serving Portion Size _____ oz.

Cost/Case $_____

2. BACON

How Often Used: _____ Times/Week   or   _____ Times/Month

How Many Slices/Pound _____   Quantity Used/Month _____

Cost/Pound $_____

3. SAUSAGE

How Often Used: _____ Times/Week   or   _____ Times/Month

Form of Sausage Used: Patties_____ Links _____ Quantity Used/Month_____

No. of Servings: _____

Cost per Serving: $_____

4. BREAD

Type of Loaf Used: Fresh _____ Day Old _____

White Sandwich: Qty Used/Month____ No. Slices/Loaf____Cost/Loaf_____Cost/Slice _____

White Sliced: Qty Used Month____No. Slices/Loaf____Cost/Loaf_____Cost/Slice

Whole Wheat: Qty Used/Month____ No. Slices/Loaf____Cost/Loaf_____Cost/Slice

5. COFFEE

Type Used _____

Brand Used_____

Size Container (bag, box, etc.) Purchased _____

Quantity Used/Month_____

How Many Times/Day Does Facility Make Coffee _____

Cost/Pound $ _____

Cost/Case $ _____

6. TEA

Brand Used _____ Quantity Used/Month

Are 1 oz. Bags Used_____

How Many 1 oz. Tea Bags/Gallon of Water Used: _____bags/_____gallon of water

Do You Re-use Tea Bag_____

Cost/Case $_____

No. Bags/Case $_____

7. MILK

Size "Glass" Used _____

Quantity Used/Month_____: 1/2 Pints_____Gallons_____

2%_____ 1% _____ Whole _____

Exhibit 4-4 Scrambled Eggs Deluxe

Yield: Approximately 120 2-ounce portions
Saves ½ flat or 15 eggs per recipe

3½ Flats of medium eggs (105 eggs)
12 Slices white bread
2 Cups milk (2%, skim or whole milk)

1. Blend bread and milk together and add to broken eggs. Whip, preferably in a mixer, until well blended.
2. Scramble in normal fashion and serve with #16 portion control scoop, which will yield one 2-ounce portion or 1 egg.

In reviewing invoices in one 100-bed institution, it was determined that an average of 19 cases of large eggs per month were being purchased. Without using the nutritional extension recipe, only 12 cases per month should have been purchased and, based on an average cost of $.60 per dozen, a per annum savings of $1,512 was projected. This projection became reality by implementing the following recommendations.

- They established an average monthly purchasing ceiling of 12 cases per month. When the nutritional extension recipe was used, the facility was able to reduce its egg purchases to 11 cases per month, saving an additional $216 per year or a total of $1,728 annually. Justification should be made for deviations.

- They ordered only medium eggs.

- The food service director supervised allocation of eggs for breakfast and for other purposes.

- They used number 16 scoop (2 ounces) for each serving of scrambled eggs. (Patients should receive additional portions on request.)

- They evaluated the number of eggs used in cooking. (Is it really necessary to use 1- to 2-dozen eggs per cornbread recipe? How many eggs are used in chicken salad, potato salad, or casserole items. Are they necessary or noticed?)

- They locked the refrigerators and scheduled times for opening them to control inventory as well as to conserve energy.

Bacon and Sausage

Be certain that 18 to 22 slices of bacon per pound are actually being delivered as specified. Literally count them. Ordering slab sliced bacon or slab bacon that your kitchen slices (18 to 22 slices per pound) is the most economical means of purchasing bacon.

Regardless of how many strips of bacon and/or how many times per week it is offered, food service directors and administrators must be aware of how much the decision actually will cost. How can policy changes affect the food service budget? Bacon is a graphic example of the financial ramifications that rarely are considered when institutional policies are changed.

Quantity v. Cost

Bacon

	Quantity/month	Cost/lb.	Cost/month	Cost/year
1.	300 lbs.	$1.50	$450.00	$5,400
2.	150 lbs.	1.50	225.00	2,700
3.	75 lbs.	1.50	112.50	1,350
4.	43 lbs.	1.50	64.50	774

1. 2 strips bacon/100 patients/each morning
2. 1 strip bacon/100 patients/each morning
3. 1 strip bacon/100 patients/every other day
4. 1 strip bacon/100 patients/twice weekly

Sausage

Six pounds (or 66—1½-ounce patties) at $8.76 yields a cost of $.13 per pattie, twice the cost of bacon per serving.

Quantity v. Cost

	Quantity/month	Cost/lb.	Cost/month	Cost/year
1.	26 lbs.	$1.50/lb.	$39.00	$468.00
2.	6 lbs.	1.50/lb.	9.00	108.00
3.	433 links	8.34/box of 96 (.087 each)	37.67	452.05
4.	100 links	8.34/box	8.70	104.40

1. One 1½ ounce sausage pattie per 100 patients, one breakfast per week
2. One 1½ ounce sausage pattie per 100 patients, one breakfast per month
3. One sausage link per 100 patients, one breakfast per week
4. One sausage link per 100 patients, one breakfast per month

Recommendations

• Evaluate cost of number of slices of bacon per portion and number of times per week your facility can provide bacon, considering the ramifications of economics and public relations.

- Verify that the facility is receiving quality and number of slices specified per pound of bacon.
- Serve sausage links instead of sausage patties, if the per serving cost continues to be less expensive.
- Contact a local slaughtering company to purchase directly instead of purchasing through a distributor, if possible.

Oleo

If oleo solids were whipped prior to use, an increase of 7.5 pounds per 30 pound case could be realized.

unwhipped: $10.90/30   lbs.=$.36/lb.
whipped: $10.90/37.5 lbs.=$.29/lb.

Incorporate 1½ cups of whipped oleo solids or 1 cup of unwhipped oleo solids for recipes. However, the whipped oleo solids are primarily to be used for general cooking purposes as in glazing rolls, adding to grits, and buttering toast.

With an estimated 5 pounds of oleo used per day in a 100-bed facility for general cooking purposes, a maximum of 150 pounds of oleo should be ordered monthly. This represents approximately 2.5 teaspoons per patient per day. However, if the oleo solids were whipped, only 4 cases per month would be needed, given the increased volume of whipped oleo solids. Therefore, at $.36/lb. and a minimum savings of 30 pounds per month, a per annum savings of $129.60 would be realized merely by whipping the oleo solids.

Milk

To comply with the Recommended Daily Dietary Allowances established by the National Research Council, the facility should purchase a minimum of 16 ounces per patient per day for beverage and/or cooking purposes. An average of 16 ounces of milk per patient per day equals 12.5 gallons per day (based on 100 patients). This means 375 gallons of milk per month is needed, including all types of milk.

When a milk utilization study was effected for one institution of approximately 100 beds, the administrator and food service director were amazed to learn that an average of 600 gallons of milk per month had been ordered. This was 225 gallons in excess of the proposed level. After careful analysis, it was determined that patients were not receiving the extra milk and that the quantity ordered could be greatly reduced. The extra milk could have been used excessively in cooking or could have been "removed" from the premises. Since a cost per half-pint carton that approximated the cost per 8 ounces of dispensed milk could be arranged with the vendor, greater portion control could be instituted by using milk cartons. When monitoring systems were coupled with purchasing ceilings, approximately $4,320 was saved by implementing this one recommendation.

Other recommendations that can offer significant cost reduction as well include the following.

- The food service director should detail the exact amount and kinds of milk that the vendor is to leave rather than permitting the quantity of milk to be "built up" to a standard level.
- Quantity and charges on milk invoices should be monitored carefully.
- In the interest of economics the facility could prepare its own buttermilk for cooking only. (Use ½ cup commercial buttermilk to 1 quart of reconstituted nonfat dry milk.)
- Consider using 2 percent milk exclusively if there is a substantial cost differential. There is little difference in taste and the lower cholesterol level could also be beneficial.
- Use nonfat dry milk powder for cooking in the interest of economics. It is generally one-third the cost of fresh milk.
- Charge employees for milk if not already doing so. The ultimate charge should be approximately 2.5 times the actual raw food cost of the milk to recoup the labor and extraneous costs. However, the administration may wish to consider this to be a fringe benefit and charge less.

Exhibit 4-5 is an example of a form that would clarify the difference between a purchasing ceiling and the actual rate of use for the items discussed in this section.

RECEIVING

Establishing good receiving control systems is essential to the natural progression from purchasing to realizing budgetary goals. There are basic rules to initiating good receiving controls.

1. Designate and train one primary employee to be responsible for receiving food service supplies. (Periodically intersperse management and/or a substitute as the "receiving" employee for security.)

Exhibit 4-5 Purchasing Ceiling versus Use Comparison

FACILITY _____   MONTH _____

FOOD ITEM	CEILING	USE	DIFFERENTIAL
Eggs			
Bacon			
Sausage			
Oleo Solids			
Oleo Reddies			
Milk			
Ice Cream			

2. Establish specific receiving hours (Example: Monday through Friday between the hours of 7:00 A.M. and 4:00 P.M.)

3. Keep respective purchase orders, specifications, count and cost of delivery records in close proximity of the delivery area.

4. Keep a meat scale and other measuring devices necessary for verifying the orders delivered. (Several food service equipment suppliers sell an inexpensive meat scale—approximately $50.00—that could pay for itself in a short period of time if properly used.)

Improper receiving of goods may actually be doubling purchasing expenditures. In one 200-bed facility that periodically utilized meat scales to verify orders delivered, the dietary consultant was weighing freshly delivered meat to assist the food service director when the consultant determined that 20 pounds of meat had been delivered, although the institution had ordered and had been billed for 40 pounds. At $1.33 per pound a loss of $26.60 would have occurred had the discrepancy not been identified. Purveyors soon recognize deficiencies in purchasing procedures and alert delivery men can profit by your mistakes. If this loss occurred only once a week for a year, $1,383.20 would have been lost. Therefore, the facility would have spent $2,766.40 per year for merchandise valued at $1,383.20 in order to recoup the initial loss by replacing the quantity of food not delivered. The importance of proper receiving procedures cannot be overemphasized.

Delivery Discrepancies

Economic loss can occur in ways other than discrepancies in quantities delivered. Loss can occur in discrepancies in quality as well. Produce and all perishable goods should be carefully checked on delivery. Cases of canned items should be opened to return unusable cans. Expiration dates, particularly on milk, should be verified before accepting delivery. Indiscriminately signing invoices for expediency ultimately can reflect in total food cost when unusable goods are accepted. Signed invoices represent accepted inventory and money owed.

The invoice stamp indicated below is a simple, yet effective, verification that proper receiving procedures have been followed.

Date Rec'd _____   Rec'd by _____
                       Checked By:
Quantity   _____
Quality   _____
Prices   _____
Extension   _____
Approved for payment by _____

If further documentation of receiving procedures is desired by administration, a daily receiving report may be appropriate (refer to Exhibit 4-6).

STORING SPECIFICS

Proper food storage is the final step prior to preparation to insure quality, yet cost-effective food service. The fi-fo (first in-first out) system of storage is important to maintain and protect the financial and nutritional investment made in goods received.

Increasing Storage Capacity Economically

Emphasis has been placed on the benefits of volume purchasing. However, the storage capacity of most health care facilities is limited. The following are several simple, inexpensive ways to increase storage capacity without adding square footage.

Exhibit 4-6 Daily Receiving Report

DATE: _____   VENDOR: _____   INVOICE NO. _____

_____

_____

_____

_____

_____

_____

_____

_____

_____

_____

_____

_____

- Recapture any "extra space" between items stored and the next shelf by adding shelving in reach-in and walk-in refrigerators and freezers.
- Fabricate pallets on casters to place on the floor beneath bottom shelves in the storeroom and in the walk-in coolers. Sanitation codes are met as pallets can be moved for cleaning.
- Use pallets on casters for center of the storeroom floor to serve as a "landing area" for newly delivered goods. (Pallets can be eased out of the way as necessary.)
- Hang all possible utensils to free drawers.
- In the interest of organization, safety, and sanitation, fabricate drawer dividers from two lengths of wood or metal wedged into drawer.
- Mount spice rack on the back of the storeroom door.
- Use space between tops of equipment, but no closer than 18 inches to the ceiling, for infrequently used items.
- Consider increasing the depth of present shelving in relation to items stored. (12 inch shelving can become 24 inch shelving, inexpensively doubling the present storage capacity.)
- Add shelf between tubular legs of dish tables for additional rack

Exhibit 4-7 Sample Summary of Utilization and Cost Savings

ITEM Fiscal year 1 Sept. to 31 August	ANNUAL USAGE Fiscal Year 1976-77	UNIT COST Fiscal Year 1977-78	TOTAL COST ANNUAL 1977-78 CONTRACT	UNIT COST 1976-77	TOTAL COST 1976-77	DIFFERENCE IN UNIT COST	TOTAL ANNUAL SAVINGS	MONTH USAGE
Eggs Extra large	1740 doz.	.60	1044.00	.67	1165.80	.07	121.80	145 doz
Sliced apples	15 cs	14.08	211.20	15.60	234.00	1.52	22.80	2+
Green beans cut 6/10 Blue Lake	53 cs	7.69	407.57	10.64	563.92	2.95	156.35	4+
Peach Halves 6/10 light syrup	26 cs	11.33	294.58	13.24	344.24	1.91	49.66	2+
Pear Halves 6/10	26 cs	12.12	315.12	13.47	350.22	1.35	35.10	2+
English peas 6/10	53 cs	10.43	552.79	12.37	655.61	1.94	102.82	4+
Sweet Potatoes	26 cs	12.43	323.18	14.64	380.64	2.21	57.46	2+

storage. Shelves also can be built on the wall in the dish room for dish and/or rack storage as well.

These suggestions are just a beginning in an effort to enable you to take a fresh look at the storage possibilities of your kitchen, which are limited only by your imagination. Increased storage can bring reduced costs (Exhibit 4-7).

SELECTED REFERENCES

Buchanan, Robert D. "Food Service Purchasing '78—What Are the Trends?" *Food Service Marketing* 40:64, 67-68.

Buchanan, Robert D. "How to Save Money in Receiving." *Food Service Marketing* 40:53-55.

Dawson, Elsie H.; Dochterman, Elsie F.; and Vettel, Ruth S. "Food Yields in Institutional Food Service." *Journal of the American Dietetic Association* 34:371-377.

Ketschevar, Lendal H. "Food Service for the Extended Care Facility." *Institutions/ Volume Feeding Magazine*, 1973.

Chapter 5

Inventory Cost Control

A simple, yet effective inventory cost control system can be the next best friend to a realistic operating budget for a food service director. Time is always essential and maintaining an up-to-date record of invoice totals may be the only contact with "inventory" administration. A cost per meal and/or per patient day can easily be determined with these figures. Yet, when the food service department is given no "credit" for the thousands of dollars of items being stored, a cash basis of accounting is being used. Although the cash basis is effective for fiscal purposes, the accrual basis of accounting offers a more accurate reflection of department performance.

The accrual method reflects stock currently maintained in the storeroom, and through an inventory system, provides an accurate picture of monthly food service costs as Exhibits 5-1, 5-2, and 5-3 indicate.

PERPETUAL INVENTORIES

Perpetual inventory systems are the most informative of inventory systems, but they are also the most costly to maintain in terms of time and labor. Exhibit 5-1 represents the perpetual inventory card that can be coupled with Exhibit 5-2, the storeroom check out sheet. However, there is a simplified version of the perpetual inventory that should be considered. The results are similar in that the quantity purchased can be compared to the quantities prepared, yielding the value-on-hand. The time and labor required to maintain the modified version of the perpetual inventory system is reduced, yet it provides the following services.

Exhibit 5-1 Perpetual Inventory Card

Item:							
Date	On Hand	Received	Unit Cost	Total Cost	Amount Used	Cost	Value On Hand
6/10	2 cans		$1.90	$ 3.80			$ 3.80
6/12		2 cases (12 #10 cans)	$2.00	$24.00			$27.80
6/13					2 cans	$3.80	$24.00

1. Reflects quantity on hand.
2. Indicates progression or regression of prices.
3. Guides purchasing.
4. Provides a current value of items-on-hand.

Exhibit 5-3 is a simplified version of the perpetual inventory system that reflects the beginning inventory as well as the progression and/or regression of prices and enables the food service director to keep a current account with the storeroom check out sheet of the items remaining on hand pertaining to quantity as well as cost. This system is relatively simple to initiate as detailed below.

1. Arrange the storeroom items as much as possible in accordance with various categories in the order shown on the inventory form.
2. Take an inventory at the end of one month that subsequently becomes the beginning inventory of the next month.
3. Record food service supplies as they are received, indicating the quantity received as well as the cost. These entries are made in the respective weekly columns.
4. Note the cost per case *and* per can or per package of each item directly on the item when shelving. This will facilitate taking inventory and tallying the monetary value of the item maintained.
5. Initiate the storeroom checkout sheet at the beginning of the month.

Exhibit 5-2 Storeroom Checkout Sheets

Facility _____   Date_____

Quantity	Food Item	Cost/Unit	Total

For inventory as well as security purposes, consider "pulling" food items only twice daily. Foods needed to be prepared for the noon meal could be pulled immediately after breakfast, and foods for the evening and breakfast meal of the following day could be retrieved after completion of the noon meal. Perishable items naturally would be stored in one section of the refrigerator designated for subsequent meal preparation. Periodic supervision by the food service director and a direct comparison of the food items pulled against the storeroom checkout sheet should be made for verification purposes. The storeroom should remain locked between "official pulling" times unless specifically authorized by the food service director or other recognized authority. As the food items have been recorded on

Exhibit 5-3 Modified Perpetual Inventory System

Beg. Inv.	Item	Unit	1st Qty.	1st Cost	1st Unit Cost	1st On Hand	2nd Qty.	2nd Cost	2nd Unit Cost	2nd On Hand	3rd Qty.	3rd Cost	3rd Unit Cost	3rd On Hand	4th Qty.	4th Cost	4th Unit Cost	4th On Hand	End Inv.	Total Cost
1 cs	Apple Rings	6/10	1 cs	15.88		1 cs													1 cs	15.88
1 cs	Applesauce	6/10	1 cs	11.00	11.00	1 cs					2 cs	22.00	11.00	2 cs					1 cs	11.00
2 cs	Fruit Coctail	6/10					1 cs	13.60	13.60	1 cs					1 cs	13.60	13.60	1 cs	1 cs	13.60
1 cs	Peach Halves	6/10	1 cs	11.77	11.77	1 cs	2 cs	24.00	12.00	3 cs	1 cs	12.00	12.00	1 cs	1 cs	12.00	12.00	2 cs	1 cs	12.00
1 cs	Peach Slices	6/10	1 cs	11.77	11.77	1 cs					1 cs	15.50	15.50	1 cs					1 cs	12.00
1 cs	Pineapple Sl	6/10																	—	

the checkout sheet, the inventory form can then be updated in the column indicating food-on-hand. Naturally, food would be subtracted from the "on hand" column when "pulled" and would be added as newly delivered goods are received. These forms are maintained throughout the month and, in order to complete the system for its maximum effectiveness, an ending inventory at the close of the month is taken as final verification of balance-on-hand. The subsequent figures are entered on the inventory cost control report indicated in Exhibit 5-4. Total purchases are added to the beginning inventory of the month as the closing inventory is subtracted from that total, leaving the total cost of raw food and supplies consumed.

Exhibit 5-4 Inventory Cost Control Report

RAW FOOD COST FOR THE MONTH OF   :

    Beginning inventory $2,045.00
    Plus total purchases $4,822.00 $6,867.00
    Less closing inventory $3,040.00
TOTAL COST OF RAW FOOD CONSUMED $3,827.00

SUPPLIES:

    Beginning inventory ....$ 150.00
    Plus total purchases ....$ 300.00
    Less closing inventory ....$ 180.00 $ 270.00
TOTAL COST OF SUPPLIES CONSUMED ....$ 270.00

SUMMARIZATION OF EXPENSES:

    Raw Food $3,827.00
    Labor $4,222.00
    Supplies ....$ 270.00
    Other operating expenses ....$ 385.00
    Total $8,704.00
    Less Revenue ....$ 400.00
    Net Cost $8,304.00
    Number of meals served, total 4750
    Patient 4000
    Staff 700
    Guests 50
    Raw Food ....$3,827.00 $.805/meal
    Labor ....$4,222.00 $.888/meal
    Supplies ....$ 270.00 $.057/meal
Total Cost per meal $1.75

Inventory Levels

Setting goals to maintain appropriate inventory levels cannot be over-emphasized. Detailed below is a listing of recommended maximum monthly inventory ceilings.

Each facility should adopt its own maximum monthly inventory ceiling with specific accountability to the administration if the current inventory level exceeds the maximum. These ceilings generally reflect the minimum that should be maintained on hand at any one time to assure compliance with regulations and efficiency. Thus, the necessary minimum should be considered as the maximum ceiling, since there is usually no need to over-stock the storeroom. Occasionally, there may be specific reasons for exceeding the maximum monthly inventory ceilings, including special purchasing opportunities or unexpected increases in patient census. However, justification of deviations should be made.

Maximum inventory ceilings should be established by each institution according to its patient and staff needs, coordinating purchasing capabilities and storage capacities to regulations in areas which require a minimum three-day supply of food and ancillary items. In states requiring a full one week's supply of food, the maximum ceiling levels would increase accordingly.

Economic Indicators

Inventories are more than money represented by shelved cans in the storeroom; inventories can yield economic indicators. Although it is important to determine the value of items in the storeroom, it is even more significant to evaluate the data in terms of food inventory turnover. Food inventory turnover[1] is derived by dividing the value of food-on-hand into the cost of the food used per year.

$$\frac{\text{cost food used per year}}{\text{approximate value of food inventory}} \quad \frac{\$62,458}{\$\ 2,000} = \$31.23$$

Optimally, food inventory turnover of three to five times per month by needs is indicative of efficient storeroom management. An elevated food turnover rate can imply minimal quantity buying and the inability of the facility to afford volume purchasing. Although the food inventory turnover rate may go undetected by administration as pertinent to the economic well-being of the department, maintaining a policy of small quantity purchasing can be self-defeating and can significantly escalate expenditures and cost per patient day.

The opposite side of the coin—too low a food inventory turnover—can be equally deadly economically because the assets shelved in the storeroom are essentially being ignored. This requires that additional goods be purchased and increases the storage cost.

Economic Regulators

Perpetual inventory systems with internal controls can also become economic regulators by reducing personnel pilferage. The National Restaurant Association reports that Carl Klump, President of the Chicago Professional Polygraph Center has stated that "40 percent of all employees in any business can be expected to steal."[2] Among this group 23 percent are considered borderline, and 17 percent are classified as significantly dishonest. The employees who are deemed "borderline" steal an average of $45 a year, whereas those considered "significantly dishonest" steal $175 each year. Klump contends that even the remaining 60 percent of employees who are basically honest steal an average of $5.50 per year. "They do this in ways which they don't really consider stealing such as giving discounts to friends, taking pencils home or damaging or wearing out merchandise or equipment so that it will have to be discarded and they can claim it."[3]

The National Restaurant Association further notes that Mark Lipman, private investigator of a national firm in Memphis, Tennessee, indicates that stealing is a three-step process. "The temptation to steal is there in all of us. So when the opportunity is given by management, the employees will steal. Next, greed sets in when employees see how easy it is."[4] Examples of pilferage are common and each food service director has stories to tell. Several of the following may sound familiar.

- The food service director signed for a delivery of food and returned to duties. The driver reloaded the truck and left, leaving the facility with a signed invoice of undelivered goods.
- Although forty pounds of chicken had been ordered and invoiced, a substitute "receiving" employee discovered only twenty pounds were delivered when the order was weighed.
- Food or equipment is sold by an employee to an outside source at considerably less than the original price to net a substantial profit to the employee. Some employees have been known to start their own businesses on goods stolen from employers.
- Hams, turkeys, silverware, etc., have found their way to the outside parking lot in garbage cans, purses, dirty linen, and other innovations too numerous to mention.

- The institution's policy is to permit employees to carry any leftovers home. Gradually, the quantity of leftovers increases as employees, taking advantage of the standard operating procedure, purposely prepare far more than necessary. This too, can lead to other opportunities.
- Cash register thefts occur with "no sale" entries on the tape.
- Money is pocketed from the drawer used by several cashiers to "hide" the actual thief.
- An employee accepts kickbacks from suppliers for business.

Safeguards

The administration should investigate the economic extent of personnel pilferage and institute appropriate safeguards to minimize theft that may be small initially but can substantially pervade every department in time. Listed below are several guidelines.

- Institute a perpetual inventory system to protect the institution against a majority of its potential losses.
- Conduct unexpected inventories by employees other than storeroom personnel.
- Secure all storage areas, maintaining a close check on keys.
- Recommend that the food service director periodically check storage areas unannounced.
- Lock the kitchen at night.
- Maintain tighter security near the loading dock.
- Restrict nonfacility personnel from wandering through the premises.
- Prohibit employees from storing personal belongings such as purses in the kitchen.

NOTES

1. James R. Keiser and Elmer Kallio, *Controlling and Analyzing Costs in Food Service Operations* (New York: John Wiley & Sons, Inc., 1974).
2. Bob Curtis, "Thwart Thieves With Tough Goods Control," *Nation's Restaurant News* (April 11, 1977).
3. Ibid.
4. Ibid.

SELECTED REFERENCE

Kobert, Norman. "Inventory Control: Time to Get Tough." *Boardroom Reports* 7:9.

Chapter 6

Preparation Practicalities and Serving Standards

The preparation and serving of food offers a golden opportunity to satisfy all factions of a health care facility. Properly executed, food service can provide patients with appetizing, highly nutritious food that offers three stimulating interludes eagerly awaited each day. Food served according to the diet prescribed and with consideration of each patient's needs, helps to coordinate other professional services to the patient. Effectively planned food preparation and serving also embody the culmination of administrative efforts. Food properly planned, prepared, and portion controlled is an ultimate tribute to the food service manager and virtually assures the realization of therapeutic and economic goals while enhancing patient enjoyment of the food.

PURCHASING GUIDELINES

Purchasing guidelines, production sheets and standardized recipes are three tools basic to economically efficient quality food service.

Exhibits 6-1, 6-2, and 6-3 indicate approximate quantities of food to be ordered for the number of meals served. As a guideline, they provide parameters for purchasing and/or for establishing a monitoring system of food utilization.

Production Sheet

How many cans of green beans do the cooks really prepare per meal? The production sheet (Exhibit 6-4), used with the purchasing guidelines,

Exhibit 6-1 General Purchasing Guide: Meats

FOOD ITEM	25 meals	50 meals	100 meals	150 meals	200 meals
POULTRY					
Chicken pieces	20# (8 birds)	40# (16 birds)	80# (33 birds)	120# (49 birds)	160# (66 birds)
Shredded	16# (3 hens)	32# (6 hens)	64# (12 hens)	96# (18 hens)	128# (24 hens)
Canned	2# (1/2 gal)	4# (1 gal)	8# (2 gal)	12# (3 gal)	16# (4 gal)
Sliced Turkey Raw Cooked	12-1/2# 5#	25# 10#	50# 20#	75# 30#	100# 40#
Turkey Sandwich	3-1/4#	6-1/2#	13#	19-1/2#	26#
Turkey Roll	7#	14#	28#	42#	56#
BEEF					
Beef Stew Meat	7#	14#	28#	42#	56#
Meatloaf (grd. beef)	5#	10#	20#	30#	40#
Corned Beef Hash	6#	12#	24#	36#	48#
Cubed Steak	12#	24#	48#	72#	96#
Beef Sandwich	5#	10#	20#	30#	40#
Beef-a-roni Beef Macaroni	3# 1#	6# 2#	12# 4#	18# 6#	24# 8#
MISCELLANEOUS					
Luncheon Meat (1 oz. portion)	1# + 8 oz.	3# + 2 oz.	8# + 4 oz.	9# + 6 oz.	18# + 12 oz.
Salmon Patty (3 oz. portion, raw)	4# + 11 oz.	9# + 10 oz.	19# + 4 oz.	29# + 14 oz.	37# + 8 oz.
Tuna Salad (2 oz. portion)	3# + 2 oz.	6# + 4 oz.	12# + 8 oz.	18# + 12 oz.	25#

offer simple yet effective tools for the food service director to prepare and for the cooks to use.

The portion size of all foods to be served should be determined before preparation so that an accurate number of portions can be prepared to minimize waste. Simple as this may seem, few facilities make a conscious effort to forecast the actual number of servings to be prepared.

Standardized Recipes

Standardized recipes, those that continually produce good products, are excellent tools to assure a sufficient quantity of high quality food. (Refer to Exhibit 6-5). Although some cooks may pride themselves on not needing recipes, standardized recipes offer the following undisputed benefits to all. They

- eliminate guess work,
- guarantee repeated quantity and quality of product,
- require less skill from employees,
- reduce the amount of supervision required, and
- serve as a continuing cost control procedure.

Exhibit 6-2 General Purchasing Guide:* Vegetables

FOOD ITEM	25 meals	50 meals	100 meals	150 meals	200 meals
Beets #10 can	1 can	2 cans	3+ cans	5 cans	1 cs + 1 can
Broccoli Frozen Chopped	1.5 bxs	3 + bxs	6 + bxs	10 bxs	1 + cs
Brussels Sprouts Frozen	1.5 bxs	3 + bxs	6 + bxs	10 bxs	1 + cs
Cabbage Fresh (for cooking)	8#	16#	32#	48#	64#
Carrots #10 can Frozen	1 can 1.5 bxs	2 cans 3 + bxs	3 + cans 6 + bxs	5 cans 10 bxs	1 cs. + 1 can 1 + cs
Cauliflower Frozen	1.5 bxs	3 + bxs	6 + bxs	10 bxs	1 + cs
Coleslaw	4#	7#	14#	21#	28#
Creamed Corn	1 can	2 cans	3 + cans	5 cans	1 cs + 1 can
Greens, Spinach #10 Can Frozen	1 can 1.5 bxs	2 cans 3 + bxs	3 + cans 6 + bxs	5 cans 10 bxs	1 cs + 1 can 1 + cs
Green Beans #10 can Frozen	1 can 1.5 bxs	2 cans 3 + bxs	3 + cans 6 + bxs	5 cans 10 bxs	1 cs + 1 can 1 + cs
Lima Beans #10 can Frozen	1 can 1.5 bxs	2 cans 3 + bxs	3 + cans 6 + bxs	5 cans 10 bxs	1 cs + 1 can 1 + cs
Mixed Vegs. #10 can Frozen	1 can 1.5 bxs	2 cans 3 + bxs	3 + cans 6 + bxs	5 cans 10 bxs	1 cs + 1 can 1 + cs
Okra #10 Frozen Fresh	1 can 1.5 bxs 6#	2 cans 3 + bxs 12#	3 + cans 6 + bxs 24#	5 cans 10 bxs 36#	1 cs + 1 can 1 + cs 48#

*All estimates based on 2 ounce portions. If 4 ounce portions are used for cafeteria and/or patients, then the amount ordered would be doubled.

Exhibit 6-2 General Purchasing Guide: Vegetables (Continued)

FOOD ITEM	25 meals	50 meals	100 meals	150 meals	200 meals
Peas, Blackeyed					
#10 can	1 can	2 cans	3 + cans	5 cans	1 cs + 1 can
Dried	3#	6#	12#	18#	24#
Peas, Crowder					
#10 can	1 can	2 cans	3 + cans	5 cans	1 cs + 1 can
Dried	3#	6#	12#	18#	24#
Peas, Field					
#10 can	1 can	2 cans	3 + cans	5 cans	1 cs + 1 can
Dried	3#	6#	12#	18#	24#
Peas, Green					
#10 can	1 can	2 cans	3 + cans	5 cans	1 cs + 1 can
Frozen	1.5 bxs	3 + bxs	6 + bxs	10 bxs	1 + cs
Peas, White Acre					
#10 can	1 can	2 cans	3 + cans	5 cans	1 cs + 1 can
Dried	3#	6#	12#	18#	24#
Potatoes					
Hash Brown	1#	3-1/2#	7#	10-1/2#	14#
(dehydrated)					
Rice, Raw	2#	4#	8#	12#	16#
Rutabagas					
#10 can	1 can	2 cans	3 + cans	5 cans	1 cs + 1 can
Fresh	6#	12#	24#	36#	48#
Squash, Yellow					
#10 can	1 can	2 cans	3 + cans	5 cans	1 cs + 1 can
Frozen	1.5 bxs	3 + bxs	6 + bxs	10 bxs	1 + cs
Succotash					
#10 can	1 can	2 cans	3 + cans	5 cans	1 cs + 1 can
Frozen	1.5 bxs	3 + bxs	6 + bxs	10 bxs	1 + cs
Sweet Potatoes					
#10 can	1 can	2 cans	3 + cans	5 cans	1 cs + 1 can
Frozen	1.5 bxs	3 + bxs	6 + bxs	10 bxs	1 + cs

Standardized recipes and experienced cooks are an incomparable combination, but both require time to develop. The following pointers should increase the cooks' productivity and experience.

PRACTICAL PREPARATION POINTERS

Eggs

- Add salt to water when boiling eggs; it reduces cracking and makes them easier to peel.
- Crack hard-cooked eggs when hot and put in cold water to cool, then peel.

Exhibit 6-3 General Purchasing Guide: Fruits

FOOD ITEM	25 meals	50 meals	100 meals	150 meals	200 meals
Applesauce #10 can	1 can	2 cans	3 + cans	5 cans	1 cs + 1 can
Appricot Halves #10 can 75/80 count (4 per serving)	1 + can	3 cans	5 cans	8 cans	10 cans
Cranberry Sauce #10 can (1 oz. portion)	1/4 can	1/2 can	1 can	1-1/2 cans	2 cans
Fruit Mix #10 can	1 can	2 cans	3 + cans	5 cans	1 cs + 1 can
Peach Halves 40/50 count (1 peach half/serv.)	1/2 can	1 can	2 cans	3 cans	4 cans
Peach Slices (31 serv/can)	1 can	2 cans	3 + cans	5 cans	1 cs + 1 can
Pear Halves 40/50 count (1 pear half/serv.)	1/2 can	1 can	2 cans	3 cans	4 cans
Pineapple Slices 100/110 count #10 can (2 sli/serv.)	1/2 can	1 can	2 cans	3 cans	4 cans
Prunes 190/200 count #10 can (2/serv)	1/4 can	1/2 can	1 can	1-1/2 cans	2 cans
Apple Rings #10 can	1 can	2 cans	3 + cans	5 cans	1 cs + 1 can
Plums 80/90 count (2/serving)	1/2 can	1 + can	2 + cans	3-1/2 cans	5 cans
Apple Slices #10 can, pre- heated or solid pack 30-35 serv/can	1 can	2 cans	3 + cans	5 cans	1 cs + 1 can
Blueberries 30-35 serv/can	1 can	2 cans	3 + cans	5 cans	1 cs + 1 can
Citrus Sections 25-30 serv/can or gal. jar	1 jar	2 jars	4 jars	5 jars	7 jars

All portions based on approximately 2 ounce portions with the exception of cranberry sauce, which is used as a garnish.

Quantities noted above represent approximate quantity needed per serving.

Exhibit 6-4 Production Sheet

DATE: _____   HOSPITAL CENSUS: _____
MENU CYCLE: _____   NURSING HOME CENSUS: _____
WEEK NO.: _____   CAFETERIA: _____

FOOD ITEMS	QUANTITY TO PREPARE																
	General			Soft		Bland (4)		Low Salt		Low Fat		Diabetic		Blended		Liquid	
	Cafe	H	NH	H	NH	H	NH	H	NH	H	NH	H	NH	H	NH	H	NH	COMMENTS

- Peel hard-cooked eggs by slipping a spoon under the cracked shell at the large end.
- Cover unused egg yolks with cold water before storing in refrigerator and they will not dry out.
- Break eggs into a small funnel to separate the yolks from the whites.
- Have a pan ready in which to drop the shells when opening eggs. This saves rehandling the shells when you are ready to dispose of them. (Break an egg in each hand simultaneously.)

Exhibit 6-5 Standardized Recipe: Fruited Chicken Salad

YIELD: 50 – 1 cup portions = 25 pounds		PORTION SIZE: 1 cup			
PAN SIZE: not applicable		TEMPERATURE:		no final cooking necessary	
INGREDIENTS	Gram Wt. per 50 Serv.	COMMON WEIGHT OR MEASURE			PROCEDURE
		50	100	150	
Macaroni	.562 kg.	1 lb. 4 oz.	2 lb. 8 oz.	3 lb. 12 oz.	Cook macaroni till tender yet firm drain well.
Cooked Cubed Chicken	1.13 kg.	2 1/2 lb.	5 lb.	7 1/2 lb.	
Diced Celery	.960 kg.	1 qt.	2 qt.	3 qt.	Combine macaroni
Salad Dressing	.480 cc.	1 pt.	1 qt.	1 1/2 qt.	chicken, celery,
Minced Onion	60 g.	1/4 cup	1/2 cup	3/4 cup	salad dressing, onion
Lemon Juice	60 cc.	1/4 cup	1/2 cup	3/4 cup	lemon juice and salt.
Salt	15 gm.	1 Tbstp.	2 Tbsp.	3 Tbsp.	Cover and chill
Mandarin Orange Sections	.9 kg.	2 lb.	4 lb.	6 lb.	thoroughly.
Grapes, Halved	.960 kg.	1 qt.	2 qt.	3 qt.	
Heavy Cream, Whipped	480 cc.	1 pt.	1 qt.	1 1/2 qt.	Before serving, fold in drained oranges,
Almonds, Slivers	120 g.	4 oz.	8 oz.	12 oz.	grapes, whipped cream and almonds
Lettuce Leaves		50	100	150	

GARNISH WITH: PLACE ON LETTUCE LEAF AND PLACE ALMOND ON TOP

PORTION CONTROL SERVINGS WITH: 1 No. 4 Scoop, or 2 – No. 8 Scoops

---

- Spin a whole egg. If it spins like a top, it is hardcooked.
- Prepare scrambled eggs in double boiler for a tender, fluffy product. This seems to increase labor efficiency by reducing the necessity for continuous supervision of the product.
- Prepare the following recipe to eliminate the necessity of purchasing commercial whipped topping. Yes, one egg white does yield one gallon of Miracle Topping.

MIRACLE TOPPING

1 Egg White

1 Cup Granulated Sugar

1 Cup *Heavy* Fruit Syrup (from can of peaches, fruit cocktail, or plums)

1. Place all ingredients in mixing bowl at same time.
2. Mix at high speed for 5 to 7 minutes or until topping forms stiff, white peaks.

Yield: One gallon
Serves 125

This topping may be browned (for banana pudding). Topping may also be used as a complete dessert by folding or whipping in drained fruit pieces. Adding leftover cake crumbs, graham cracker crumbs, or broken cookie pieces makes a delightful dessert treat as well. Jello cubes folded with the topping are excellent as a "Jello Fluff."

Prepare the Miracle Topping before serving. Tripling the recipe facilitates whipping and will provide topping for the future. Cover and store in the refrigerator. Whip again, and it is ready to use.

Cheese

- Store cheddar cheese, grated or cubed, in plastic bags and freeze. Thaw and use as needed for such dishes as scrambled eggs and casseroles. Be sure to mark the amount of cheese in each bag.
- Apply a thin coat of butter to the cut surface of cheese to prevent its drying out under refrigeration.
- Dip a loaf of cheese in hot water for easy removal of the wrapper.
- Use a dry vegetable brush for removing cheese from a hand grater before washing it. This also works well for lemon and orange rind.
- For easy separation alternate corners of sliced cheese or meat when stacking the slices.
- Grate cheese and add to mayonnaise to give zip to salads made with peaches, pears, or apples.

Milk and Cream

- Coat the inside of a steam-jacketed kettle with butter when heating milk. This will prevent milk deposits and scorching, making the cleaning job easier.
- Prevent formation of skin on milk during heating by:
    1. covering the pan,
    2. floating a small amount of butter or cream on the surface of the milk, or
    3. beating the milk during the heating time.
- Do not add salt to large quantities of milk or cream sauce until the last minute or it will curdle.
- Mix the sugar with the egg rather than the milk for best results when making custards or other dishes that call for hot milk to be added to eggs. Add hot liquids to beaten egg and sugar a little at a time. Do not overcook.

- Chill bowl, beater, and cream when whipping cream. The cream will whip in half the time. Should the cream seem too thin to whip, put the chilled dish in a pan of hot water, then whip.

Cereals and Pastas

- Butter sides and bottom of a pan in which noodles, spaghetti, or rice is to be cooked. This prevents them from boiling over and/or from sticking to pan.
- Add butter or cooking oil to boiling water before adding macaroni or spaghetti. Bring to a boil and turn off heat. Keep covered to finish cooking.

Gelatin

- Heat only enough liquid to dissolve the gelatin when using flavored gelatin for molded salads or desserts. To hasten the congealing, use ice water to make up the total amount of liquid.
- Do not soften plain gelatin if there is sugar in the recipe. Simply mix the gelatin and sugar together and dissolve in hot liquid.
- Use dried fruit flavored gelatin granules as a garnish for salads, puddings, cookies, and in combination with shredded coconut.
- Dip individual molds of gelatin salad in warm water, turn out trays, and place in the refrigerator to firm before serving.
- Grease jello molds with mayonnaise rather than oil prior to pouring in gelatin. This gives a "frosted" appearance.

Baking

- Start and end with dry ingredients, when adding dry ingredients and liquid alternately to a batter.
- Add moisture and flavor to a chocolate cake mix by adding a small amount (¼ cup per 2-layer cake) of salad dressing. For extra tenderness, add ½ cup cooking oil to any cake mix for full size sheet pans.
- Mix all dry ingredients together and all liquid ingredients together before blending into each other.
- Add some of the liquid called for in the recipe when creaming butter and sugar. The contents will cream faster with less sticking to the bowl.

- Bake cakes in individual paper cups for variety. This will save pan washing, make desserts attractive, make it easier to count the servings from a given recipe, and control portions.
- Avoid soggy bread crust by removing bread from pans immediately after baking. For a tender crust, brush with butter immediately after baking; for a crisp crust, do not butter.
- Roll out biscuit or roll dough in the bun pan; then cut into squares, diamonds etc., using a knife instead of a biscuit cutter. This saves reworking and rolling the dough scraps.
- Roll yeast or quick-bread dough to about a ¼ inch thickness, spread generously with softened butter, then fold in half and cut out the rolls. When baked, the rolls are already sliced and buttered.
- Roll out and bake cobbler crust on a cookie sheet and then cut into squares and place on warm fruit which has been cooked, thickened, and portioned into serving dishes.
- Prepare a pan-coat from flour and shortening to grease cake pans. Apply with a 3 inch brush.
- Make bread crumbs.
  1. Place dry bread in plastic or paper bag and roll with rolling pin.
  2. Place dry bread in mixer bowl and use flat paddle to crush it.
  3. Shred dry bread with food chopper or grater.
  4. Freeze soft bread and then grind.
- Is opening sugar or flour sacks a problem? Stand the sack perpendicular to you with the double stitching on your right. Cut end of string nearest to sack. Pick first stitch or two carefully and the rest will unravel easily.
- Use an ice cream scoop to portion muffin mixture in pans.

Fruits

- Drain canned berries and fruits for fruit pies. Thicken and cook the juice before mixing with the fruit. Fill the shells. This keeps the fruit in whole pieces, firm and appetizing.
- Make fruit skid-proof (grapefruit, oranges, and melons) by cutting a slice off the bottom to make it rest solidly on the cutting board.
- Place the fruit in hot water for five minutes when preparing whole sections of oranges and grapefruit. The skin and white membrane can then be easily peeled from the edible fruit.

- Increase the amount of juice from citrus fruit by dipping fruit in hot water before squeezing.
- Grate the rind of whole oranges or lemons and store in refrigerator in a small jar for future use in frostings, etc. To remedy dry lemons, put them in a warm oven for a few seconds and see them become plump and juicy again. To keep freshly peeled fruit such as peaches, apples, and bananas from discoloring, add lemon juice or orange juice and mix.
- Coat raisins with melted shortening to permit them to go through the food chopper without sticking.
- "Plump" raisins.
    1. Cover with cold water and bring to a boil. Remove from heat and allow to stand for at least five minutes. Drain and dry raisins.
    2. Cover with fruit juice and store covered in refrigerator.

Vegetables

- Heat vegetables in steam table pans on steam table to increase labor efficiency.
- Remove skins from tomatoes.
    1. Dip them in boiling water until the skin slips. Cool immediately by placing them in cold water. Remove the skins and place tomatoes in refrigerator.
    2. Rub the back of a knife over the entire surface to loosen the skin.
    3. Insert a fork into a firm tomato and hold it over a low flame until the skin wrinkles and splits.
- Do not mix fresh tomatoes or cucumbers in combination salads until ready to place on the serving line. The acid from these vegetables will tend to wilt the others.
- Do not cut out the core of lettuce when preparing lettuce for salad cups. Grasp the core firmly, twist once, and it will come out rather easily. Let water run through the core hole into the lettuce, and it will loosen and separate the leaves.
- Make celery rings or crescents by cutting an entire bunch at one time with a cook's knife, then sweeping it all into a colander. Wash under a strong stream of water.
- Hold onions under lukewarm water when cleaning and cutting. This will help you avoid discomfort as well as the tear-stained look.

- Cut unpeeled onions in quarters from top to bottom. Remove skin from quarters by pulling skin out and down.
- Cook potatoes in their jackets. This will save food value and prevent waste in peeling. Boiled potatoes may be peeled faster by hand than uncooked potatoes.
- Scrub or scrape vegetables whenever possible instead of peeling them.
- To score a cucumber, first pare it, then run the sharp tines of a fork down the length. After the cucumber is thinly sliced, the slices will have an attractive scalloped edge.
- Add a sprig of fresh mint to water when cooking green peas and carrots. Add a pinch of nutmeg to spinach, carrots, and squash while cooking.
- Rub hands with fat before preparing squash or other vegetables to prevent roughness and irritation of hands.
- Cut a handful of celery, carrots, and/or beans together.
- Clean spinach by breaking off all stems from the leaves before washing. Wash in warm water, using two pans. Work from right to left using both hands. Put a lot of salt in the first pan of water to prevent several washings. The salt will loosen worms or bugs and cause them to rise to the top of the water.
- Fasten a plastic bag over the mouth of a shredder to receive shredded vegetables.
- Thaw frozen vegetables in the refrigerator before they are cooked to make them taste fresher.
- Let celery stand in cold water to which 1 teaspoon of sugar per quart has been added to yield delicious, crisp celery.
- Add one teaspoon vinegar or lemon juice to red beets while cooking to retain color.
- Add a little milk to the cooking water to keep cauliflower attractively white.
- Place ½ cup of vinegar on the range near cooking cabbage to absorb the odor.

Meat

- Prepare hamburger patties in quantity by using one of several methods.
    1. Spread ground meat evenly over the entire surface of a baking pan (18″ x 26″), cover with wax paper, and flatten with a rolling pin. Cut into square hamburger portions before cooking.

2. Portion ground meat with a scoop on a baking pan (18″ x 26″). Cover with waxed paper and place a second pan the same size on top. Push gently to flatten meat patties. The second pan is ready for filling.

3. Flatten patties with the bottom of a can dipped in cold water. Use both hands, a can in each one.

4. Slice frozen ground beef for hamburger patties to eliminate portioning and shaping. Place frozen beef in the refrigerator the day before it will be used. It will be thawed enough to slice the next morning.

5. Place meat patties in rows three layers deep in a baking pan, separating layers with strips of aluminum foil just wide enough to cover each row of patties.

- Grate a raw potato and add to each pound of hamburger to make a juicier hamburger.
- Use two long handled spoons to turn meat during roasting. Forks puncture the meat and cause loss of the meat juices.
- Use leftover bacon, by putting it back in the pan and frying until very crisp. When crumbled, it may be added to scrambled eggs, soups, even peanut butter sandwiches.
- Cut several pieces of uncooked bacon at the same time with scissors, or chop with a cook's knife when chopped bacon is needed.
- Place meat loaf mixture for 40 portions into a pan (12″ x 20″ x 2¼″) and portion into individual servings before cooking. This way is faster and facilitates serving.
- Sew chicken or turkey with dental floss after stuffing. The floss is strong and will not tear the flesh.
- Brush turkey with olive oil several hours before roasting to make turkey skin tender while roasting and to insure succulent, juicy meat. Frozen turkey can be brushed while thawing.
- Allow at least 15 minutes for a roast to cool before carving. This allows the juices to settle back in the meat, and less juice will be lost.

Miscellaneous

- Freeze coconut meat to make it grate more easily.
- Divide large quantities of food into several shallow containers for quick cooling. Cool cooked foods as quickly as possible, uncovered. Then refrigerate immediately.

- Remove the bottom of an empty coffee can and use it as a handy enclosure when chopping nuts, etc. Put the bottomless can on your cutting board, and it will keep the nuts corralled as you break them up. Use a spring-type cutter to chop nuts.
- Weigh ingredients instead of measuring them.
- Measure in largest size, such as one quart—not four cups; one table-spoon instead of three teaspoons.
- Take advantage of drop delivery when possible.
- Use trays or carts for bringing supplies from storage to work area.
- Keep two pans of food on serving counter. This will prevent delays in serving when first pan is empty.
- Soak dishes containing starches, sugar, and eggs in *cold* water. Soak greasy ones in hot soapy water.
- Use a wire whip for mixing flour and water for gravies and sauces.
- Cook food in serving pans when possible. The food will be more attractive, will stay warm longer, and will save dishes, time, and labor.
- Keep a mix of flour and fat (roux) in refrigerator to be used as thick-ening when needed. Whip into hot liquid.
- Grease measuring cup first to measure honey or other sticky sub-stance.
- Arrange sequence of work so there is no break in movement or wasted motion.
- Use a pair of scissors for cutting such foods as marshmallows or meat and vegetables for salads. The marshmallows will not stick to scissors if they are dipped in water.
- Use an egg slicer to cut cooked carrots, cooked potatoes, bananas, butter, and other soft foods.
- Grind such foods as cheese for sandwiches, onions, and meats. It will save time and give more uniform results.
- Use the food chopper to cut such foods as nuts, raisins, and many vegetables.
- Keep sandwiches made before serving palatable by placing a damp towel on the bottom of a flat pan and covering each layer with wax paper, stacking the sandwiches carefully. Cover the top layer with a damp towel.
- Prepare sandwiches by placing bread on a tray or waxed paper, using a #30 scoop to portion filling on each slice of bread, spreading the filling with a 1-inch spatula. Place two pieces of bread on top of the spread and proceed as before to speed assembly.

- Do not add fresh spice to old spice. Never mix the two. Discard the old, then place the fresh spices where they will be handy for everyday cooking.
- Make economical syrup using maple flavoring. A little bottle makes 24 pints of syrup; add only hot water and sugar. Allow sugar to dissolve in boiling water before adding flavoring.
- Stir a teaspoon of flour into a carton of sour cream before adding it to a sauce that must boil. The flour will prevent the sour cream from curdling.
- Use only one-third to one-half as much when substituting dried herbs for fresh ones.
- Quarter a potato and add to gravy or soups that are too salty to remove some of the salty taste.
- Substitute leaves of celery for celery salt for added fresh flavor.
- Do not measure spices and herbs by the handful or pinches. A measuring spoon should be used to obtain exact amounts, and the cook who takes the time to do this can be proud of this skill.
- Do not leave the lid off a spice container because volatile oils are lost when spices and herbs are exposed to the air. It is important to keep spice containers tightly sealed. Spices that are kept in paper sacks and partly opened cardboard containers will lose their potency of flavor quickly.
- Prepare soft crumbs in the mixer by using mixer bowl, splash cover, and wire whip. Put soft bread slices in the bowl and operate at moderate speed until bread is cut into the size pieces desired. Remove any crusts that are not cut up and chop them separately. As a guide to the approximate yield when cutting up bread, one ⅝-inch slice makes about one cup of soft bread cubes or soft bread crumbs. It will also make about ¾ cup of dry or toasted bread cubes or about ⅓ cup of dry bread crumbs.
- Do not reconstitute nonfat dry milk solids or powdered eggs if they are to be used for cooking or baking.
    1. Combine these with flour and other dry ingredients.
    2. Add the liquid used in reconstituting these products with the other liquid ingredients in the recipe.

Portion Control

Coordinating proper portion control with careful food preparation translates into major savings. Portion control scoops are paramount to cost control; serving spoons provide inaccurate portions at best. By providing only one extra ounce of vegetable per serving twice daily, the department loses an estimated $1,941.80 per year! For example, if one case of vegetable costs an average of $8 ($1.33/can) and the following number of portions yielded:

20 three-ounce portions/can = 6 cases or $7.98
30 two-ounce portions/can = 4 cans or   5.32

Total additional cost/meal   2 cans or $2.66 (resulting from at least one extra ounce per serving due to lack of portion control)

$2.66 × twice/day = $5.32 × 365 =$1,941.80 additional cost per year would be incurred due to lack of portion control. Portion control is important!

Determining Scoop Size

Using portion control scoops is one of the most effective ways to maintain proper control of serving sizes. To determine the size portion per the scoop number used, divide 32 ounces by the serving size. For example, to determine the scoop number for a 2-ounce portion:

$$\frac{32 \text{ ounces}}{2 \text{ ounces}} = \#16 \text{ scoop}$$

To determine the size portion a specific scoop yields, divide the number of the scoop into 32:

$$\frac{32 \text{ ounces}}{\#8 \text{ scoop}} = 4 \text{ ounce portion}$$

Portion control scoops can even be used for serving liquid-retaining vegetables such as spinach or peas by drilling holes in the bottom of the scoops to permit the drainage of liquid. By using portion control scoops, the server is always aware of the quantity that constitutes one serving. If a patient requests double or triple servings, then these can be provided accurately and included in the number of servings to be prepared.

SERVING STANDARDS

Serving Efficiency

Efficiency in serving specifically relates to productivity and patient satisfaction.

There are numerous examples. One that is particularly interesting relates to a new facility whose staff took exceptional pride in the meals, but whose patients were complaining of cold food and extremely delayed meal service. A superficial observation revealed that the brand new steam table and other equipment were laden with 100 plus trays on which the cook was dutifully dishing up one food item at a time. When questioned as to why the steam table was not being used as intended, the reply came, "We've always done it this way and it works fine." The steam table was immediately revitalized and employees were amazed at the speed with which the tray service assembly line moved. Patients and staff alike were delighted with the improvement.

The assembly line method is not the only labor-efficient method of tray service. Facilities with limited space may find it more effective to preset trays for the next meal. Trays may be cross-stacked or placed directly in the food cart depending on tray accessibility during meal time.

Greater distribution of work load can also be accomplished by using a second set of trays to preset breakfast trays in the afternoon. This may enable the morning shift to be reduced by one employee or permit an employee to come in several hours later, thereby reducing the ultimate number of labor hours.

Preportioning juice, racking bacon, breaking eggs, advance preparation of jello or desserts, and any other pre-preparation that can be accomplished maximizes food service productivity by achieving a more evenly distributed work load.

Appetite Appeal

Providing appetizing meals need not be expensive in terms of time or money. Meals that appeal can be created with the proper combinations of color, taste, texture, and temperature with the added touch of a simple garnish. The following provides a list of garnishes to improve appetite appeal.

Soup: Just before serving top with

- croutons,
- grated parmesan cheese,
- diced or julienned meat or poultry,
- vegetables cut in various sizes and shapes, or
- parmesan toast strips.

Vegetables:

- lemon or grated cheese on cauliflower, broccoli, spinach, asparagus
- grated hard-cooked eggs on any vegetable
- halved or quartered maraschino cherries
- minced parsley or dill on carrots
- melted cheese
- bread crumbs

Meats:

- pink cinnamon apples, apple rings, applesauce (with pork)
- cranberries, cranberry sauce, cranberry relish, orange slices (with turkey or chicken)
- sauteed mushrooms, watercress, broiled tomato (with beef)
- canned pear halves filled with mint jelly, mint sprigs, apple jelly (with lamb)
- spiced peaches
- parsley

Fish:

- minced pimiento, green pepper
- dill
- lemon wedges, lemon juice
- cheddar cheese—grated
- rye crackers
- tomatoes: wedges, slices, filled with buttered peas
- spiced peach
- parsley

Fruit or Gelatin Salads:

- dry gelatin
- nuts
- sprays of watercress or mint
- cherries: fresh, maraschino, bing
- grapes: fresh—halved or whole
- raisins
- prunes

- whipped cream, cream cheese, cottage cheese, sour cream
- "Miracle" topping

Other Salads:

- hard-cooked eggs: chopped, sliced, wedged, deviled, with paprika
- parsley: sprigs, chopped, grated
- celery: sticks, stuffed
- carrot: curls, sticks, rings, shredded
- radishes: sliced, rosettes
- beets: pickled, sliced, chopped
- pimiento: strips, chopped
- tomatoes: sliced, diced, wedges, rings, with salad fillings, i.e., tuna, cottage cheese, chicken salad, coleslaw, potato salad
- green peppers: strips, rings
- olives: green, stuffed, black
- pickles: whole, sliced, sticks, sweet, sour, dill, relish
- dehydrated sweet red peppers: chopped, diced

Desserts:

- "Miracle" topping
- dry gelatin: various colors
- nuts: chopped, slivered, or whole
- tinted coconut
- toasted coconut
- whole or sliced berries to top puddings
- granola
- raisins

SELECTED REFERENCES

Gordon A. Friesen International, Inc. "The Ready Foods System for Health Care Facilities." *Institutions/Volume Feeding Magazine.* Chicago: 1973.

Sheridan, John F. "Planning Food Service Facilities for Health Care Institutions." *Ross Dietetic Currents* 5:7-12.

West, Bessie B.; Woods, Levelle; and Harger, Virginia F. *Food Service in Institutions.* New York: John Wiley & Sons, Inc., 1966.

Chapter 7

Food Service Costs and Maximizing Reimbursement

The mid-1960's brought revolutionary changes to the health care delivery system, principally through federal and state programs initiated by Congress. The health care industry rejoiced assuming that institutions would be paid for care that in the past had been furnished, in many instances, free. The one part of these programs, that was not really understood, was that the health care facilities were to be paid for the cost of furnishing these services. Cost reimbursement had arrived on a large scale. But what exactly is cost reimbursement as it is related to health care programs?

COST REIMBURSEMENT PROGRAMS

Cost reimbursement is a program that pays a hospital or skilled nursing facility for the cost of providing services as opposed to the charge that the hospital or skilled nursing facility puts on these services. Examples of cost reimbursed programs are: the Title XVIII or Medicare Program, the Title XIX or Medicaid Program, the Title V or Crippled Children's Program, Blue Cross, and many private pay insurance companies.

The largest and most costly of these programs, the Title XVIII or the Medicare program, was established by an act of Congress in 1965. It started as a federal health insurance program for people aged 65 or older. Congress felt that this group needed federal help more than any other. A large portion of this segment of the population had retired. On retirement they had lost the group insurance coverage they had while employed.

They were now having to live on a fixed income from retirement plans and/or social security benefits. This income was generally much lower than they were accustomed to having and the adjustment was difficult. In many instances one long spell of illness could wipe out a family's life savings. Medicare was expanded to include disabled persons and those with chronic renal disorders. The program is divided into part A, hospital insurance, and part B, medical insurance. Only part A is relevant to the discussion in this chapter. The program started paying benefits to beneficiaries on July 1, 1966.

Title XIX or Medicaid

The Title XIX or Medicaid Program was established to enable each state, as far as practicable given the conditions in each, to furnish (1) medical assistance to families with dependent children and to aged, blind, or permanently and totally disabled individuals, whose income and resources were insufficient to meet the cost of necessary medical services, and (2) rehabilitation and other services to help such families and individuals attain and retain capability for independence or self-care. Congress authorized to be appropriated for each fiscal year a sum sufficient to carry out the purpose of this program.

Since Medicaid is administered by the states, it is not as uniformly applied as the Medicare program, which is administered by the federal government. The benefits paid and the administration of the program are drastically different in various states. The federal government had to approve the state Medicaid program for each individual state and, therefore, the state programs went into effect at various times.

Grant Programs

Besides these federal and state programs, the federal government offers various grants to help the elderly and needy. These are generally allocated to the states based on the percentage of persons in some age groups to the total percentage of population in the state. One example of this is Title VII of the Old Americans Act of 1965. This is a grant given to various non-profit agencies to provide food for elderly people. The real purpose is to encourage these people to get out of their homes and socialize with others of their own age group. This is not a cost reimbursed program. The agency knows exactly how much money they are getting from the specific grant, and when that runs out, the program ceases.

COST REIMBURSEMENT

Reimbursement for the cost of services rendered is usually adjusted annually, using a cost report filled out by the facility to arrive at the reimbursable cost. Usually retroactive adjustments are made at that time, adjusting for overpayments or underpayments that have occurred during the year.

Food Service Costs

What food service costs are recognized by cost reimbursed programs? All reasonable costs incurred and accrued by the hospital, skilled nursing facility, and combination hospital–hospital-based skilled nursing facility are recognized. A reasonable cost is one that is proper and necessary to the operation of the hospital for the patients. This, in most instances, excludes the cafeteria cost that applies to visitors and guests. An example of a cost that would not be allowed would be the cost of extraordinary meals in a patient environment, or the cost of the food, preparation, and delivery of meals that were for nonpatients of the facility.

The food service department in a hospital or nursing facility is considered a support department and the cost of the food service is allocated to revenue producing departments. Support department, means one that services one or more revenue-producing departments. Generally, the food service department services the routine area of a hospital or nursing facility as food is served to the patients. It also furnishes service to the special care units, such as the intensive care ward or the coronary care ward or various other special care units in the facility. In some facilities food and nourishment come from the food service department and go to the nursery. However, since the advent of the Medicare program, hospitals were quick to realize that when this happened, considerable overhead and direct cost were also allocated from the food service department to the nursery; since the nursery generally is not utilized by Medicare patients, hospitals found that they were losing this cost, and therefore, added revenue. Now, most nurseries order and store all supplies for the nursery.

The food service department also services ancillary departments in a hospital such as laboratory, x-ray, and pharmacy through the cafeteria. In most hospitals the employees will eat in the hospital cafeteria. The cost of a food service department is generally allocated between strictly patient food service and cafeteria, based on the number of meals served. Therefore, the cost of the cafeteria is then allocated to the various ancillary departments, based either on the number of meals served to employees of each department or, if almost everyone eats in the cafeteria, on the number of employees in each department.

Documenting Differences

One of the difficulties that hospitals and skilled nursing facilities encounter is the inability to document the difference, if in fact there is any, in the cost of preparing and delivering the meals to patients as opposed to meals served in the cafeteria. In larger facilities this can be done a little more easily since these facilities have employees who spend 100 percent of their time preparing and serving meals in the cafeteria and other employees who spend 100 percent of their time preparing and serving meals to patients. In the smaller facilities, however, where an employee's time is used in both the preparation of cafeteria meals and preparation of patient meals, this can prove to be a major costing problem. In many instances the food served in the cafeteria and to the patients is the same. However, the major cost differential would be delivering meals to the patient rooms and returning plates and utensils to the food service department. A consulting dietitian with experience in many facilities could help to design, to conduct, and to analyze tests in order to document the difference between patient food service and cafeteria costs. It is sometimes difficult to convince hospital personnel that the small amount of time spent performing a small duty is important. As an example, a chore that takes a food service employee only five minutes a meal to perform for a specific area in the hospital translates into 5,460 minutes (91 hours) or 2 and ¼ weeks' salary and benefit costs that should be allocated to that particular area. Five minutes a meal on a particular duty does represent a substantial cost.

PER ANNUM COST OF FIVE MINUTE TASK

Number of Minutes Per Year	MINIMUM WAGE RATES		
	$2.90 hr.	$3.10 hr.	$3.35 hr.
5460 (91 hrs.)	$263.90	$282.10	$304.85
25% benefit cost	$ 65.98	$ 70.53	$ 76.21
TOTAL	$329.88	$352.63	$381.06

The exhibits in this chapter can be adapted for gathering data to be used in allocating food service costs. Exhibit 7-1 is a means of costing out servings of raw food. It is simply a list of the food served for that meal and whether it was served to hospital patients or in the cafeteria to visitors or employees. The cost per serving of each menu item can be determined by the dietitian and/or the food service director. The latest invoices should be used for costing. These costs should be extended and totaled for all meals served during the day at the end of each day rather than permitting them to accumulate. After the cost of each food item has been determined, totaling can be done by clerical personnel.

Exhibit 7-2 can be used to develop ratios of how personnel labor cost can be divided between the cafeteria and patient food service to the hospital and/or nursing home. It is a listing of all employees responsible for a specific duty. Each separate routine should be on a separate sheet for each meal. The employee should be made aware of the importance of these tests and shown how to complete the form properly. (Exhibit 7-3 can help in developing Exhibit 7-2.) Exhibit 7-4 is simply a means to compile and summarize the labor cost incurred.

Hospitals and/or skilled nursing facilities that do not have employees who work in and cook solely for the patient or cafeteria food service will find that using these exhibits will reflect a more accurate way to cost meals between the cafeteria and patient food service than merely by dividing the cost of meals served in the two areas. It is recommended that at least a two-week test be conducted in each quarter of the year and that these tests be held at different times during each quarter. Please note that it was suggested that the total labor cost be allocated based on the ratios developed during these tests since it does not account for down time. The fiscal intermediary will insist that down time costs be allocated as well since that is the purpose for documenting time spent in each. It is essential that time spent in *each* separate area be documented in order to receive proper reimbursement.

Cafeteria Costs

If these tests prove that cafeteria meals cost less, the hospital will benefit from the higher cost in the patient areas in a cost reimbursed program. However, in the cafeteria there are some special problems.

Often employees pay less for cafeteria meals than visitors and guests. The discount generally is offered to encourage employees to eat their meals in the facility, which encourages a shorter lunch break. It is also advan-

Exhibit 7-1 Cost / Serving of Raw Food

FOOD ITEM	CAFETERIA				HOSPITAL				NURSING HOME			
	Size/Serving	No. Serving	Cost/Serving	Total Cost	Size/Serving	No. Serving	Cost/Serving	Total Cost	Size/Serving	No. Serving	Cost/Serving	Total Cost
Orange juice					4 oz.	25	.050	1.25	4 oz.	60	.050	3.00
Egg					1	20	.047	.94	1	65	.047	3.06
Cereal					4 oz.	20	.050	1.00	4 oz.	55	.050	2.75
Toast					1	22	.025	.55	1	70	.025	1.75
Milk					8 oz.	20	.094	1.88	8 oz.	60	.094	5.64
Coffee												
Fried Chicken	4 oz.	35	.31	10.85	4.oz.	15	.31	4.65	2 oz.	46	.155	7.13
Baked Chicken					4 oz.	5	.29	1.45	2 oz.	14	.145	2.03
Rice	4 oz.	25	.03	.75	4 oz.	20	.03	.60	2 oz.	55	.015	.83
Carrots	4 oz.	29	.110	3.19	4 oz.	20	.123	2.46	2 oz.	60	.055	3.30
Roll	1	34	.04	1.36	1	17	.04	.68	1	50	.04	2.00
Banana Pudding	4 oz.	28	.10	2.80	4 oz.	15	.10	1.50	2 oz.	45	.05	2.25
Banana						5	.106	.53		15	.106	1.59
Swiss Steak					4 oz.	15	.51	7.65	2 oz.	46	.255	11.73
Plain Steak					4 oz.	5	.41	2.05	2 oz.	14	.206	2.88
Mashed Potatoes					4 oz.	20	.04	.80	2 oz.	60	.020	1.20
Mixed Vegetables					4 oz.	20	.104	2.08	2 oz.	60	.046	2.76
Roll					1	17	.04	.68	1	46	.04	1.84
Fruit Cup					4 oz.	15	.163	2.44	2 oz.	45	.081	3.65
Diet Fruit Cup					2 oz.	5	.214	1.07	2 oz.	15	.214	3.21
TOTAL				$18.95				$34.26				$62.60

Note: Breakfast and evening meals are not served to cafeteria clients in this institution. Nursing home patients may receive additional servings on request.

Exhibit 7-2 Documentation of Labor Hours Per Duty

DATE _____

ROUTINE: Washing Dishes

MEAL Breakfast

Employee	Hrly Wage	Cafeteria			Hospital			Nursing Home		
		Start	Stop	Total	Start	Stop	Total	Start	Stop	Total
Jane Doe	2.35	9:00	9:10	:10	9:10	9:40	.30	9:45	10:30	:45
John Doe	2.25	9:00	9:35	:35				9:45	10:30	:45
Mary Smith	2.40				9:00	10:20	1:20	10:20	11:00	:50
Sally Jones	2.37	9:30	9:45	:15	9:45	10:10	:25	10:15	11:00	:45

tageous to the facility because the employee is essentially "on call" should an emergency arise.

The difference between the actual cost of the cafeteria meal and the charge made to the employee can be allocated to employee health and welfare. Whether this would be advantageous would not be clear until the cost report is worked using both methods. It can be beneficial when a hospital or skilled nursing facility's payroll cost in departments with a high Medicare involvement is much greater than the ratio of employees who work in other areas. This is because employee health and welfare is generally allocated on gross salaries and the cafeteria cost is allocated on either the number of employees in the various areas or on the number of meals served in the cafeteria to employees of the various departments. In a free-standing skilled nursing facility there will be less chance for any cost differential between cafeteria meals and patient meals. As in skilled nursing facilities, the patients who are generally more mobile are encouraged to go to a common eating area where their meals are served along with any guests, visitors, and/or employees.

Reimbursement to Nursing Facilities

The hospital and hospital-based skilled nursing facility situation offers probably the greatest opportunity for reimbursement savings than any other setting. Normally, Medicare utilization in a skilled nursing facility is far less than in a hospital. This is due mainly to tightened regulations

Exhibit 7-3 Work Schedule Form

Name:

Position:	Food Service Aide I (position #3)
Hours on Duty:	6:00 a.m. - 2:30 p.m.
Days off:	Saturday and Sunday
Relieved by:	Part-time Food Service Aide (weekends)
Supervisor:	A.M. Cafeteria Superivsor

Time	Duties
5:55	Clock in, in correct uniform
6:00	Assist cooks as necessary in breakfast preparation
6:45	Set breakfast trays
7:00	Help dish up breakfast
7:15	Take breakfast carts to floors
7:30	Break - 15 minutes
7:45	Wash pots and pans
8:15	Set up trays for lunch
8:30	Assist cooks in lunch preparation
9:45	Break - 15 minutes
10:00	Clean: Refer to assigned duties on cleaning schedule
11:30	Assist cooks in setting up steamtable for lunch
12:00	Help dish up for lunch
12:15	Take carts for floor
12:30	Wash pots and pans
1:00	Lunch break - 30 minutes
1:30	Sweep and mop dining room
2:30	Clock out

— Any other duties as assigned by supervisor.

Exhibit 7-4 Summary of Time Spent

DATE _____

Routine	Cafeteria	Hospital	Nursing Home
Washing Dishes	3:00	4:15	5:45
Preparing & Checking Menus	0:35	1:45	2:00
Cooking Food	4:30	5:05	6:10
Preparing Salad	1:15	2:00	1:30
Baking	1:20	2:05	3:30
Cleaning	2:02	3:35	4:30

regarding skilled nursing care and to stringent limitations Medicare places on the length of stay in skilled nursing facilities.

The Medicare program states that a patient is entitled to a maximum of 100 days of skilled nursing care for each spell of illness. Once these days have expired, the patient is no longer a Medicare patient. If, during this time, the patient no longer needs "skilled nursing care" then the patient is no longer covered under the Medicare program. The program does not pay for any level of care except skilled nursing care. The program requires that a physician certify the need for skilled care before the patient enters the skilled nursing facility. This certification and treatment plan must be submitted before the end of the second day after admission. The certification must include an estimate of how long the patient will require skilled care. A recertification is required as of the last day of the presumed period of coverage. Subsequent recertifications are also required that are re-evaluated periodically by a utilization review committee.

Therefore, the more cost retained in the hospital, the higher reimbursement generally received by the facility. Since there will normally be a very high Medicaid utilization in the skilled nursing facilities, and since both programs are cost reimbursed programs, one would think that if Medicare did not pick up the hospital cost, it would in the nursing facility. However, it is not quite that simple. Although the Medicaid program and payment levels vary radically from state to state, states have set ceilings on the amount per day that they will pay for skilled nursing care during an interim period. In many instances, there is no retroactive settlement for Medicaid programs. This is why it is vital to document any differences in cost between meals served in the hospital and those in the skilled nursing facility. Some states set limitations on the routine costs per day that they will pay to nursing facilities regardless of the cost to the institution. If the facility has a high Medicaid utilization, the state is basically setting the price for the institution. For this type of institution, controlling cost is critical. Exhibit 7-5, Patient Day Cost, illustrates examples of how a nursing facility with a high Medicaid utilization in a state that has a payment limitation can get into serious financial difficulty. In this example, in a nursing facility whose allowable costs per day exceeded the $25 a day cost allowed, the total cost above the $25 per day would be lost as indicated. The unreimbursed costs would have to be made up by private-pay patients or the facility eventually would have to close.

Meal Cost Differential

Several national organizations have proven that the cost of meals in skilled nursing facilities is less than the cost of meals served in hospitals. There are many reasons for this. First, skilled nursing facilities generally have older patients who usually require smaller portions. There is also the fact that the majority of these patients are more mobile and, consequently, do not need to be served or fed meals in their rooms. Although the data on the cost differences between the two types of facilities are overwhelming, the fiscal intermediaries do not accept them universally. They insist on documentation by each individual facility arguing that the Provider Reimbursement Manual (HIM-15) requires that the statistics used to allocate cost must be documented so that the intermediary may audit them.

Periodic tests conducted in the food service department can provide documentation. Most intermediaries insist on at least four two-week test periods. First, the actual cost of the food sent to the nursing facility should be identified. Then the labor involved in time of preparation, serving, dishwashing, and materials used should be identified and documented. When the cost is identified for the two-week period, the number of meals served should then be divided into this cost to determine the cost per meal. This should be done once a quarter and at the end of the last quarter, and the information should be summarized to arrive at a per meal cost. A sample form is shown in Exhibit 7-6.

These tests can be conducted using the same forms shown as Exhibits 7-1, 7-2, and 7-4 by adding a column entitled "skilled nursing facility." The procedures described previously should be followed. With this documentation one facility proved that the cost of their meals in a hospital-

Exhibit 7-5 Patient Day Cost

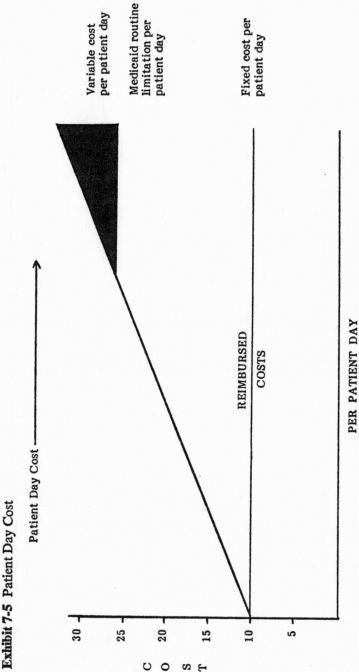

Patient Day Cost

Variable cost
per patient day

Medicaid routine
limitation per
patient day

Fixed cost per
patient day

REIMBURSED
COSTS

PER PATIENT DAY

C
O
S
T

30
25
20
15
10
5

Exhibit 7-6 Summarization of Raw Food Cost/Meal For Cafeteria, Hospital and Nursing Home

DATE (January)	CAFETERIA		HOSPITAL		NURSING HOME	
	RAW FOOD COST/MEAL	LABOR COST/MEAL	RAW FOOD COST/MEAL	LABOR/COST MEAL	RAW FOOD COST/MEAL	LABOR COST/MEAL
1						
2						
3						
4						
5						
6						
7						
8						
9						
10						
11						
12						
13						
14						
SUB-TOTAL						
TOTAL COST/MEAL						

This form need be completed only once quarterly to serve as the culmination of data received during the quarterly two week test periods.

based skilled nursing facility was approximately 35 percent less than the cost of meals in the hospital. Since their Medicare utilization in the hospital was much greater than in the nursing facility, this 110-bed facility received approximately $14,000 more in Medicare reimbursement at the end of its fiscal year than it would have had by allocating the cost based on the number of meals served. The administrator of this facility estimated the cost of the time spent on the tests to be $1,000. Although this would not be true in every facility, the possibility is certainly worth exploring.

Costs and Benefits

In addition, overhead cost should be allocated to the skilled nursing facility. However, once this direct cost is identified, it is a fairly simple matter to allocate overhead based on the number of meals served in the hospital. Undertaking these tests, however, is costly and the ultimate benefits must be weighed against the cost in each facility to determine if the expense is justified. At least one should be conducted to see if the nursing facility meals cost less.

What Constitutes a Meal?

Another problem that hospitals and skilled nursing facilities encounter is what actually constitutes a meal. This question is particularly relevant to the cafeteria. When an employee or guest goes to the dining room and through the cafeteria and buys only a partial meal, how is this counted? Some facilities simply count the number of people going through the cafeteria line, and this figure becomes the number of meals served. From a reimbursement standpoint, this is not advantageous. It tends to increase the meal cost to the cafeteria rather than to the patient areas. What can be done to alleviate this problem? Probably the simplest solution is to determine a dollar amount that would be considered as a meal. At the end of the day, gross receipts from the cafeteria can be divided by the predetermined amount to resolve the number of meals served in the cafeteria for the day. The figure set for the cost of a meal, however, will be somewhat arbitrary and could be disputed by the fiscal intermediary when they audit after the fiscal year's end. Another approach uses a meal equivalent, for example, a meat, two vegetables, and beverage would constitute a meal. This again, is somewhat arbitrary, and if there are many instances of people passing through the cafeteria line picking up only an item or two, the fiscal intermediary could ask what was being done with this cost if it were not being counted as a cafeteria meal. This further identifies one of the underlying problems with the current Medicare program.

Intermediaries interpret various regulations in the Medicare law differently. Differences sometimes exist among individual auditors working for the same fiscal intermediary. If a statistic is accepted one year by the auditors of a fiscal intermediary, it does not necessarily mean that it will be accepted the next year. This presents major problems for the hospitals and skilled nursing facilities, as there is a lack of consistency of application throughout the program in almost all areas of statistics and allowable costs. A dietitian should know exactly what duties each staff person performs. These duties should be documented and reviewed periodically since new or different duties are assigned people as they gain experience. Written job descriptions and duty schedules are good vehicles for the review, which will be available to all employees. A sample of a duty schedule is shown as Exhibit 7-3.

If specific people prepare or deliver food to any specific area, the cost for this should end up in that specific area, not pooled with the rest of dietary costs and allocated in that manner. This can be accomplished by monthly journal entries posted to the general ledger rather than reclassifications of the cost at the end of the year. This seems to be more readily acceptable to fiscal intermediaries than year end reclassifications. The adage, "If it is not documented, it is not done," applies specifically to maximizing third party reimbursement. Again, this is not an easy task and can be costly. However, it is one that is necessary for the proper allocation of cost for both the cost report and management. Therefore, it is necessary for the person in charge of food service, whether it is a full-time dietitian, consulting dietitian, or food service director, to have a general knowledge of cost reimbursement. This is also true of all other department directors. They should be aware of the high cost reimbursed areas in the facility and the limitations that are placed on these facilities by cost reimbursed programs. Some of these limitations are routine, such as the lower of cost or charges limitation, certain drug limitations, and physical therapy cost limitations. More limitations are being placed on facilities every year, and to be unaware of these limitations can be financially disastrous. Awareness can be emphasized through a simple educational program for all department heads. This program either can be managed internally by someone thoroughly familiar with cost reimbursement within the hospital or, if there is no qualified person, then experts can be brought in.

Many large certified public accounting firms with extensive health care experience have developed such programs and will generally conduct them for facilities for a nominal cost in relation to the benefits received. Consulting firms offer the same services. One of the benefits of such a program, other than that the department heads and employees are aware of their part in the cost reimbursed program, is that it tends to create a spirit of competitiveness between department heads. This can result in department heads searching for new ways to cut costs and to improve management throughout the facility. Some hospitals and nursing facilities have offered incentives to their employees for any ideas resulting in either a cost saving or higher cost reimbursement to the institution. These incentives can come in the form of cash payments, a percentage of cost saved, or additional reimbursement obtained throughout the year. Administrative incentives of recognition in the local or institutional newspaper can further encourage cost-effective suggestions. Some professional associations also give awards for cost-saving suggestions.

One example of simple, cost-effective employee suggestions, occurred when an employee of one large institution suggested placing three trash can liners in a trash can at the same time in the administrative area. When the administrative office employees leave in the afternoon, they simply pick up the top liner along with any trash in it and deposit it on the way out of the building. By doing this the housekeeping department does not have to go into every office every day to empty trash. The savings to this facility for this one simple idea is estimated at $5,000 a year. Another simple idea that saved money required cafeteria patrons to remove paper and disposable items from their trays before putting them up to be washed. Employees often propose ideas that save time, money, and material when they are challenged.

Properly managed, the entire health care team can be an invaluable resource to reduce costs, as well as to maximize reimbursement.

SELECTED REFERENCES

B.H.I. Pub. No. 066. *Introduction to Medicare.* February 1977: 23.

Federal Register 43:25869-25876.

U.S. Department of Health, Education and Welfare. *Provider Reimbursement Manual.* July 1967, Chapter 23, Section 2300.

U.S. Department of Health, Education and Welfare. *Title XVIII of the Social Security Act.* B.H.I. Pub. No. 034, July 1977: 3.

Chapter 8

Controlling Labor Costs

The cost of labor is a major consideration in planning and controlling total food service costs. Labor currently represents approximately 50 percent of total food service costs, and present conditions such as the scheduled minimum wage increases indicate that labor costs will continue to be the major cost component.

LABOR COST FACTORS

Labor costs involve two factors.
1. time required to perform the job, and
2. rate of pay designated.

The following food service areas must be carefully evaluated when labor budgets and staffing needs are determined.

- Amount of labor-saving equipment available
- Physical plan of the kitchen area (Does the placement of the preparation and serving areas require extra walking or movement?)
- The use of china as opposed to disposables
- Menu pattern (selective or nonselective menus as well as menu size and complexity)
- Form in which food is purchased (convenience or "homemade" foods)
- Number of meals served per day, seating capacity

- Working conditions in the kitchen (including temperature, humidity, lighting, and noise)
- Personnel training programs, motivation, and skill of employees
- Amount and adequacy of supervision
- Current wage rate
- Rate of labor turnover
- Personnel productivity
- Performance standards required in production and service (Maintaining high standards will require more supervision.)
- Employee morale (low morale may result in substandard performance, low productivity, and/or absenteeism)
- Number and complexity of therapeutic diets
- Quantity of nourishments and/or between-meal feedings to be prepared and served
- The department that dispenses trays to patients
- The department that is responsible for maintaining sanitation standards in the dining room
- Type of food service (self-service, length of daily operation, number and type of special services provided)

Determining Actual Labor Costs

It is important to remember that the hourly employee wage rate is only the beginning of actual labor costs incurred by the employer. Although this cost may be considerable, especially with the rising minimum wage, it can become the least costly component of labor when the hidden costs are considered.

Exhibit 8-1 graphically presents the expenses incurred by the employer on an hourly basis per employee. Assuming that an employee is paid $2.90 per hour, the following expenses incurred by the employer yield an actual productive cost of $8.46 per hour, almost triple the base wage.

- FICA (employer's share)
- Workmen's Compensation
- Unemployment Compensation (hospital insurance)
- Uniform allowance
- Meals (2 each costing employer $1)
- Meal breaktime (30 minutes) optional

Exhibit 8-1 Actual Hourly Employer Costs Per Employee

BASE RATE PAID TO EMPLOYER PER HOUR	$2.90	$3.10	$3.35
FICA (employer's share)	.18	.19	.20
Workmen's Compensation	.06	.06	.07
Unemployment Compensation	.09	.10	.11
Medical and Hospital Insurance	.12	.12	.13
Uniform Allowance	.05	.05	.05
Meals (two, each costing employer $1.00)	.23	.25	.27
Meal Breaktime (30 minutes)	.21	.22	.24
Coffee Breaks (2 @ 15 minutes each)	.21	.22	.24
Vacation (one week)	.06	.06	.07
Time Off for sickness (7 days)	.06	.06	.07
Holiday Pay (7 days)	.06	.06	.07
Total Cost Per Hour	4.23	4.49	4.87
Total Productive Cost Per Hour (50% Productivity)	$8.46	$8.98	$9.74

The figures above do not include additional employer costs incurred for supervision, pilferage, payroll preparation, bookkeeping, overtime, institutional maintenance for employees, life insurance, or other employee benefits.

- Coffee breaks (2 at 15 minutes) optional
- Vacation (1 week)
- Time off for sickness (7 days)
- Holiday pay (7 days)

In addition to these expenses, food service productivity has been estimated at approximately 50 percent—compared to other industry productivity of 80 percent. As Exhibit 8-1 indicates, the minimum wage employee is an expensive commodity to the employer.

Labor Turnover

Employer costs continue with labor turnover. The cost of replacing employees is one of the greatest expenses the employer incurs. Evaluating the employee turnover rate could yield reduced turnover and greater cost efficiency.

Formula For Figuring Cost of Employee Turnover

A ratio of "leavers" to "stayers" is used. The relative frequency rate is the number of employees who have left divided by the number who did not leave, plus the total number employed during the year.

These are approximate rates . . . obscuring differences in length of service and dissimilarities in characteristics of personnel. Therefore, there should be a stability rate as well.

$$\text{Turnover rate} = \frac{\text{Total terminations}}{\substack{\text{Average number} \\ \text{persons employed} \\ \text{in specified time}}} \times 100 = \underline{\quad}\%$$

$$\text{Relative frequency turnover} = \frac{\text{Total terminations}}{\substack{\text{Total persons} \\ \text{employed during} \\ \text{specified time}}} \times 100$$

$$\text{Instability Rate} = \frac{\substack{\text{Number terminations among employees} \\ \text{on payroll at beginning of period}}}{\substack{\text{Number of persons employed at} \\ \text{beginning of period}}} \times 100$$

The optimum turnover rate is 10 percent or less per year. The greatest turnover occurs usually within the first two weeks of employment. The following costs are associated with turnover.

- Break in cost: the cost incurred due to substandard performance by new employees as they are learning
- Breaking in cost: the cost of the time lost by supervisors as they train new workers
- Lost production and extra burden cost: the cost of running a food service on low or below normal staffing as well as overtime costs

- Extra social security tax cost: the employer's cost when tax payments are resumed with each new employee
- Extra unemployment tax cost: cost when a former employee collects unemployment insurance and increased burden of insurance for each new employee
- Bookkeeping cost: the cost to complete necessary paperwork when an employee is terminated or hired

Improving Employee Satisfaction

It is evident that the cost of turnover is a major one, and a look at what causes employees to leave is justified. Sometimes the fault lies with the person responsible for hiring: an applicant's work record, qualifications, and recommendations may not have been examined well; many new employees may not have been qualified for their jobs, or they may have been placed in jobs not compatible with their capabilities, leading to boredom and frustration. Perhaps the orientation program did not adequately define the job and its requirements, leading the new employee to· misunderstand what was expected of him. Poor or inadequate supervision is also a cause of employee failure.

Proper wage structures must be defined. If new employees are hired at higher wages than current employees doing the same job, morale is decreased. If a grievance outlet is not available, employees may become discontented. Frustration may also occur due to apparent lack of supervisory interest. This can be prevented by providing a way that employees can communicate with supervisors or their representatives (such as employee councils or staff meetings). Lack of motivation may result if a definite means of advancement or financial incentive is not apparent. For many employees, a periodic wage increase is not enough to satisfy their potential as productive leaders of the organization, and a definite path toward more responsibility is necessary.

Working conditions are a major consideration in employee satisfaction. Excessive heat, humidity, or noise may result in poor performance and employee discontent. Many employees are subject to long hours of standing. Resilient flooring, antifatigue mats, and footstools on wheels may help relieve some of the tiredness. Proper ventilation should be maintained, especially around heat-producing equipment such as ranges, ovens, fryers, and the dish machine. Noise control is also an important factor, and soundproofing materials in ceilings and floors are helpful.

Since turnover cost is such an important expense to control, what causes turnover must be discovered to reduce this unnecessary outlay of funds.

Exhibit 8-2 Termination Interview

Name:_____   Termination Date:_____

Position:_____   Department:_____

RATING AT TERMINATION

	Superior	Above Average	Average	Below Average
Ability				
Quality of Work				
Attendance				
Physical Health				
Emotional Disposition				
Appearance				
Attitude				

Comments:_____
_____

Reason for leaving:_____
_____

Recommended for reemployment: Yes_____   No_____

Comments:_____
_____

Forwarding address:_____

Forwarding telephone:_____

Date:_____   Signed:_____
                                              Supervisor

One effective means of establishing reasons for turnover is the termination interview. This can be done either upon the exit interview or via mail as indicated in Exhibit 8-2.

Absenteeism

Absenteeism is yet another labor cost factor that must be considered. Whether the absent worker is compensated or not, his fellow workers must bear the consequences of his absence and low morale may result. An absenteeism rate above 2 percent is considered excessive, so the need arises to monitor it closely. Three basic causes of absenteeism are:

1. On the job (poor supervision, kitchen heat fatigue, dirty working conditions, poor morale);
2. Community (poor transportation, inadequate police protection, lack of child care facilities); and
3. Personal (illness, alcoholism, family responsibilities, psychological problems).

The most effective way to combat absenteeism is to show concern. Check on the absentee and communicate that the absence is important to the coworkers. The decision to stay away from work is a symptom that something is wrong. Preventive medicine, such as the requirement of a yearly physical, may reduce absenteeism due to illness. Some employers include bonuses for attendance as an incentive against absenteeism. A control program involving the use of various social agencies could be established for those who are chronically absent. Employees or unions should be made aware that such a program would be utilized. Percent of absenteeism can be established by the following formula.

$$\frac{\text{no. of daily absentees during pay period} \times 100}{\text{average no. of employees} \times \text{no. of working days}}$$

Example

$$\frac{2 \text{ employees absent} \times 100}{\text{average 6 employees} \times 14 \text{ working days}} = 2.38\%$$

Overtime

Uncontrolled overtime can be a considerable labor cost. The key to controlling overtime is constant awareness of its cost, since overtime may be created to pad an employee's paycheck. Among the devices that have been developed in an attempt to control overtime are

- requisitioning overtime in advance when absence due to illness or vacation is anticipated (Refer to Exhibit 8-3) and,
- requiring an explanation for any overtime within 24 hours after it has been incurred.

It is important to compare the cost of hiring an extra part-time employee to paying continuous overtime for one or more full-time employees. A full-time employee receiving a minimum wage of $2.90 receives $17.40 for 4 hours of overtime. A part-time minimum wage employee receives $11.60 for 4 hours of work. On a daily basis, this is a substantial cost differential

Exhibit 8-3 Report for Overtime or Extra Wages

Department: _____

Date Overtime Occurred: _____

Number of Persons Required for Overtime: _____

Total Number of Hours Overtime:_____

Employee	Hours Overtime Incurred	Rate
_____	_____	_____
_____	_____	_____
_____	_____	_____
_____	_____	_____
_____	_____	_____

Reason for Overtime: _____

_____

_____

_____

Signature – Department Head

even without including the additional 30 to 40 percent employer costs. If overtime on this basis continued three times per week for a year, the additional costs would pyramid to $904.80. This cost could have been saved by merely hiring a part-time employee.

DETERMINING STAFFING NEEDS

Accurately estimating staffing needs directly affects the labor budget and indirectly affects employee morale, absenteeism, and overtime. This section will examine several methods of determining specific staffing needs.

One of the most helpful indices used in determining staffing needs is the number of meals served per labor-hour or the number of labor-minutes per meal. *A Guide to Nutrition and Food Service* (U.S. Department of Health, Education, and Welfare) offers two ways to estimate food service staffing needs in a health care facility.

1. one food service employee, including relief personnel, per eight patients
2. 4.29 meals served per labor hour or 14 minutes of labor required for each meal (This can increase to 17 minutes per meal or 3.53 meals per labor hour with a high level of complex therapeutic diets and a restricted use of convenience foods.)

However, these are merely guidelines based on a national average. Many institutions are able to provide high quality food service at a considerably reduced labor-minute per meal ratio (10 to 14). Naturally, this depends on individual variables, but increased labor efficiency can make this a reality. Exhibit 8-4 details the method of determining labor-minutes per meal.

Exhibit 8-4 Method of Determining Labor Minutes per Meal

$$\frac{\text{Number of employees on duty x hours actually worked x days worked}}{\text{meals served during the period}} = \text{hours per meal}$$

Hours per meal x 60 (minutes) = labor minutes per meal

Example: $\frac{10 \times 8 \times 7}{100 \times 3 \times 7}$ = 0.27 hour or 16 minutes-- (100 beds x 3 meals x 7 days)

$$\frac{8 \times 8 \times 7}{60 + 10 \times 3 \times 7} = \frac{448}{1470} = 0.30 \text{ hour or } 18.3 \text{ minutes per meal}$$

(60 beds plus ten employees x 3 meals x 7 days)

Small Hospitals: 25 - 100 beds.........17 - 18 minutes per meal (average)

Medium Hospitals: 100 plus.............14 - 17 minutes per meal (average)

The Public Health Service has prepared estimates in regard to food service personnel required in institutions of 100 beds or less, as indicated in Exhibit 8-5. One way to determine specific staffing needs is to establish the number of positions to be filled and multiply by 1.5 employees per position. Although meals must be served 365 days per year, full-time employees are available only an average of 236 days per year (as detailed below) requiring the number of full-time positions to be multiplied by .55 to determine the number of relief personnel necessary.

$$
\begin{aligned}
&\text{365 days/year} \\
-\ &\text{104 days off/year (2 days off/week)} \\
-\ &\text{10 vacation days/year} \\
-\ &\text{8 holidays} \\
-\ &\underline{\text{7 sick leave days}} \\
\end{aligned}
$$

Total number of days   236
actually worked/year

Once the staffing needs and labor budget have been determined on a monthly basis, it would be helpful to monitor the daily personnel schedule to minimize overtime and stay within the established budget. If the monthly budgeted wages are $5,000 (excluding salaried employees), then the daily budgeted wages approximate $166.00. The daily budgeted wages are

---

Exhibit 8-5 Suggested Levels of Personnel in Hospitals

Number of Beds	25	30	40	50	60	75	80	90	100
Number of Full-Time Employees	4	4-5	5-6	6-7	7-8	9-10	9-10	10-11	11-12

EXTENDED CARE FACILITIES, NURSING HOMES AND SHELTERED CARE

Number of Beds	25	30	40	50	60	75	80	90	100
Number of Full-Time Employees	3	3	3-4	4-5	5-6	6-7	7-8	8-9	9-10

Source: Public Health Service.

divided by the average hourly rate to yield the number of daily labor-hours required.

$$\frac{\text{Budgeted wages}}{\text{Average hourly rate}} = \text{Daily hours required}$$

$$\frac{\$166.00}{\$2.90} = 57.24 \text{ hours}$$

This will maintain a close check on the number of labor-hours (therefore labor dollars) being expended, and adjustments can be made quickly before serious over runs in time and money occur.

PROFICIENCY IN PRODUCTIVITY

Labor costs are significant considering the additional employer costs (FICA, employee benefits, etc.), overtime, absenteeism, and labor turnover and these costs are multiplied by reduced productivity. In addition to inflation and the rash of legislative and health care industry proposals to contain or control costs, high labor costs have prompted administrators and departmental managers to concentrate on the concept of productivity improvement.

Essentially, these questions are being asked:

- How can I get *more* for the *same* level of resource input, or
- How can I get the *same* level of output by using *fewer* resources?

Due to the added need for financial management brought about by the federal funding of hospital care and the decline in philanthropy, most institutions are now doing an adequate job in managing their "nonpeople" resources (cash, accounts receivable, inventories, etc.). However, the area of personnel productivity only recently has begun to receive the emphasis it deserves.

For most hospitals, labor accounts for 55 to 60 percent of the direct expense and can be a major contributor to any overall cost control effort. In turn hospital food service, by its very nature, represents an area where productivity improvement can have a highly visible impact. While relatively small in terms of overall direct expense (5 to 7.5 percent), it is highly labor intensive (approximately 50 percent is tied up in salary expense). Also, problems with the preparation, quality, and timely delivery of meals or nourishments can have a rippling effect throughout the patient care areas.

Other current developments as well are exerting upward pressures on food service payroll costs. Minimum wage increases are escalating and there is a growing movement toward unionization of health care employees. Coupled with this is the downward trend in employee productivity.

In this section, an approach for implementing a productivity improvement project in the food service department is discussed. While items such as inventory control, facility layout, food preparation techniques, and equipment considerations obviously contain their own productivity implications, these aspects are considered in other chapters of the book. Emphasis is on those areas where immediate short-term benefits can be realized through manpower utilization, control, and reporting, and on those functions over which the food service director has direct responsibility and authority to implement change.

Review Current Operations

The impetus for a food service productivity project can come from any number of sources—administration, an already functioning cost-control committee, or the food service director. The reasons can be equally varied —complaints regarding service or quality, concern over the cost per meal of the facility compared to similar institutions, or simply a vague "feeling" that the food service could be more efficient.

If the review and implementation of subsequent recommendations is to succeed, the project must be carefully controlled and monitored. Responsibilities must be delineated along with a definite timetable for achieving project stages and the reporting of results.

The selection of a project staff is also critical. Although the food service directors may have the expertise and necessary credibility, their availability is limited, and project time gets eroded under the press of daily duties. If the health care facility employs management engineers, they are usually adept in the techniques of problem analysis and definition. Where possible, their skills and time should be included.

Outside consultants generally know the techniques and process of a food service productivity project and are expert in project control and management. However, additional costs must be expected in connection with their use. While no definitive answer is available, successful projects usually contain a mix of skills, depending on each institution's circumstances.

Consideration must be given to the food service employees. They must understand the concepts and reasons behind the program and have their job security fears allayed. It is almost certain that the most perfect conceptual design will fail without their support and participation. In this connection, many institutions adopt a policy of using normal attrition and transfers to other departments to realize any staff savings identified in a productivity project. Although this may mean that savings are somewhat deferred, it can pay real dividends in terms of employee cooperation, yielding ultimate monetary savings as well.

Once the team has been selected and the project management and reporting mechanisms are in effect, the initial reviews can begin. At this juncture, two methods can be employed. The first is a general review and documentation of all areas. This would involve interviews with food service, nursing, and other personnel; flowchart analysis of the food service cycle from ordering, storage, and issue through preparation, assembly, delivery, and cleanup; and detailed analysis and measurements of staffing and scheduling.

Good interviewing and flowcharting techniques are not difficult to learn and there are several good texts on management engineering and systems analysis.*

Focused Review

A second method, a "focused" review, has usually proven to be a better approach. The first step involves gathering of "rough" work measures and statistics. These may include, but certainly are not limited to the following.

- trays assembled per minute (including error ratios)
- dietary hours per patient meal
- cost per meal
- number of late meals or meals not served
- overtime hours by employee skill type
- number of special diets ordered

These measures can then be compared to available predetermined standards such as those published by the Hospital Administrative Services (HAS), the Commission of Administrative Services in Hospital (CASH), and the American Society for Hospital Food Service Administrators. Although these general industry averages are not always applicable, they can identify quickly areas requiring a more detailed review and analysis.

---

*Note: For example, *Business Systems,* published by the Association for Systems Management.

In addition to those items identified for a more in-depth review, several other areas or functions can be analyzed and their impact on departmental productivity documented. These may include the following.

- An initial survey should be undertaken of the quality of the meals by using available formats and worksheets (CASH or the Tennessee Hospital Association, for example) or by designing a patient questionnaire.

- An in-depth survey of personnel scheduling should also be effected. One intermingled nursing facility realized a $13,000 per year savings on labor alone through careful analysis of personnel scheduling. Although recommendations were made to combine the two kitchens in a centralized system, the employees voluntarily increased productivity and reduced the number of personnel to retain the autonomy of two separate kitchens.

- The cycle menus should be reviewed in detail. This can yield three benefits. First, items requiring complex preparation and assembly such as a meat casserole requiring 15 ingredients, a hand-rolled crust, and 21 preparation steps have obvious productivity implications. Second, a wide range of menu choices neutralizes the benefits of mass preparation and assembly. Finally, an excessively long cycle may not allow the employees to become familiar enough with the individual items and preparation requirements.

- Simply being alert can help identify problems. Bottlenecks in the tray assembly procedures, observed "idle" times in the work schedule, or obvious facility layout problems can often be corrected easily.

- Distribution of nourishments should also not be neglected. In one hospital, by instituting control and accountability on the nursing units, the cost per patient dropped from $.51 to $.27 and yielded over $30,000 in annualized savings.

- The employees' cafeteria operations should be subject to the same rough measurement and documentation techniques. In many cases, the productivity gains due to more efficient scheduling (food service employees and hours of operation) and improved procedures can result in significant benefits. For example, a major teaching hospital achieved a savings of $80,000 by adopting various measures to eliminate idle time between meals.

Another note in this area should be added. In many instances, what initially appears to be a problem in the food service area is really a symptom of systemic problems in other departments. A slow or inaccurate census system may really be the cause of an inordinate number of late meals or meals not served. Also, a high number of special diets may mean that the dietitian has failed to educate the medical staff on the clinical indications and implications of a special dietary regimen.

Analysis and Recommendations

Once the mass of data and observations has been gathered, the next consideration obviously is what to do with it. In most cases, the process is similar to the normal management problem-solving techniques. For each function or area the following checklist is of inestimable benefit:

- Purpose: WHAT is being done?
- Place: WHERE is it being done?
- Sequence: WHEN is it done?
- Person: WHO is doing it?
- Menus: HOW is it being done?

And last, but usually the most important, WHY? This may be the most difficult question, especially when one is confronted with the old sacred cows, "We've always done it that way," or "We can't change that!"

Using this detailed examination of the issues and other possibilities such as brainstorming, consultants and/or a literature review to discover others' methods, a set of alternative solutions to address whatever problems may be present should emerge.

This list should, in turn, be subject to further analysis to evaluate the efficiency of the proposed alternative methods or procedures. For each, documentation should be developed showing

- strengths and weaknesses
- identification of costs to develop and install
- determination of benefits to be achieved (dollar savings, improved quality, and/or improved service level)
- the reactions and comments of the personnel who will be affected by the change

Once the preferred solution has emerged, but prior to obtaining formal approval to implement any changes, it is usually beneficial to separate the various projects into long-term and short-term categories. Long-term items, which must in turn be tied into the dietary long-range plan, include

- major equipment acquisitions such as ovens, steam kettles, or a dishwasher;
- major layout modifications such as a scatterline cafeteria versus a single straight line;
- a change to a new food delivery system;
- a change to convenience foods requiring only reconstitution or microwave warming;
- a change to centralized preparation with decentralized assembly or reconstitution for outlying buildings; and
- modifications to systems external to the food service department (included here because they usually require a separate project).

The short-term items, those that can be implemented rather quickly with no capital outlays, could include

- minor modifications to the menu complexity to distribute the daily workload more evenly;
- institution of a quality control program necessary to allay fears that a productivity improvement project is synonymous with a reduction in quality);
- modification to the tray delivery and pickup schedule;
- modifications to the cafeteria menu to tie it more closely to the patient menu;
- changes in scheduling to minimize idle time of cafeteria personnel;
- changes to the mix of personnel, for example, clerical support for the dietitians to allow them more time with patients, or for medical staff education or for initiating and monitoring cost-effective measures; and
- modifications to the tray assembly procedures.

Once the various solutions or proposals are selected, costed, and prioritized, the final step before implementation is to obtain approval from the project steering committee. If the reasons for the proposals are well documented, this should be one of the easier steps.

Implementing the Recommendations

After the recommendations for improvement have been approved, a detailed implementation plan should be prepared. In fact, some preliminary planning already will have been done in analyzing the costs of proposed alternatives. However, successful implementation of the recommendations requires a work plan that breaks the implementation down into a series of detailed steps, each of which should contain a maximum of four or five labor days of effort. In addition, the work plan should clearly indicate the person responsible for completing each task and the date by which it is to be completed. A plan that is prepared in this way will serve as an effective tool in monitoring the progress of the implementation effort. The implementation team should include food service supervisory staff and specific tasks should be assigned to them for completion.

When the recommendations involve new or modified forms and procedures, it is important to allow sufficient time in the work program for their review and approval. The procurement of forms from suppliers can be a lengthy process, and it is extremely frustrating to have to delay the final implementation of a recommendation because the required forms are not available.

Well-written procedures are not only an essential input to the training process when new work methods are introduced, they also become an on-going training tool for new employees.

The training program is another element that should not be neglected. Training should begin well in advance of implementing new procedures, but not so early that employees have time to forget what they have learned. The supervisory staff should participate in training their personnel as much as possible.

Progress meetings should be held at regular intervals with the project steering committee to report on work completed as compared to the original plan and to discuss any major problems encountered in the implementation.

Work Measurement

In order to achieve staff savings and to monitor labor productivity on a continuing basis, labor standards are essential. Their development requires not only technical expertise, but also the exercise of managerial judgment in connection with one or two key issues.

The first is the timing of the work measurement. In theory, it is desirable to delay the beginning of work measurement until the recommended methods of improvements have been implemented and are operating successfully. In this way, the standards reflect the most efficient manner of performing each task.

On the other hand, there may be certain aspects of the food service operation that will not be affected by the new methods. In these areas, work measurement could begin at an early point in the implementation process. It may also be possible to structure the work measurement so that the amount of time that will be reduced or eliminated, once the recommendations are implemented, is clearly identifiable.

The rationale for conducting work measurements during the implementation is to reduce the overall length of the project and to demonstrate results at an earlier date. Naturally, this approach assumes that the required resources can be made available to the project team.

Another key issue is the degree of accuracy to be attained in the standards development process. Most experienced practitioners in this area have found that it is far more important in the long run to have standards that are reasonably accurate and are accepted by supervisors and staff than to have 100 percent accurate standards that are viewed with hostility by department personnel.

Contrary to the popular image that pictures the management engineer with a stopwatch and a clipboard, this traditional "time study" technique is only one of many approaches to standards development.

One group of techniques can be applied quickly and with a minimum of effort. Historical averages use available figures on output per period compared to the hours used in each period to produce that output. It may be difficult or impossible to obtain the required statistical data, however, and the resulting standards will, of course, include any inherent inefficiencies in the production or delivery process.

Supervisory estimates are prepared by experienced personnel who are conversant with the operations of the department. Although these estimates are very subjective, they may provide a useful yardstick against which to measure the results of other techniques. They may also bring out a significant difference between the time required to perform various tasks as perceived by supervisory personnel, and the time these tasks actually take.

Available Standards

Depending on the area being measured, it may be possible to find available standards for various tasks. These may be obtained from state or regional management engineering groups. The term "predetermined standards" is sometimes used to describe them and this may lead to confusion with predetermined motion time systems, which are described below. Available standards are simply standards that are developed in one organization and transplanted to another, with appropriate allowances made for different conditions such as layout, food preparation methods, or patient mix. Careful judgment is necessary in determining to what extent available standards apply in a given situation.

As suggested above, these approximative techniques are most useful when quick preliminary results are required, or when used in conjunction with the more precise techniques to be described.

Logging

In logging, the employee keeps track of his own time on a special form or time log. This is usually a multi-columned sheet with a time scale on which the employee indicates the start and stop time together with a description of the activity, either by the name of the activity or with an appropriate code. It is important that the activity list be brief (not more than 10), clear, and comprehensive. The form may also provide a record of the units of work produced for each activity period, or these may be separately counted. The activity may be such that direct outputs can not be associated with it, as in the case of some professional and managerial tasks.

The chief advantage of this approach is that good coverage can be achieved with a minimum of direct involvement by the project team in the actual measurement. It is also well-suited to the measurement of paraprofessional and supervisory time. However, it is not always reliable, since employees can cover up a certain amount of idle and unproductive time. It also requires a certain amount of discipline to make entries in the logs on an hour-by-hour basis and not to wait until the end of the day to complete them. Logging is actually a self-measurement technique and requires employee time, effort, and motivation.

Batching

Batching is most frequently used to measure high volume clerical paperflow operations. As such, it probably has limited applicability in the food service environment. In this technique, work is grouped into batches of predetermined size and handed out to the employee by a supervisor or other control person. The time that the batch is handed out is recorded, as well as the time when it is returned. Since the number of items in the batch is known, it is a simple matter to calculate the standard time per item for that batch or for a series of batches over a number of days. The batch size should be such that it involves about an hour's work. One advantage of batching is that it can be used on an on-going basis to provide supervisory control over repetitive clerical operations.

Work Sampling

Work sampling is performed by recording observations of the work being performed at random time intervals. The observer determines what activity is being performed and records the activity code beside the specified time. This is repeated until a sufficient number of observations has been made. The percentage distribution of the total number of observations in the sample among the various activities is then calculated and these percentages are applied to the total time available. The resulting times are compared to the work units produced during the time period to derive the standard times per unit.

This technique produces reliable results and the sampling approach allows for a high degree of precision and confidence levels with a limited number of observations. On the other hand, it is necessary to have some training in sample size determination and the interpretation of sample results. It may also be time-consuming and awkward to set up the random time intervals. Because of the randomizing, this technique is employed on only one or two employees at a time, and it is necessary to choose employees whose skill and experience is representative of the entire group.

Another drawback is that the observer must be able to identify the activities being performed at the time the observation is made. This should normally pose no problem for physical tasks such as tray assembly, but it is more difficult for clerical tasks such as menu summarization.

Group Timing

Group timing is very close to work sampling in many respects except that instead of random observation times, a fixed interval is used (perhaps 5, 7, or 10 minutes) often with a random start. In theory, this makes it less precise than work sampling, but the difference is insignificant for practical purposes. The fixed interval makes it easier to record observations and allows observations to be made on groups of 5, 10, or even 20 individuals. For example, it has been successfully applied to a group of about 20 dietary aides engaged in tray assembly, cart stripping, and dish washing.

Predetermined motion-time systems (PMTS) rely on elaborate tables and catalogues relating various motion elements to standard times. The best-known of these systems is Methods-Time Measurement (MTM). The various motion elements, such as grasp, reach, and move are associated with distances in inches and in some cases with the weight of the objects being manipulated. The tables give predetermined times for each of the combinations of the variables. The total of the standard times for each motion element in a complete operation is the standard time for that operation. Since this technique yields highly precise standards but depends on a careful analysis of the movements that make up a given operation, hiring a trained MTM practitioner is usually recommended.

Pace Rating

The three previous techniques—work sampling, group timing, and PMTS—share a common advantage, namely, that they can be carried out with a minimum amount of disturbance to the employee in the course of his duties. The same could be said of the final technique, stopwatch or traditional time study, but most employees object to working against a stopwatch. This technique also requires special training for the observer, particularly in "pace rating." This refers to the assignment of a factor (e.g., .75, .95, 1.1) to each observation or series of observations. This factor is an expression of the observer's judgment as to how hard the employee was working as compared to a "normal" work pace. Pace rating may also be used in connection with work sampling or group timing, when it is obvious that workers' performance is much faster or slower than normal.

In applying logging, work sampling, and group timing, sufficient time must be included in the work program for the clerical effort involved in summarizing the observations. Staff can also be trained to act as observers in the case of group timing and work sampling.

The selection of an appropriate technique list enumerated above depends on a number of factors, such as

- the nature of the work being measured
- the degree of precision desired
- employee and supervisory attitudes
- the availability of trained management engineering resources
- the availability of hospital staff to assist in work measurement

Another key area is the selection of the work measurement period. This applies in the case of logging, batching, work sampling, and group timing. It is important to have a representative mix of weekdays and weekends, busy, and slack periods. Since work expands to meet the time available for its completion (Parkinson's Law), standards based entirely on low or high demand situations may be misleading.

Staffing and Scheduling

Once the standards have been developed and approved, the next step is workload analysis. By applying the standard times for each operation to forecasted activity, a simple graph can be developed that shows the hour-by-hour and day-by-day fluctuations in the workload. These hourly statistics will probably have to be developed separately if PMTS or traditional time study is used. In most cases, it is a good idea to do separate analyses for weekdays and weekends. On the same graph, the total labor hours available to do the work can be plotted by using the staffing schedule. The idle time that occurs at various points in time is readily identifiable.

PFD Factor

In preparing the workload analysis, allowance must be made for what is known as the personal, fatigue, and delay factors (PFD). PFD is really allowable and expected idle time for breaks, personal needs, unavoidable delays, and end-of-shift slowdowns. While each situation requires careful analysis, most studies have shown that between 10 percent and 15 percent is a reasonable range. It is preferable to consider PFD in the workload analysis and in the ongoing reporting rather than to build it into the stand-ard. In this way, it retains visibility.

The heart of a productivity project is in the next step: placing the people where the work is. The two basic approaches are to adjust the staffing or to manipulate the workload. In the food service environment, smoothing out the peaks in the workload may be possible to a limited extent only. A tight schedule of meal delivery must be adhered to and the patient care implications of delays and backlogs are considerable. The focus must, therefore, be on staffing adjustments.

One obvious technique is the use of part-time and casual staff, bringing them in when the work is at its peak. Maintaining a staff of trained people who will work part-time or who are available on a few hours notice may pose a problem, however.

Another approach is the use of float staff or pool staff. Float staff are specially designated employees who move from one section of the depart-ment to another as the need arises. This is most useful if different areas have their workload peaks occurring at different times of the day. Pool staff are similar to float staff except that they have no "home section" and are a separately identified group who are assigned on an "as needed" basis.

Cross-training of employees is another approach that allows for more flexibility in work assignments. Employees should be trained to perform all or most of the positions required in the department.

Staggering the times at which various groups start and finish their work day may also provide a better distribution between employees and respon-sibilities required during the day.

In preparing the revised staffing schedule, careful consideration must be given to vacations, holidays, and sick time. Deciding what allowance to make for these factors is based partly on facility policies, but it may also be necessary to research payroll records to determine actual sick leave experience. (An initial guide was discussed earlier in this chapter.)

It is at this point that the impact of changes in the level of services offered must be considered. For example, replacing cafeteria service by vending machines for staff breakfasts and coffee breaks may provide quick payoffs in staff savings. A consensus must be reached among the project team, food service management, and administration as to the savings to be realized. In fact, the analysis process may demonstrate the necessity to increase staffing in some areas.

Reporting Systems

Developing standards, identifying staff savings, and achieving them are still only part of the picture. In order to ensure that the savings are not lost as time goes on, it is necessary for the project team to design and initiate a productivity reporting system. The reports, which compare the actual hours worked to the hours earned (activity volume times the standard), are the tool by which management monitors the level of manpower utilization. Coupled with this measure of efficiency, preferably on the same report, should be an indicator of quality or level of service.

The actual hours worked are taken from the payroll records, so it is usually advisable for the reporting period to coincide with the payroll period or some multiple thereof. The reports should start at the level of the first-line supervisor with summaries for high management levels. Besides reflecting the PFD allowance, the reports should also include fixed as well as variable time.

Fixed time is time that does not fluctuate based on some activity such as the number of meals served. An example would be supervisory and clerical time. The standards cover the variable segment of the total workload and the utilization percentages really reflect the efficiency in performing the variable work.

Reports should be summarized in graph form for management.

Of course, report preparation is not the essential purpose of a manpower reporting system. If reports vary from the targeted objective, the reasons should be carefully analyzed by management and corrective action should be taken.

Management must also be willing to accept the additional clerical time required to prepare these reports. If the worksheets used are well designed, this should take one half to one labor day per reporting period.

Since the reports are only as good as the standards on which they are based, the standards should be reviewed every six months and revised when necessary. The need for revision may arise from the purchase of labor saving equipment, layout or space modifications, or changes in food preparation methods.

Long Range Considerations

The above discussion of manpower reporting systems assumes a completely manual environment. It would be possible to develop a computer-based productivity reporting system using data from the payroll system for actual hours worked. The activity standards would be stored in a master file and the activity volumes would be input each reporting period. All summarization and reporting could be done by the computer.

Another potential use of the computer in increasing food service productivity would be the use of a computer-based patient information system with terminals at each nursing station to enter physicians' diet orders. The computer could then summarize the orders, run them against the menu cycle master file, and generate portion requirements and even ingredient lists.

Productivity is only one factor in controlling the major cost in food service—labor. With the ever-escalating minimum wage and employer costs of labor, maximizing productivity is the key to minimizing labor expense.

SELECTED REFERENCES

"Productivity: Why Employees Don't Produce More" *Boardroom Reports* 7:3-4.

Buchanan, Robert D. "How to Control Turnover." *Food Service Marketing* 40:49-50, 55.

Cotton, Bruce C. "Minimum Wage Hike Means Changes Are Ahead." *Food Service Marketing* 40:34, 36.

Chapter 9

Energy
Cost Management

Energy management can be one of the primary keys to unlocking the door of economically feasible institutional health care. According to the American Hospital Association, there are 7,200 hospitals in the United States. Annual hospital construction is projected to increase approximately 1 million square feet per year or will increase from about 76 million square feet valued at $4.75 billion in 1978 to 80 million square feet valued at $5.85 billion in 1981. In addition, according to the American Health Care Association, there are more than 25,000 nursing homes (1.5 million beds) in the United States.

Hospitals and nursing homes are energy intensive and projections indicate that the cost of energy will continue to increase at approximately double the inflation rate for at least the next ten years. As reported by the Air Conditioning and Refrigeration Business Journal:

> Energy accounts for an average 2.5 percent of a hospital's total operating cost. This figure varies widely in direct proportion to differences in energy costs throughout the country. In the northeastern states, for example, a hospital may well pay up to 7 percent of its total operating costs for energy.
>
> Experience suggests that whenever this figure rises to the 3-5 percent range, hospital administrations are inclined to start viewing energy management as an idea whose time has come.[1]

ENERGY EFFICIENCY AREAS

However, new attitudes concerning energy conservation must develop before significant changes can occur. Three primary areas directly relate to proper energy efficiency for the dietary department:

1. installation and monitoring of efficient heating, ventilation, and air conditioning (HVAC) as well as lighting equipment;
2. selection of energy efficient equipment; and
3. essential operation and maintenance of equipment.

Before reviewing energy considerations specific to the food service, an analysis of overall institutional energy efficiency should be undertaken.

INSTALLATION OF EFFICIENT HVAC AND LIGHTING SYSTEMS

Most institutional facilities were designed and built during times of inexpensive energy that were often marketed on the premise that increased use resulted in lower unit cost. Diminishing energy supplies and more stringent controls on environmental pollution have dramatically increased unit costs for energy. Because of this, many attempts currently are being made to modify buildings that must continue to operate in an economy that has changed considerably from the days of inexpensive and plentiful energy.

Energy management is based on the premise that to effect energy savings in buildings, one must make the building's energy system as efficient as possible, so that the smallest amount of energy will be consumed to perform the functions required. By considering all elements of a building's energy system, one can pinpoint several areas where savings can be achieved. Therefore, well designed energy management can conserve energy and cut costs while meeting health care and related requirements.

Most energy-consuming systems in institutional buildings are there because people are there. Lighting, for example, allows use of the building at night and in places where insufficient natural light is available. If people never entered parts of the building, the need for lighting systems would not exist. The same is true for heating, ventilation, and air conditioning systems. Granted, the storage of certain materials requires temperature and humidity control to avoid damage or rapid aging, but the largest proportion of interior space is environmentally controlled because people use that space.

Therefore, effective energy management must begin with people. The users of a building should be made aware that they exercise as much control over the efficient use of energy as the thermostat, because they control the thermostat and because the thermostat is there for their benefit. The same is true for light switches and many other controls on energy-using equipment. A good energy management program should, therefore, start with a sound staff awareness program designed to make each employee more thoughtful about ways to save energy. For example, domestic hot water that is primarily used for handwashing, baths, and showers need not be hot enough to scald. There is no benefit to be realized from heating water excessively, then mixing it with cold tap water for handwashing. Generally, leaving lights on in unused areas is again unnecessary. A few degrees warmer in summer and cooler in winter can usually be tolerated with little or no discomfort, and the resultant savings in energy use is significant.

Developing a strong awareness of what can be done operationally to save energy is the logical first step toward economizing and is without doubt the least expensive to implement. After that, the physical makeup of the building and its systems should be evaluated to determine additional ways to save.

ENERGY MANAGEMENT PROGRAM

This guide offers ideas on how to organize and implement an energy management program and is applicable to institutional facilities. The following is an outline and discussion of tasks needed for a comprehensive and effective energy management program under which the institution takes the initiative to set goals to implement energy management techniques that realistically reduce energy consumption and then monitors the results.

1. Initiate an energy management program
2. Conduct an energy audit and building survey
3. Utilize a guideline for energy conservation opportunities
4. Monitor an energy management program

ENERGY CONSUMPTION

In any venture the first step is critical and often sets the tone or character of the activity. The first step in energy management is to initiate and promote energy conservation. To conserve energy consistently, an institution's administration must be committed to the concept of energy management. This commitment, will set into motion the management techniques and team efforts that are needed. Management, operating personnel, maintenance, and members of all other departments must cooperate to establish and maintain the program, realizing that their cooperative efforts will result in reduced energy consumption.

Before any decisions can be made about what energy conservation measures will be taken, an energy audit and building survey must be made of the institutional facility. Initial efforts involve review of the facility's past energy consumption characteristics and development of an Energy Utilization Index (EUI) that indicates—in British Thermal Units (BTUs) —how much energy the facility consumes per gross conditioned square foot in a given period of time. Based on the EUI and on a review of possible conservation procedures, an initial energy conservation goal can be established.

BUILDING SURVEY

Once the energy consumption data is gathered, a comprehensive building survey should be undertaken to determine where opportunities for energy conservation exist. In many cases, significant energy waste can be eliminated by repairing faulty equipment and by improving maintenance and operating practices. Several other options are available, some requiring little change, others involving substantial modification. A good reference source for evaluating options that are available is the *Standard 90-75 Workbook* published by the American Society of Heating, Refrigerating and Air-Conditioning Engineers.

CONSERVATION METHODS

After surveying how energy is being used, an analysis of the total operation is required to find energy conservation opportunities. The following guidelines are presented to help identify specific energy conservation methods that can be utilized to reduce energy consumption in the major areas of heating and air conditioning, lighting, ventilation, and electrical systems. This information can be especially helpful when there will be little or no outside consulting. However, in some cases, the information provided is not fully sufficient to provide the detailed instruction that may be required. Other potential sources of information include manufacturers, distributors, and their representatives, outside engineering consultants, textbooks, and other publications on the specific subject involved. The following discussion focuses primarily on components of various systems.

HVAC

The temperature control effectiveness of a heating and air conditioning system depends on many factors beyond the size or capacity of the mechanical equipment alone. The system must add heat to the interior spaces in the winter and must remove heat during the summer to maintain a comfortable temperature range. Also, the characteristics of cold air are generally such that less moisture can be retained than is true for warm air. Moisture in the air translates as humidity; therefore, this third factor must be controlled as well by the mechanical system. Comfort is affected by both temperature and humidity so that deviation beyond a relatively narrow range of these factors often results in conditions that can be unpleasant to the occupants of a conditioned space. Remember that any lost conditioned air that has been mechanically heated, cooled, or dehumidified must be replaced with outside air requiring reconditioning at the expense of BTUs.

Another factor that affects energy costs is the building itself. The amount of glass area in windows and doors, for example, and the directional orientation of that glass significantly affects the amount of heat that enters or leaves the building. Windows that face west add natural heating in the winter, but become additional loads on the air conditioning systems in the summer. Cracks and crevices around windows and doors allow air to pass in or out and the heating or cooling system must make up for this heat loss or gain.

Insulation, one of the single most influential factors in energy conservation, limits the amount of heat that can cross the barrier between the interior and exterior of a building. Frequently, older buildings can have additional insulation installed. New buildings should always be designed with adequate insulation included.

The proper installation and monitoring of efficient heating, ventilation, and air conditioning (HVAC) as well as lighting equipment can represent significant reductions in energy expenditures. The following guidelines are presented as an initial listing of specific energy conserving possibilities.

- Do not heat buildings excessively when they are unoccupied. Make certain that heating energy is used on people, not vacant buildings.
- Consider package units or auxiliary service to serve a small area

or rooms in a large building where there is a round-the-clock operation. This could allow major systems to be shut down although other hospital departments must remain operational 24 hours a day, such as emergency rooms, possibly some surgery suites, specific patient care, and nursing service areas. By the same token HVAC systems should be engineered to be shut down or minimized in areas that are needed less than 24 hours a day.

- Do not heat or cool unoccupied space, such as halls, passageways, lobbies, and storage rooms to the same degree as work task areas. In winter temperatures of 60°-65°F. (15°-19°C.) and summer temperatures of 80°-85°F. (27°-30°C.) are adequate.
- Reduce the environmental requirements as much as possible.
  1. Maintain a lower temperature in the winter (68°F. or 20°C.) and a higher temperature (78°F. or 25°C.) in the summer.
  2. Reduce, where possible, the number of air changes in your building.
  3. Take advantage of blinds, shades, and draperies on the sunny sides of buildings to reduce the air conditioning loads. Adding shade on the building exterior, outside of glazing, is most effective.
- Use only the number of boilers or chillers to do the job effectively. Operating boilers in summer for minimum load is wasteful. Consider smaller equipment for summer load.
- Maintain and operate boilers at a maximum efficiency to obtain the greatest fuel savings.
- Consider selective switching of air handlers to turn off units that are not absolutely required at night, on weekends, and on holidays.
- Install and control truck and dock doors to prevent costly loss of conditioned air.
- Install and maintain insulation on steam lines properly. One foot of noninsulated 8″ steam line could result in an annual loss of literally millions of BTUs that must then be purchased anew to replace the loss.
- Reduce the use of HVAC systems that require simultaneous heating and cooling within building zones.
- Examine and upgrade existing facilities with central HVAC systems, using insulation and exterior "skin" treatment. For example, consider installing an "economizer" on central air conditioning systems. This feature allows the equipment to sense the condition

of outside air, and to use it instead of mechanically cooled air if the outside air is cooler than inside air. A qualified mechanical engineer can determine if this capability is appropriate for a particular location and climate.

- Consider the use of exhaust air to precondition incoming air.
- Ensure good pipe insulation on all steam or hot water lines that pass through air-conditioned areas, as well as all chilled water lines that pass through areas not air-conditioned.
- Check periodically the condensate return lines in a steam heating system to ensure that they are not corroded and that they do not permit the condensate to be lost.
- Maintain good caulking, weather stripping, and door seals.
- Install vestibules at entrances to reduce unnecessary loss of conditioned air. This is especially important for frequently used doors, such as delivery doors and public entranceways.
- Reduce the chimney effect in multi-story buildings by keeping all stairwell openings and roof hatches closed.
- Install insulation and storm windows on all conditioned spaces. Annual fuel savings may pay for the insulation and/or storm windows in one year depending on difficulty of installation and existing insulation levels.
- When heating is required, set the thermostat to 68°F. (20°C.). For cooling, set thermostat at 78°F. (25°C.). After closing, the thermostat can be set for 55°F. (13°C.) to 60°F. (15°C.) during the winter, and 80°F. (27°C.) to 82°F. (28°C.) during the summer.
- When cooling, each degree the thermostat is raised will result in approximately 5 percent reduction in energy consumption. When heating, each degree lower will result in approximately 3 percent reduction in energy consumption.
- If you anticipate that a room will be vacant during the summer months, turn the air conditioning off. In some areas of the country, however, high humidity would prevent this practice.
- Stagger equipment start-up times to avoid heavy electrical demand at one time. This could save money on the electrical bill since many utility companies charge according to peak demand for each hour in addition to total power usage.
- Balance registers properly for the best heat distribution between the kitchen and dining room.

- Inspect and clean all HVAC system filters at least monthly (remember makeup air units).
- Clean and maintain the cooling system well. The National Bureau of Standards estimates that a general energy reduction of 10 percent could be realized if systems are kept in condition.
- Inspect all heating and cooling air ducts for cleanliness, proper insulation, and leaks.
- Install adequate insulation on all pipes and vents whose thermal control is important (hot water, steam, air conditioning, etc.).
- Check the accuracy of HVAC system thermostats and have them calibrated if found deficient.
- Locate compressors away from heating units.
- Check size and speed of exhaust fans and limit to actual needs.
- Check doors, windows, openings, and walls for tightness. Caulk all fixed openings.
- Install adequate insulation above ceilings and walls. Concrete block walls should be covered with insulation board.
- Ventilate attic areas during hot weather.
- Install fresh air dampers in HVAC return air ducts to reduce the need for air conditioning (except for fans) during off-peak seasons.
- Fresh air makeup units should be designed so that the damper is closed when the unit is shut down.
- Install drop-panel screening to reduce solar heat accumulated through glass windows and walls in summer.
- Close the damper on unused fireplaces to prevent room heat from escaping.
- Maintain adequate humidity to eliminate the extra heat needed to ensure patient and staff comfort during winter months.
- Install water treatment system on hot water and steam systems if needed. (Chemical deposits reduce heating and cooking efficiency.)
- Balance ventilation and exhaust systems to maintain the rate of air turnover at the lowest number consistent with adequate ventilation and safety.
- Close off dining areas not in use and turn off their heating or cooling systems. (High humidity areas may require some air treatment.)
- During cold weather, draperies should be open during daylight hours to allow increased light and absorption of heat. They should be closed during the night hours to conserve heat.

LIGHTING

A light source is also a heat source inside a building. In fact, a light source approaches 100 percent efficiency in converting its energy input, at the source, to heat. This means that every 1 kilowatt (KW) input to a light results in almost 3,400 BTUs of heat. This can help in winter when heat is needed, but can be a problem in summer when the air conditioning system is working to remove heat.

Since lighting affects so many other important factors in institutional operations such as productivity and safety, a compromise must be achieved to make optimum use of the lighting system for both heat and light. It should be emphasized that one should not consider a kilowatt of power used in lighting as equivalent to a kilowatt of heating power from a furnace or boiler unless the furnace or boiler is totally electrically powered. Electrical power generated by a remote powerplant and sent many miles over transmission lines and transformers to a consumer only delivers about 30 percent of its energy to the user. Therefore, the 1 KW of lighting that results in 3,400 BTUs of heat (1 KW=3,400 BTUs actually requires many more BTUs to generate because of this low efficiency. An oil-fired boiler, on the other hand, is about 65 percent efficient, meaning that approximately 65 percent of the fuel energy that goes into the boiler actually comes out as usable heat for a building. It would, therefore, be unwise to turn an oil-fired heating system off, relying on electrical lights for heat when the light is not needed.

Nature helps to solve this problem somewhat, by providing more hours of generally brighter sunlight during the summer when the air conditioner is needed (allowing for reduced operation of interior lighting systems). During winter months the hours of available daylight are reduced; more lights are needed, and more heat is produced to help warm the building. Nevertheless, because this heat that results from light sources is generally more expensive than other sources, it is good practice to conserve where possible and to consider the availability of fuel oil or gas compared to electricity. If the building's geographical location is subject to fuel shortages, the lights provide a built-in standby heat source.

The following checklist offers suggestions for achieving maximum efficiency in lighting.

- Do not light nontask areas at the same level required for task areas. Uniform lighting in any facility can represent wasted energy.

- Take advantage of outside natural light in daylight hours, wherever possible, to reduce the need for artificial lighting indoors.
- Consider small-area switching where an individual task area may be only intermittently used.
- Limit lighted areas when only custodial work (cleaning) is being done. Lighted areas should be limited to no more than what the custodial team can clean in one hour.
- Replace incandescent lamps with flourescent or high intensity discharge lamps.
- Turn lights off when the area will be vacant for longer than thirty minutes.
- Turn all exterior lights off during the daylight hours.
- Place interior lights used for facility security on separate switches to avoid using other lights that are on the same switch.
- Maintain your lighting system to achieve maximum efficiency. Several suggestions to reduce energy consumption further include:
  1. cleaning lamp fixtures;
  2. painting ceilings and walls white or other light color;
  3. replacing fluorescent lamps whose ends have turned black;
  4. using more efficient light sources and fixtures when designing new lighting and applications.
- Disconnect ballasts if fluorescent or high intensity discharge lamps are removed from fixtures as a conservation measure. Otherwise the ballasts could still waste some electricity and could be damaged.

VENTILATION

Institutions generally require certain minimum levels of ventilation to maintain hygiene, odor control, and general comfort. These requirements are clearly stated in the various codes, standards, and other guidelines that are legally applicable. Some equipment and practices, however, result in excessive ventilation that allows conditioned air to be lost unnecessarily. Exhaust hoods over cooking equipment, for example, have been developed to minimize the amount of air discharged from the building, while adequately exhausting undesirable odors and vapors. Smoking increases the need for ventilation and results in a higher BTU demand on heating and air conditioning equipment. The following are points to consider in minimizing excessive waste of conditioned air.

- Reduce outdoor air requirements where possible in buildings, especially in high ceiling areas. Ventilation rates should not be reduced in toxic or hazardous environmental conditions or atmospheres.
- Reduce the rate of ventilation in many areas and maintain air quality by using odor-absorbing devices and better filtration.
- Examine the entire facility to eliminate all unnecessary exhaust hoods and roof ventilators.
- Turn off exhaust hoods when not in use. These are often operated on a continuous basis without performing a continuous function. Evaluate size of hoods to satisfy environmental and safety requirements.
- Size vent hoods properly. Many hoods are too large and move excessive quantities of unnecessary air.
- Utilize direct air supply on exhaust hoods wherever possible to eliminate heating and cooling large quantities of fresh makeup air, then exhausting it outdoors. This is discussed in detail in the chapter on selection of energy efficient equipment.
- Consider restricting smoking in buildings because this could further reduce the number of air changes and ventilation requirements.
- Consider preheating fresh air for ventilation in the winter with available waste heat.
- Install automatic controls to ensure operation only when needed.
- Consider connecting ventilation fans in restrooms, kitchens, etc., with the light circuit.

ELECTRICITY

Careful attention to electrically-operated equipment can help ensure that the institution not only uses less electricity, but also that the rate of computation of the electric bill is the lowest possible. Many utility companies base their charges on at least two factors:

1. the quantity of electricity used, and
2. the peak or highest demand used by the institution at any one time.

Again, many of the following points on decreasing electrical costs depend as much on careful supervision and staff awareness as on the equipment.

- Identify peak load periods and reschedule for off-peak periods. This is especially true with large motors, ovens, furnaces, and battery chargers.

- Ensure that power wiring is properly sized to prevent line losses.
- Take adequate steps to make sure that equipment is not running during lunch periods when the operator is gone, after working hours during the work week, and/or on weekends. This not only includes major equipment, but minor items as well, such as: fans, heaters, calculators, typewriters, coffee pots, desk lamps, etc. Preventive measures in this category would include the following:
   1. Assign responsibilities to supervisors.
   2. Inspect facilities at random.
   3. Instruct night supervisors to turn off items running unnecessarily during their rounds. Draft "turn off" list to be checked by volunteers under staff supervision.
- Add timeclock controls on some pieces of equipment to turn them off when they are not needed.
- Consider updating or replacing equipment that is not efficient.
- Repair or replace leaky faucets immediately. A leaky hot water faucet dripping one drop a second can drip as much as 650 gallons in a year's time. At \$.05/1000 gallons that is not alarming, but add to that a sewage charge, if applicable, as well as energy wasted to heat, pump, purify, store, and dispose of it. It all adds up.
- Turn water heater down to 75°F. (24°C.) on closing and turn to 140°F. (60°C.) two hours before opening (adjust warmup time to fit the particular units).
- Drain water heater every six months.
- Use hot water only when necessary.
- Limit general domestic use hot water to 110°F. (44°C.). Domestic hot water often consumes from two to four percent of the total energy used in health care facilities. A separate source of 130°F. (54°C.) water may be needed for special applications such as laundry.
- Clean during daylight hours, if possible.
- Mop from buckets to conserve hot water.
- Accumulate trash for full load burning frequencies when incinerators are used.
- Inspect water supply system and repair all leaks, including those at the faucets.
- Inspect and test hot water controls to determine if they are working properly. If not, regulate, repair and replace.
- Avoid using fresh, hot, or warm water for dish scraping.

- Clean and maintain refrigeration water chillers and cold drink dispensers. Disconnect refrigeration systems of water fountains, if acceptable.

- Train employees to conserve hot water. Supervise their performance and provide additional instruction and supervision as necessary. Cold water, provided in drinking fountains also is a factor in total energy consumption.

- Inspect insulation of storage tanks and piping. Repair or replace as needed. Increase the amount of insulation installed on hot water pipes or storage tanks and replace existing insulation with a type having better thermal properties ("R" value).

- Consider replacing existing hot water faucets with spray faucets with flow restrictors where practical. However, the infection control committee should be consulted before making modifications.

- Consider installing spring activated hot water taps.

- Consider having a plumber install a pressure reducing valve on the main service to restrict the amount of hot water that flows in the tap, if water pressure exceeds 40 to 50 pounds.

- Reduce generating and storage temperature levels to the minimum required for washing hands, usually about 110°F. (44°C.). Boost hot water temperature locally for kitchens and other areas where it is needed, rather than provide higher than necessary temperatures for the entire building.

- De-activate the hot water heating system, including the gas pilot if installed, if isolated cooking facilities are used only on occasion, as for conferences or meetings.

- Turn off the pump supply of hot water in noncritical areas when they are unoccupied if hot water is distributed through forced circulation.

FOOD SERVICE ENERGY CONSIDERATIONS

General considerations of overall institutional energy efficiency have been discussed, but additional energy conservation can be achieved by evaluating each department individually. As an example, the following guidelines are submitted in evaluating energy consumption and conservation in food service.

Energy conservation of fuel, therefore dollars, preferably begins before construction. Environmental requirements in planning food service departments are specifically based on two primary factors:

1. Asepsis in food service is necessary.
2. Comfortable working conditions are pertinent to obtaining and maintaining competent cooks and food service personnel.

Compliance with these two basic premises are integral components of energy management. The following recommendations are made to maximize the utilization of energy in food service.

- Locate the kitchen preferably in an area with no occupied areas above so that service equipment can be located on the roof where a source of fresh air is available and where facilities can be installed for treating and expelling the exhaust directly into the atmosphere.
  1. Provide a clear ceiling height of twelve feet with a three foot plenum above to accommodate ducts, piping, wiring, and equipment.
  2. Recess the lighting in a smooth, nonporous ceiling.
  3. Locate the dishwashing facilities and scullery together in one area in the kitchen so the common exhaust ducts can serve the dishwasher and pot washer as well.
  4. Provide partitions between the rows of ovens, griddles and steam kettles in the main cooking area. Design for efficient grouping of heat-producing equipment and hoods. (Refer to chapter on selection of energy efficient equipment for a detailed discussion of an energy efficient vent hood.)
- Reduce the heat from equipment and other sources to a minimum before designing the cooling system to handle the residual heat gain.
  1. Initiate a cost analysis to determine if the utilization of disposable dishes, cooking utensils, and tableware, could be cost effective in terms of labor so that the number of heat and steam-producing dishwashing facilities could also be reduced.
  2. Design the air distribution system so the supply air to all areas does not pass over warm equipment and then impinge upon personnel before being drawn into exhaust hoods or exhaust grills.
  3. Provide shields between equipment and cooks where the radiant effect from hot surfaces cannot be reduced by insulation.
  4. Reduce the window glazing areas to a minimum and provide solar control for all remaining glazing on an east, west, or south exposure.

- Ventilate all areas in the kitchen and maintain a negative room pressure. Provide a supplementary cooling system whenever ventilation alone cannot maintain a maximum of 82°F. (28°C.) dry bulb temperature and 60 percent relative humidity. Where practical, evaporative cooling of outdoor makeup air should be used to supplement mechanical cooling.

ALTERNATE ENERGY SOURCES

Diminishing fuel sources and rising energy costs have forced consumers to take a closer look at alternate sources of energy. Many potentials can be found for tapping the earth's vast supplies of natural and freely-occurring energy from winds, tides, and the sun, and technology is constantly moving closer to the day when these sources will become economically feasible.

Solar Energy

Energy from the sun—solar energy—is one of these sources that shows great promise for inexpensive future use. Much has been achieved already in developing the means to capture and utilize this abundant source, and some of these means are available today for practical applications. Unfortunately, a significant span still remains between total solar adequacy and today's technology, but there is reason to believe that it will soon be feasible to heat and cool most buildings from this nearly-inexhaustible supply.

The most practical application of solar devices to today's institutions is in the area of domestic hot water. Systems are available to collect solar heat for this purpose and are coupled with some additional auxiliary equipment for cloudy days. It provides an inexpensive supply of hot water.

However, before undertaking any program to install a solar domestic water system, it would be highly advisable to consult with a mechanical engineer who is qualified to assess whether a particular application is feasible. Solar energy is, as noted above, an emerging technology that is complicated by many considerations. Suitability of solar applications for existing buildings can be offset by high costs incurred by long piping systems if the building's roof structure cannot bear the additional load of solar collectors. The location of a building and its exposure to direct sunlight must also be considered. In some cases, preexisting factors will preclude solar energy applications, but in many others dramatic cost savings can result.

The trend toward more extensive use of solar energy is consistent with an overall trend to increased efficiency in all energy intensive buildings and equipment. The technology that provides economically feasible means for improving solar systems often is applicable to certain parts of mechanical systems as well. As the race continues between manufacturers and suppliers to meet this increasing competition for energy efficiency in equipment, the user benefits by having a wider selection of options available for heating and cooling a building.

The following chapter on selection of energy efficient equipment describes some of the relatively new equipment that has emerged from this trend. Hopefully, those suggestions and recommendations will provide additional ideas for "fine-tuning" the energy demands of today's institution.

NOTE

1. American Society of Heating, Refrigerating and Air-Conditioning Engineers. *Standard 90-75 Workbook* (1975).

SELECTED REFERENCE

U.S. Department of Health, Education, and Welfare. *Total Energy Management for Hospitals*. DHEW Publication No. (HRA) 77:613: 39-40.

Chapter 10

Selecting
Energy-Efficient Equipment

Although energy conservation is becoming a primary concern for nursing home and hospital administrations, innovations in energy efficiency and more economical use of equipment are essentially theories on the drawing board.

Operating food service equipment is expensive. For example, typical operating costs per hour include:

Griddles	$.31 - $ .44/hr.
Fryers	$.22 - .60/hr.
Broilers	$.33 - .60/hr.
Ovens	$.33 - .65/hr.
Ranges	$.45 - .70/hr.
Coolers	$.01 - .06/hr.
Dishwashers	$.65 - 2.80/hr.

Any reduction in energy consumption of such energy-intensive equipment translates into dollars saved.

Engineering of the future promises even more durable, more energy-efficient equipment than ever before. Three current examples of engineering of the future in vent hood, refrigeration, and dishwashing equipment are discussed in this chapter. Several other examples of ingenuity in equipment design are also reviewed to further efforts in energy conservation.

VENT HOODS

Vent hoods, which traditionally exhaust 100 percent of conditioned air within close proximity, have become a major target of energy conservation due to the high energy demand placed on other equipment to recondition air that replaces that which has been exhausted. An example of an energy conserving hood exhausts 20 percent of conditioned air from within the kitchen while the remaining 80 percent of exhausted air is supplied from unconditioned outside air.

The energy conservation attributes of this system are graphically illustrated in Exhibit 10-1.

As noted below, a kitchen is basically a box. In order to remove cooking smoke, odors, steam, or grease, air must be exhausted from the box. The amount of air exhausted from the box must be "let in" to the box. This is called makeup air and must be reconditioned, which requires energy.

Supply air leaves the slot at a high velocity. The width of this air stream is adjusted to keep it inside the filters.

The high velocity jet stream causes a reduction in air pressure inside the hood. This causes the air outside the hood to flow into the hood and provide positive capture of all cooking fumes.

Since 80 percent of the exhausted air is being supplied as unconditioned outside air, only 20 percent of the exhausted air is makeup air from the space.

For a wall-mounted hood, most codes require that 100 cubic feet of air per minute (CFM) be exhausted for every square foot of hood opening. As an example, assume the size of the hood is 10 feet long by 4 feet wide.

10' $\times$ 4' = 40 square feet of hood opening
40 square feet $\times$ 100 CFM = 4,000 CFM exhaust air required
This means that 4,000 cubic feet of air per minute must be made up.

As most food service facilities are not air-conditioned, the following examples are for winter only. In the winter, this makeup air must be heated by the building heating system. It does not matter how it is introduced into the kitchen. It must be heated before it enters or it will be heated after it enters. Either way it uses heating fuel.

The following example shows how much heating fuel will be lost in the winter with a 100 percent exhaust hood:

Exhibit 10-1 Energy Saving Vent Hood

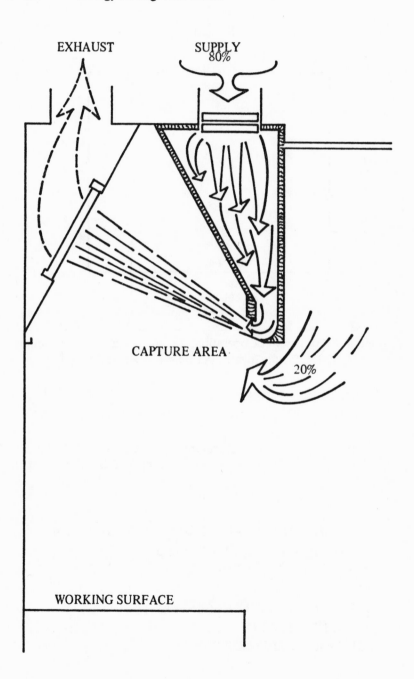

Exhibit 10-1A

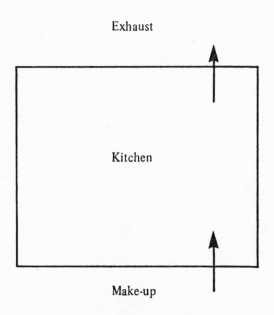

Exhaust

Kitchen

Make-up

Assume a 7 day per week operation, 12 hours per day, six months of winter temperatures, facility located in Louisville, Kentucky.

> 6 months = 182 days
> 182 days × 12 hours per day = 2,184 hours of operation.

The mean winter outside temperature for Louisville, Kentucky, is 44 degrees F. (7°C.) Inside temperature to be maintained is 72°F. (22°C.).

The formula to calculate BTUs per hour is:

> BTU/hour = Difference in temperature × 1.087 × **CFM**
> = (72°F. − 44°C.) × 1.087 × 4000
> = 28 × 1.087 × 4000
> BTU/hour = 121,744
> BTU/winter = BTU/hour × hours of operation
> = 121,744 × 2,184
> BTU/winter = 265,888,896 lost

The formula for the derivation of air constants is:

$$1.08 = .244 \times \frac{60}{13.34}$$

where .244 = specific heat of moist air at
55 F db, Btu/(deg F) (lb dry
air)
60 = min/hr
13.34 = specific volume of dry air
(cu ft/lb)

All of the following figures are based on current fuel rates and the efficiency of the system. The initial cost of the energy for new installations of the energy saving hood will be greater than that of the 100 percent exhaust hood. The cost of the 100 percent exhaust hood is subtracted from the cost of the energy saving hood to arrive at any additional cost.

(Refer to Appendix B for calculations detailing the cost per fuel of the energy saving vent hood system.)

- Gas
    Cost installed = 40¢ per cfm
    Savings = 20¢ per cfm
    Payback + 40¢ − 20¢ = 2 years.
- Oil
    Cost installed = 40¢ per cfm
    Savings = 23¢ per cfm
    Payback = 1.7 years
- Electric
    Cost installed = 40¢ per cfm
    Savings = 73¢ per cfm
    Payback = 4 months

Conversion Installations

Using a conversion package on an existing system

- Gas
    Cost Installed = $1.00 per cfm
    Savings = 20¢ per cfm
    Payback = 5 years
- Oil
    Cost Installed = $1.00 per cfm
    Savings = 23¢ per cfm
    Payback = 4.3 years

- Electric
    Cost Installed = $1.00 per cfm
    Savings = 73¢
    Payback = 1.4 years

If the kitchen area is air-conditioned or if makeup air is pulled from an air-conditioned space, the savings increase significantly. Another way to look at this is to realize that since this system requires only 20 percent makeup air from the space, it may be economical to temper the kitchen air to 80°-85°F. (60°-67°C.) to increase efficiency and reduce turnover in personnel.

A word of caution. Insist that: (1) the hood system, which includes fans, is balanced by an independent test and balance contractor, who (2) furnishes valid test data, verifying that only 20 percent makeup air is being pulled from the kitchen.

By considering the maximum payback of only two years with the energy saving vent hood in a new installation, the alternative of reduced initial costs but rising costs of energy leads to an obvious determination.

REFRIGERATION EQUIPMENT

It has taken several years for industry to become conscious of the type, availability, and cost of energy sources required to operate refrigeration units. Refrigeration is the one system that operates on a 24-hour basis. When operating properly, refrigeration accounts for 2 percent of the total operational energy budget. However, refrigeration equipment is often inefficiently used and poorly maintained. Unless carefully monitored by dietary personnel, energy consumption by refrigeration units can easily become 10 percent and even 30 percent of the operational energy budget. Unfortunately, because refrigerators and freezers are simple to operate, the basic techniques for utilizing and conserving energy are often neglected.

As with the principles behind vent hoods, electrical energy is consumed by refrigeration and freezing equipment in the process of heat removal. Refrigeration heat is introduced from four sources: the product load, ambient air, the physical structure of the cabinet, and the mechanical components that are always operating. Naturally, the size of the product load, and the total area of the product zone that must be cooled, are prime factors in determining the amount of energy that will be required to remove the heat produced by the refrigeration unit. Other factors that boost energy consumption in the unit include warm air leakage into the cabinet area (the more doors into the unit, the more areas for leakage); and the size of the compressor motor, fan motors and other heat removal apparatuses.

Because the sole purpose of the refrigeration unit is to combat warm air and heat from displacing the cooler air of the product zone area, energy conservation for refrigeration requires that there is conscious management of the units for operation, maintenance, and planning (as well as renovations.) In selecting a refrigeration system to ensure energy conservation:

- Evaluate N.S.F. Standards. What does the National Sanitation Foundation require for operational conditions? "Running time" is the important factor (compressor running time vs. compressor off time). Determining the "running time" can provide a direct rating of the electrical consumption performance of the system. Established NSF standards are based on the maximum permissible compressor running times in refrigeration units that are not loaded. Systems that can operate efficiently on less than the maximum are considered to be energy conservative. Exhibits 10-2 and 10-3 illustrate the electrical consumption of various NSF-approved refrigeration units.

- Consider the capacities. Remember that a system too large wastes energy and too small a system prevents proper air circulation. The basic guidelines to determine the capacity of refrigeration equipment to meet a facility's needs are 35 lbs. of food stored per cubic foot of freezer space and 1 to 1½ cubic feet of refrigeration space allotted per person to be served. When speaking to the manufacturers, knowledge of these capacities demonstrate that energy conservation is a priority of kitchen-planning.

- Evaluate door design. The smallest door that is practical means a reduction in the amount of heat that can enter when doors are open.

- Evaluate insulation: As with anything else that requires insulation, the better the insulation, the less energy consumed. Unlike what is expected, the main role of insulation is not to contain the cold, but to prevent warm air from penetrating the unit and elevating the temperature. This is why the term "heat transfer" is important. Insulation can range from a metal-clad foam urethane panel to a fiberglass sheet. The choice between these materials is comparable to the temperature retention of Styrofoam as compared to cardboard. The reduction in continuing costs of energy utilization overshadow the higher initial costs of effective insulation.

- Assess new energy design features. Some manufacturers are including built in devices to reduce energy consumption further.

Exhibit 10-2 Total Cabinet Electrical Consumption

Upright Cabinets	Cubic Foot Capacity	Condensing Unit Size	Percent Running Time per Hour	KWH/ 24 hr. Period	Daily Elec. Cost
Product Zone Coil:					
Refrigerator					
1 section Reach-in	22	1/4 (115 V.)	25%	7.1 KWH	0.32
2 section Reach-in	47	1/3 (115 V.)	30%	11.6	0.52
3 section Reach-in	72	1/2 (115 V.)	35%	17.2	0.77
Freezer					
1 section Reach-in	22	1/3 (115 V.)	65%	23.0	1.04
2 section Reach-in	47	1/2 (115 V.)	59%	23.9	1.08
3 section Reach-in	72	3/4 (208 V.)	62%	35.0	1.58
Display Refrig. Full Glass Doors					
2 section Reach-in	47	1/2 (115 V.)	40%	14.8	0.67
3 section Reach-in	72	3/4 (208 V.)	37%	16.8	0.76
Top Mounted Coil:					
Refrigerator					
1 section Reach-in	24	1/4 (115 V.)	30%	6.8	0.31
2 section Reach-in	48	1/3 (115 V.)	40%	15.8	0.71
1 section Roll-in	34	1/3 (115 V.)	47%	18.3	0.82
2 section Roll-in	67	1/2 (115 V.)	38%	20.3	0.91
Freezer					
1 section Reach-in	24	1/2 (115 V.)	52%	17.9	0.81
2 section Reach-in	48	3/4 (208 V.)	49%	27.8	1.25
3 section Reach-in	72	1 (208 V.)	43%	25.3	1.14
Dual Temp. - Fr./Ref.					
1 section Reach-in:					
Freezer	10	1/4 (115 V.)	53%	23.4	1.05
Refrigerator	10	1/5 (115 V.)	22%	6.2	0.28

Testing conducted for 24 hour period without product load and doors closed in 90°F. (32°C.) ambient room. Current price of 4.5¢ per KWH (1-78)

1. Defogger controls regulate the heating wires built into the door frame, preventing condensation on the door opening area.

2. Hot gas-line condensate vaporizer evaporates and defrosts the water in the refrigeration system. It has been found that an older heating element vaporizer can evaporate up to 4 ounces

Exhibit 10-3 Walk-in Compressor Running Times

			Compressor Run Time
50°F.	Walk-in Meat Preparation Room		22 hrs.
35°F.	Walk-in Cooler:	Light Load	16 hrs.
		Heavy Load	16 hrs.
35°F.	Walk-in Cooler with Glass Doors		16 hrs.
28°F.	Walk-in Cooler:	Light Load	18 hrs.
		Heavy Load	18 hrs.
0°F.	Walk-in Freezer:	Light Load	18 hrs.
		Heavy Load	18 hrs.
-10°F.	Walk-in Freezer:	Light Load	18 hrs.
		Heavy Load	18 hrs.
-20°F.	Walk-in Freezer:	Light Load	18 hrs.
		Heavy Load	18 hrs.

Testing conducted for 24 hour period without product load and doors closed in 90°F. (32°C.) ambient room. Current price of 4.5¢ per KWH (1-78). *Information courtesy of Victory Manufacturing.*

Tested for 24 hour period in 90°F. ambient. *Information courtesy of Singer Climate Control Division.*

---

of water per hour, while the new hot gas-line vaporizers evaporate approximately 12 ounces per hour. This reduces the humidity of the entire kitchen considerably.

3. Magnetic door gaskets ensure tight door closing.

4. Door hinges that are self-closing provide a positive seal and prevent air leakage. Often the employee does not have "free" hands to close the door.

5. Time-activated automatic defrost controllers permit management to determine defrost periods. When coils are free of any frost, the cycle ends and the energy consumption of defrosting is shortened.

• Consider installation factors. In addition to all design features, installation considerations will affect consumption of electricity.

1. Locate the unit in the work flow pattern that will result in adequate air circulation and a cool working environment.

2. Do not install refrigeration units near heat producing or moisture venting equipment.

3. Provide the compressor with plenty of free air exchange to discharge heat.

4. Use the heat from the condensers for other areas such as heating the dishwasher water.

5. Assure refrigeration is installed on a level surface. Any tilting affects the automatic sealing of the doors, especially if they are self-closing.

DISHWASHING EQUIPMENT

Since dishwashers represent the most concentrated consumption of energy per hour (four times any other equipment), proper selection could mean the difference in considerable sums spent or saved. Selecting dishwashing equipment today involves more than the initial capital expenditure. The following considerations should be included in the selection process.

- Fuel costs:
  1. electricity to operate the dishwasher motor
  2. gas to heat the water and boost the temperature
- Ventilation system costs to remove the heat from the dishwashing area
- Water usage costs to reflect quantity of water necessary to operate the dishwasher (Few people realize they are charged for this.)
- Sewage costs to indicate the amount of water discharged into local drains (This is another less familiar cost factor.)
- Peak-demand factor costs (Dishwashing machines using 220 volts, can add to peak demand loads, increasing the rate charged.)
- Other hidden costs (These are primarily due to the high temperatures required for sanitizing purposes.)
  1. Parts wear faster and continued extreme heat further increases maintenance costs.
  2. Plastic ware and china have a shorter life expectancy under high temperature conditions.
  3. Employees can easily become burned or shocked by the 180°F. (82°C.) temperature of dishwashers, causing burns or breakage of items that are being "run through" the unit.

Cold Chemical System

The cold chemical dishwashing system, unlike the traditional hot temperature dishwashers, requires only 110 volts (normal household current) and utilizes domestic water temperature, resulting in substantial savings of energy, therefore, dollars. The sanitizing process is effectively accomplished by chemicals sanitizing every rack of dishes. Laboratory tests prove that the cold chemical dishwashing system is far more effective in destroying bacteria than its more traditional counterpart. Furthermore, local health departments have reviewed this system with enthusiasm, sanctioning its use.

Savings abound since many of the costs of dishwashing initially outlined with the hot temperature system have been eliminated.

- Electrical costs are reduced because 220 volts are not needed and a smaller primary heater is used. Booster and sustainer motors are not needed.
- Fuel costs are reduced because the water is not boosted to 180°F. (82°C.) since the chemicals are completing the sanitizing portion of the rinse cycle.
- A ventilation system is not needed since little heat is given off.
- Water usage is decreased because the cold chemical dishwasher utilizes less water.
- Sewage costs are decreased because less water is used.
- The peak demand factor cost is decreased as the machine is using 110 volts, and this is the primary level of operation for the rest of the facility.
- Hidden costs are reduced as:
  1. Lower temperatures mean parts will not wear as quickly and maintenance costs will be reduced.
  2. Plasticware and china last longer.
  3. Employees will not likely be burned, as with a high temperature system, and the dishes are cold to the touch and easier to handle, yielding essentially less breakage.

Extending the advantages of a cold chemical dishwashing system into dollars, the savings on energy expenditures are summarized as follows:

No booster heater	$ 450.00
No ventilation system	$1,500.00
Smaller primary heater	$ 500.00

No 220 volt circuit	$ 300.00
40% less water & sewage used	varies
Approximate savings on	
maintenance per month	$25-$50/month
40% longer life of plasticware	
and china	varies

Conservatively, an energy expenditure savings of $3,050 per year (without the cost of water, sewage and plasticware or china included) could be realized with the cold chemical dishwashing system. In the interest of economics and sanitation, the cold chemical system of dishwashing bears serious consideration.

In considering the cold chemical dishwashing system, the energy costs (electricity and gas) should be analyzed for each facility. Use the form indicated in Exhibits 10-4 and 10-5 to determine the cost differential between your present machine and the cold chemical dishwashing machine.

Two examples of actual calculations are given in Exhibits 10-6, 10-7, 10-8, and 10-9. The first is for a 100-bed facility using a single tank model (refer to Exhibits 10-6 and 10-7), and the second is for a 200-bed facility using a double tank model (refer to Exhibits 10-8 and 10-9). The information was calculated with the length of operation of the dishwashing machines being used 6 and 8 hours a day respectively, that allows an average of 2 hours per meal for all dishwashing. With the following information, a comparative energy analysis can be calculated for any dishwashing system and the cold chemical dishwashing system.

Explanation of Electricity Usage

1. Booster—KW or AMPs required to operate booster are on the information plate of every dishwasher. (The cold chemical dishwashing system does not require a booster unit.)
2. Sustainer—Located on the dishwasher's information plate. (The cold chemical dishwashing system does not require a sustainer.)
3. Pump motor—Located on the information plate of the units.
4. This information is then totaled and multiplied by the number of volts used for total KW used. (The KW of the booster is added at this point.)
5. Rate—This figure is what local utility companies charge per KW. This information can be obtained from the local power company. (Be certain to ask for commercial rate billing as opposed to residential rate billing.)

Exhibit 10-4 Energy Cost Analysis Form

ELECTRICITY USAGE

"Hot" Dishwasher

1. Booster _____ amps
2. Sustainer _____ amps
3. Pump Motor _____ amps

   Total Amps Used _____ amps

   Volts (220 or 110) _____ 110 Volts

   Amps x Volts = Total Watts

   Total Watts _____ watts

   Total Watts ÷ 1000 = KWH _____ KWH

4. KWH _____ KW
5. Rate (local) _____ per KW
6. Cost Per hour = KW x Rate $_____ $_____
7. Hours used per day _____

   *Cost Per Day $_____ $_____
   (hours used x cost per day)

   *Cost Per Month (year ÷ 12) $_____

   *Cost Per Year (day x 365) $_____

GAS USAGE

"Hot" Dishwasher   vs.   "Cold" Dishwasher

Cold Chemical Dishwasher

1. Gas Rate (local) $_____ $_____
2. Cost per M (gallons) 100° rise–primary heater $_____   150°$_____

   Taken from Column G (A.O. Smith)
3. Cost per M (gallons) 30° rise–booster heater $_____   180°$_____

   Taken from Chart 3 (A.O. Smith)
4. Total Cost per M Gallons $_____ $_____

   (Line no. 2 and Line no. 3 added together)
5. Gallons per Hour – Usage by machine _____

   (date for NSF Food Service Listing)
6. Operating Hours per Day _____
7. Gallons Used per Day _____

   (Line no. 5 x Line no. 6)
8. Number of M Gallons _____

   (Line no. 7 ÷ 1000)

   *Cost Per Day $_____ $_____
   (or Line 4 x Line 8)

   *Cost Per Month (year ÷ 12) $_____ $_____

   *Cost Per Year (day x 365) $_____ $_____

Exhibit 10-5 Energy Cost Analysis Recap Form

Energy costs have doubled in the past 24 months. All experts in the field say that this trend will continue at an ever-increasing rate. Being on top of "Energy Costs" can mean the difference in staying in business for many in the years ahead.

The savings noted below do not take into account the elimination of the vent for exhaust systems which can increase air conditioning and heating costs. Nor is the savings for 40% less water usage, and the resulting reduced sewage bill calculated here.

The amp information is found on the data plate of all dishmachines and booster heaters. The costs for heating water with natural gas are based on data prepare by A. O. Smith, a manufacturer of commercial hot water heaters. Water consumption data is taken from the NSF food service manual for commercial dishwashers. This analysis for gas computes the cost of raising the temperature of tap water to the required 180°for warewashing, based on an estimated running time. There is no provision in this analysis for determining the cost of the gas powered sustainer heater which is built into the dishwasher for the purpose of maintaining the wash temperature at the required 140°throughout the day. Instead, only the primary and booster heating costs can be readily calculated.

	"Hot" Dishwasher	Cold Chemical Dishwasher	Savings Differential
Electricity Cost per Year	_____	_____	_____
Gas Cost per Year	_____	_____	_____
Total Energy Cost per Day	_____	_____	_____
Total Energy Cost per Month (Year ÷ 12)	_____	_____	_____
Total Energy Cost per Year (Day X 365)	_____	_____	_____

Prepared for:_____ Prepared by:_____

---

6. Cost per hour—Calculated by multiplying KW × rate.

7. Hours used per day—This varies with the operation. Analyze the dishwashing machine operation for accurate determination.

The cost per day, per month, and per year is then calculated and the results are shown on the summarization sheet (Exhibit 10-5).

Exhibit 10-6 Energy Cost Analysis Form

Energy Cost Analysis Form
100 Bed Facility

Single Tank Models
Cold Chemical Dishwasher

ELECTRICITY USAGE

	"Hot" Dishwasher	Cold Chemical Dishwasher
1. Booster	12 amps	N/A amps
2. Sustainer	5 amps	N/A amps
3. Pump Motor	2.75 amps	13 amps
Total Amps Used	2.75 amps	13 amps
Volts (220 or 110)	220 Volts	110 Volts
Amps x Volts = Total Watts		
Total Watts	605 watts	1430 watts
Total Watts ÷ 1000 = KWH	.6 KWH	1.4 KWH
4. KWH	17.6 KW	1.4 KW
5. Rate (local)	$.04 per KW	$.04 per KW
6. Cost Per hour = KW x Rate	$ .70	$ .056
7. Hours used per day	6	6
*Cost Per Day (hours used x cost per day)	$ 4.20	$ .366
*Cost Per Month (year ÷ 12)	$127.75	$ 10.22
*Cost Per Year (day x 365)	$1533.00	$122.64

GAS USAGE

	"Hot" Dishwasher	"Hot" vs. "Cold" Dishwasher
1. Gas Rate (local)	$ 1.90	$ 1.90
2. Cost per M (gallons) 100° rise-primary heater	$ 2.51 150°	$ 2.51
Taken from Column G (A.O. Smith)		
3. Cost per M (gallons) 30° rise-booster heater	$ N/A 180°	N/A
Taken from Chart 3 (A.O. Smith)		
4. Total Cost per M Gallons (Line no. 2 and Line no. 3 added together)	$ 2.51	$ 2.51
5. Gallons per Hour – Usage by machine (date for NSF Food Service Listing)	91	48
6. Operating Hours per Day	6	6
7. Gallons Used per Day (Line no. 5 x Line no. 6)	546	288
8. Number of M Gallons (Line no. 7 ÷ 1000)	.546	.288
*Cost Per Day (or Line 4 x Line 8)	$ 1.37	$ .72
*Cost Per Month (year ÷ 12)	$ 41.67	$ 21.99
*Cost Per Year (day x 365)	$ 500.05	$ 263.85

Exhibit 10-7 Energy Cost Analysis Recap Form

100 Bed Facility
Single Tank Model

Energy costs have doubled in the past 24 months. All experts in the field say that this trend will continue at an ever-increasing rate. Being on top of "Energy Costs" can mean the difference in staying in business for many in the years ahead.

The savings noted below do not take into account the elimination of the vent for exhaust systems which can increase air conditioning and heating costs. Nor is the savings for 40% less water usage, and the resulting reduced sewage bill calculated here.

The amp information is found on the data plate of all dishmachines and booster heaters. The costs for heating water with natural gas are based on data prepare by A. O. Smith, a manufacturer of commercial hot water heaters. Water consumption data is taken from the NSF food service manual for commercial dishwashers. This analysis for gas computes the cost of raising the temperature of tap water to the required 180° for warewashing, based on an estimated running time. There is no provision in this analysis for determining the cost of the gas powered sustainer heater which is built into the dishwasher for the purpose of maintaining the wash temperature at the required 140° throughout the day. Instead, only the primary and booster heating costs can be readily calculated.

	"Hot" Dishwasher	Cold Chemical Dishwasher	Savings Differential
Electricity Cost per Year	$ 127.75	$ 10.22	$ 117.53
Gas Cost per Year	$ 41.67	$ 21.99	$ 19.68
Total Energy Cost per Day	$ 5.57	$ 1.06	$ 4.24
Total Energy Cost per Month (Year ÷ 12)	$ 169.42	$ 32.21	$ 137.21
Total Energy Cost per Year (Day X 365)	$ 2033.04	$ 386.52	$ 1646.52

Prepared for:_____ Prepared by:_____

Explanation of Gas Usage

1. Gas Rate—This local rate, per BTU, is for the cost of natural gas per/1000 cu. ft. Information can be provided by the local gas company for commercial use facilities.

2. Cost per M(gallons)
   100 degree rise—primary heater—This information was taken from an A. O. Smith copper-coil gas heater chart prepared by A. O. Smith

Exhibit 10-8 Energy Cost Analysis Form

Energy Cost Analysis Form
200 Bed Facility
Double Tank Models
Cold Chemical Dishwasher

ELECTRICITY USAGE

	"Hot" Dishwasher	
1. Booster	45 amps	N/A amps
2. Sustainer	15 amps	N/A amps
3. Pump Motor	2.75 amps	26 amps
Total Amps Used	2.75 amps	26 amps
Volts (220 or 110)	220 Volts	110 Volts
Amps x Volts = Total Watts		
Total Watts	605 watts	2860 watts
Total Watts ÷ 1000 = KWH	.6 KWH	.286 KWH
4. KWH	61 KW	3 KW
5. Rate (local)	.04 per KW	.04 per KW
6. Cost Per hour = KW x Rate	$ 2.44	$ .12
7. Hours used per day	8	8
*Cost Per Day	$ 19.52	$ .96
(hours used x cost per day)		
*Cost Per Month (year ÷ 12)	$ 593.73	$ 29.20
*Cost Per Year (day x 365)	$ 7124.80	$ 350.40

GAS USAGE

	"Hot" Dishwasher	"Cold" Dishwasher
1. Gas Rate (local)	$ 1.90	$ 1.90
2. Cost per M (gallons) 100° rise-primary heater	$ 2.51 150°	$ 2.51
Taken from Column G (A.O. Smith)		
3. Cost per M (gallons) 30° rise-booster heater	$ N/A 180°	$ N/A
Taken from Chart 3 (A.O. Smith)		
4. Total Cost per M Gallons	$ 2.51	$ 2.51
(Line no. 2 and Line no. 3 added together)		
5. Gallons per Hour – Usage by machine	450	92
(date for NSF Food Service Listing)		
6. Operating Hours per Day	8	8
7. Gallons Used per Day (Line no. 5 x Line no. 6)	3600	736
8. Number of M Gallons (Line no. 7 ÷ 1000)	3.600	.736
*Cost Per Day (or Line 4 x Line 8)	$ 9.04	$ 1.85
*Cost Per Month (year ÷ 12)	$ 274.97	$ 56.27
*Cost Per Year (day x 365)	$ 3299.60	$ 675.25

Exhibit 10-9 Energy Cost Analysis Recap Form

200 Bed Facility
Double Tank Model

Energy costs have doubled in the past 24 months. All experts in the field say that this trend will continue at an ever-increasing rate. Being on top of "Energy Costs" can mean the difference in staying in business for many in the years ahead.

The savings noted below do not take into account the elimination of the vent for exhaust systems which can increase air conditioning and heating costs. Nor is the savings for 40% less water usage, and the resulting reduced sewage bill calculated here.

The amp information is found on the data plate of all dishmachines and booster heaters. The costs for heating water with natural gas are based on data prepare by A. O. Smith, a manufacturer of commercial hot water heaters. Water consumption data is taken from the NSF food service manual for commercial dishwashers. This analysis for gas computes the cost of raising the temperature of tap water to the required $180°$ for warewashing, based on an estimated running time. There is no provision in this analysis for determining the cost of the gas powered sustainer heater which is built into the dishwasher for the purpose of maintaining the wash temperature at the required $140°$ throughout the day. Instead, only the primary and booster heating costs can be readily calculated.

	"Hot" Dishwasher	Cold Chemical Dishwasher	Savings Differential
Electricity Cost per Year	$ 593.73	$ 29.20	$ 564.53
Gas Cost per Year	$ 274.97	$ 56.27	$ 218.70
Total Energy Cost per Day	$ 28.56	$ 2.81	$ 25.75
Total Energy Cost per Month (Year ÷ 12)	$ 868.70	$ 85.47	$ 783.23
Total Energy Cost per Year (Day X 365)	$ 10,424.40	$ 1025.64	$ 9398.76

Prepared for:_____ Prepared by:_____

Corp. (1977). These can be obtained from anyone who manufactures or demonstrates gas heaters for fuel cost comparisons.

Specifically, the approximate cost per 1000 gallons of hot water is needed, at a 100° rise from the temperature at which the water is supplied through water lines (the water comes in at 50°F. (10°C.), and is boosted by the primary heater to 150°F. (66°C.).

3. Cost per M(gallons)

30 degree rise—booster heater—This information also was taken

from the A. O. Smith chart as according to regulations, the rinse water must reach 180°F. (82°C.); this is a 30° rise in temperature. To reach this, the cost of #2 on the form is multiplied by .3 as an adjustment factor.

The cold chemical dishwashing system does not require any "boosting" and so this cost is avoided.

4. Total cost—The addition of the costs of the 100 degree increase and the 30° rise translated into local gas rates per 100 gallons.

5. Gallons per hour usage by machine—This information is specific to the machine you use. The National Sanitation Foundation can supply this information as can the manufacturer of any dishwasher.

   Specifically needed is the final rinse usage of gallons per hour at 20 p.s.i. flow (per square inch). This is an NSF standard for each machine produced.

6. Operating hours per day—Again, this varies with the operation.

7. Gallons used per day—This gives the total number of gallons used.

8. Number of M Gallons—Since the charts for cost are calculated for M gallons (1,000 gallons), conversion must occur. The cost per day, month, and year are calculated, and the results are shown on the summarization sheet.

MISCELLANEOUS EQUIPMENT

Energy efficiency has become one of the primary considerations in selecting food service equipment. Such considerations apply to equipment requiring large capital expenditures (i.e. refrigeration and dishwashing systems) as well as smaller investment items such as griddles and fryers.

Griddles

Energy innovations in griddles have now produced a product with a trivalent chromium surface bonded to a carbon steel plate which yields an energy emission of only 10 percent of the average emission of a standard hard steel grill top. In brief, only 10 percent of the potential heating energy of the grill top is being discharged from the plate and lost to the atmosphere as opposed to the 90 percent energy lost by the standard type griddle. Obviously, much less energy is required, and when the grill is not actively being used, the surface temperature of the griddle is maintained without extra energy.

Fryers

Energy continues to be conserved in the newly designed fryers that use both infrared and conductive heating principles through heat transfer tubes. This is accomplished by using cold rolled steel and transfer tube baffles. Subsequently, an additional energy source is received by double utilization of the same BTUs.

Ovens

Saving energy, therefore dollars, is further realized with "continuous cleaning" ovens as contrasted to self-cleaning ones. Self-cleaning ovens require an energy and time-consuming procedure of turning the oven temperature to an extremely high level to burn off the baked on particles while the continuous cleaning catalytic process uses the same heat required in normal cooking cycles to accomplish the same goal. The energy differences are significant.

Hot Top Ranges

Electric hot top ranges are now designed to offer unique energy saving features as well. Utilizing two 18 inch plates, with two separate controls, one for the front and back of each plate, flexible management of the energy used in the cooking process is possible. Older models use three 12 inch plates, each with only one single control. The new ranges can cook effectively with only one-fourth of the total available energy while other ranges must use two-thirds of the total energy to accomplish the same goal.

Tilted Braising Pans

The engineering ingenuity incorporated into the new tilted braising pans provides an additional opportunity to conserve energy. For example, the gas-fired unit uses a bi-metal pan bottom to transfer heat as a cold rolled steel plate is bonded to the stainless steel bottom to hold and conduct the heat. The burner unit uses 35 miniature gas jets, firing through individually fired tunnels that run the entire length of the pan. The heat is, therefore, transferred evenly under the pan surface which creates the desired temperature and maintains the same temperature with 30 percent less gas consumption than is required by other units.

Plumbing Innovations

Innovations in plumbing have produced spout attachments that can be added to all faucets to reduce the flow of water, saving three-fourths of a gallon of water per minute. Even by reducing the water consumption up to 90 percent, a steady stream of water and economy result.

Incinerators

Some larger institutions, strangled by energy costs, have installed a trash-heat recovery incinerator that provides heat for the entire facility, yielding a per annum savings of $14,000 on the amount of natural gas conserved alone. (Electrical energy savings vary more with the locality.) This system costs approximately $175,000, but coupled with savings of $20,000 to $24,000 a year in trash compacting and trash removal bills, the initial capital expenditure could be recouped in approximately four years for larger facilities.

Careful selection of durable, energy-efficient food service equipment cannot be overemphasized. Poorly engineered products can create costly problems, and the money initially saved is insignificant when compared to the economically-oriented field of energy conservation.

PREVENTIVE MAINTENANCE PROGRAM

The proper and frequent maintenance of food service equipment can significantly contribute to energy conservation. Clean, well-maintained equipment operates at maximum efficiency and, in many cases, means a more efficient use of all energy. If a switch, thermostat, contactor, or heating element fails on a piece of electrical equipment, the equipment will not function properly until it is repaired. There are some things that can happen to electric cooking equipment that may not take the equipment out of service, but will affect its performance to the extent that energy is wasted through inefficiency and improper finishing of foods.

- Obtain exact manufacturer's specifications for each item of equipment.
- Install equipment properly per specifications.
- Fasten thermostat bulbs and capillary tubes properly in place to keep equipment from malfunctioning. These controls can be visually inspected in ovens, fryers, and broilers without any difficulty. A loose thermostat bulb on a range or griddle will cause erratic heating. Thermostats and other controls should also be checked periodically to ensure proper operations.
- Check oven doors to be sure they are closing properly.
- Replace burned out indicator lamps so that the cook can tell if the

equipment is on and when it has reached the desired operating temperature.

- Clean equipment regularly to increase energy saving and provide a longer service life for the equipment. Maintenance does mean cleaning, caring, and maintaining old equipment as well. Job breakdown cards on the proper cleaning, care and operation of each piece of equipment in the kitchen should be initiated, maintained and updated on an annual basis. Refer to Exhibit 10-10.

- Be familiar with each piece of equipment and hold in-service education programs on the proper care, cleaning, operation, and pertinent points of maintenance.

- Establish a cleaning schedule and post it in the kitchen for easy reference by employees. An example of a cleaning schedule is shown in Exhibit 10-11.

A regular cleaning schedule for dishwashing equipment specifically is also highly pertinent to energy cost reduction. Keeping equipment clean will ensure that dishes are properly cleaned the first time rather than doubling the amount of water and energy used when it becomes necessary to wash them a second time. Being certain that silverware is adequately presoaked and dishes are properly rinsed prior to washing will also reduce the length of operating time required, thereby conserving energy and dollars.

Water leakage is another costly operating factor of food service. A leak of only 60 drops of water per minute yields a monthly water loss of 210 gallons. Even this relatively minor leak can amount to many dollars "down the drain." Repairing leaky pipes and water faucets can assist in providing funds to hire a maintenance employee on a regular basis.

- Monitor cleaning and maintenance schedules of food service equipment. Monitor the performance of new equipment and have adjustments made immediately. Consider initiating a department maintenance review committee to monitor your department's equipment more closely.

- Maintain a "life history" of each piece of equipment in addition to the names and addresses of dealers and service representatives.

Drafting and maintaining a functional preventive maintenance program is a vital component to energy conservation. However, the procedures followed in day-to-day usage bear directly on energy expenditure and are discussed in the chapter on essential operation of equipment.

Exhibit 10-10 Job Breakdown Card

HOW TO CLEAN A BUNNOMATIC

Equipment and Supplies Needed: Cleaning Products Needed:
  2 cloths: Detergent:
    1 to wash   In amount needed to make one gal solution
    1 to dry   Proportion: 1 oz to 1 gal water
  2 - 1 gallon containers   Sanitizing Agent: Bleach
                                1/4 oz per gallon water
          Approximate Time: 10 minutes
          Frequency of cleaning: After each use
          Approximate Cost: Labor _____
                         Supplies _____

What To Do	How To Do It
1. Turn off.	1a. Black switch on left.
2. Remove basket and filter.	2a. Throw away filter.
3. Wash basket.	3a. Wash. Rinse. Sanitize.
4. Clean inside of unit.	4a. Press brew button once. b. With pot underneath.
5. Clean glass pot.	5a. Wash. Rinse. Sanitize.
6. Clean outside of unit.	6a. With water and detergent. b. Rinse. c. Dry.

HOW TO OPERATE A BUNNOMATIC

1. Turn on.	1a. Black switch on left.
2. Remove basket from coffee maker.	2a. Pull handle on front.
3. Place paper filter in basket.	
4. Empty coffee packet into filter.	
5. Return basket to position.	5a. Into slots b. Under the top of coffee maker in front.
6. Set glass pot on unit.	6a. After rinsing with hot water. b. Under the basket.
7. Push brew button.	7a. On right hand side of coffee maker.
8. Turn on warmer units as necessary.	

Exhibit 10-11 Sanitation Schedule

DAILY	MON	TUE	WED	THU	FRI
1. Clean all used equipment; cleaned by user					
2. Wash steam table					
3. Wash top of range					
4. Wash milk box					
5. Leave dishwasher clean					
6. Straighten and wipe out refrigerator					
7. Sweep storeroom and do any necessary straightening					
8. Wash garbage cans or have them washed					
9. Mop kitchen					
10. Mop dining room					
WEEKLY	Week 1	Week 2	Week 3	Week 4	
1. Thoroughly clean refrigerator, including top					
2. Clean storeroom - before date of deliveries					
3. Clean drawers and dish cabinets, including tops					
4. Wipe down vent hood inside. Check filters					
MONTHLY					
1. Wash back doors, inside and out; wash windows, inside and out; wash light fixtures					
2. Clean around legs of equipment and plumbing; clean vent hood inside and out					
3. Defrost freezer as needed					

DATE _____

SELECTED REFERENCES

"The Hospital Market: Great Potential for Energy Management." *Air Conditioning and Refrigeration Business Journal.* Aug. 1977, 36-38.

"How to Install and Maintain an Energy-Efficient Dishwasher." *Equipment Specialist.* June 1978, pp. 38-42.

Ley, Sandra. *Fundamentals of Food Service Refrigeration,* C.B.I. Publishing Company, 1979.

Chapter 11

Essential Operation of Equipment

Although it is desirable, it is not essential to begin with kitchen design and equipment selection to institute good energy management practices. An existing kitchen may have been designed for maximum efficiency but is not being fully utilized. To increase fuel efficiency, energy management principles for cooking equipment, refrigerated storage equipment, hot food holding transport equipment, warewashing machines, and ventilation systems will be discussed.

GENERAL ENERGY GUIDELINES

The largest part of energy used by food surfaces is for preparation and storage of food. Preparation equipment may be operated as long as 10 to 14 hours per day, although food storage equipment is operated 24 hours a day. This results in high energy consumption. More than half this energy may not be used to cook the food but can be lost in the atmosphere of the kitchen. By utilizing simple energy conscious preparation procedures such as the following, significant energy reduction can result. These guidelines, compiled from recommendations made by the National Restaurant Association and Midwest Research as well as the Federal Energy Commission, can literally become the building blocks for the construction of your food service energy efficiency program. (An energy management analysis is also included in the Appendix C to evaluate the energy utilized by your facility.

Peak Loading

Reduce peak loading. Bake a roast during off hours. Use high energy demand equipment sequentially, rather than simultaneously as many utility companies base their rates and pricing on peak load use. It is a good energy management practice to turn the cooking equipment off or set the controls back to a lower temperature that would require less energy to maintain during slack periods of the day. Menus may also need to be reevaluated to balance peak loading times, especially for heavy duty equipment.

In addition to charging for electrical energy used, electric utilities also charge a customer according to the maximum kilowatt demand established during each billing period. While keeping the kilowatt demand low may not necessarily save energy, it may save money for the food service operator. To keep the demand for electric energy as low as is practical will require determining the time of day that the peak electrical demand is established and then checking if any cooking equipment may be on during this period of time. If equipment is on during the peak, the amount this equipment contributes to the maximum demand should be determined. Finally, a decision may be made on whether it is worthwhile to change or reschedule the food production operation to eliminate using the equipment at that time. If preheating of kitchen equipment is responsible for creating the maximum meter demand, then staggering the preheating of equipment may help keep the maximum energy demand down.

Listed below are some suggestions to alternatives to peak loading:

Potatoes:

- For instant potatoes prepare by using tap water through the booster heater instead of boiling water.
- For baked potatoes do not wrap in aluminum foil while baking because that increases baking time. A metal skewer inserted lengthwise into each potato can serve to decrease baking time.

Meats:

- Roast as full a load as possible in a convection oven, starting with a cold oven. No preheating is necessary.
- Bacon can be placed in a cold convection oven, heated to temperature and turned off while it is still slightly raw. The fan can remain on and the bacon will continue to cook until it is done.

Rice:

- Instant and regular can be left to "bloom" in cold water overnight.

Instant then only needs reheating; regular will require less cooking time.

Vegetables:

- Many do not need to be boiled. Reduce cooking temperature to 180°F. (82°C.) for carrots, peas, and corn. Experiment with heating vegetables directly on the steam table in lieu of heating twice on both the range and the steam table.

Frozen foods:

- Thaw in refrigerator before cooking.

In sauces and many gravies, puddings and dessert sauces, cold water starch can be used to reduce the heat cycle.

Preheating

Minimizing preheat, reheat, and cooking times takes careful planning but can save many energy dollars. A schedule of preheating times for ovens, steam tables, grills, broilers, deep fat fryers, etc., should be determined. Generally, 10 to 30 minutes (depending on appliance) is adequate. The time required to preheat most electrical cooking equipment to operating temperature is relatively short. Only 5 to 6 minutes are required to preheat an electric fryer, 7 to 12 minutes for preheating electric griddles, and 20 to 30 minutes for preheating the most popular sizes of deck ovens. (Refer to the table in the Appendix for preheating times of specific equipment.) A cook can also determine when, or at what point in the pre-preparation process of the food, the equipment should be turned on. In many operations, because of the small amount of foods cooked, more energy is used in preheating the various equipment than is actually used in cooking the food products.

The practices in some food service kitchens is to assign one person the responsibility of turning on all cooking equipment early in the day in preparation for the cook's arrival. This practice is often wasteful and costly, as in many instances, all of the equipment is not used. If this duty were assigned to the cooks using the equipment, the waste could be reduced considerably, assuming the cook predetermines the cooking requirements for the day. It may also be possible to schedule processing of foods so that fewer pieces of equipment are used, thereby saving the energy required to preheat the extra equipment.

Staggering turn-on times for heavy duty electrical equipment by 30 minute intervals should reduce the demand load as well. Develop a schedule showing the hours and days where second fry units, broilers, and ovens, would be required for peak serving times. Good energy management practice requires that all cooking equipment be turned off anytime that doing so does not interfere with production requirements.

Whenever possible also schedule the processing or finishing of foods so that fewer pieces of equipment are used, thereby saving the energy required to preheat extra pieces of equipment. Most equipment is not needed at the same time.

Utilizing the correct size of equipment for each operation is also important and simply means using the smaller size equipment when there is a choice, rather than preheating a large piece of equipment. Only the number of sections needed with equipment such as griddles, broilers, or deck ovens should be utilized.

Full Production Cooking

Cooking at full-production capacity of the equipment means cooking full loads on every cooking cycle. It also means cooking loads repeatedly one after another. This reduces total production time and saves energy during the cooking cycle.

When is it practical and when is it not practical to cook one load following another at full production capacity of equipment. Foods cooked to order and foods having a short life in the finished state must be cooked to fit the demand. This may include such foods as fried and scrambled eggs, fried potatoes, pancakes, and steaks. It may not be practical to cook these foods at the full production capacity of the equipment. The equipment used to cook foods to order and foods with short finished life most often are fryers, griddles, and broilers. However, the largest feasible volumes of food should be cooked at one time to minimize the time and energy required.

Equipment may be used to full production capacity periodically by cooking foods that may be cooked ahead of time, or partially cooked and held in refrigerated or heated storage. This may include such foods as cakes, pies, breads and to some extent, chicken and hamburger patties. Deck ovens and convection ovens are usually used to cook foods ahead of time. Partial cooking of foods may be done on griddles and broilers and finished in ovens. Ovens are also designed to accommodate standard size bake pans properly. When smaller pans are used, the oven is not being used to its full production capacity. Capacity loading of baked goods is recommended because small loads are uneconomical.

To use a piece of equipment for a task for which it was not specifically designed is to misuse the equipment. Placing a stock pot on a charbroiler or griddle instead of a range that will cook the food in the pot with less energy would be an example. Use electronic cookers, pressure cookers, and prepared package goods to reduce the requirements of the number of heat producing pieces of kitchen equipment and to reduce the period of time that the heat-producing equipment is in operation. Consider using microwave ovens for thawing and fast food preparation whenever they can serve to reduce power requirements.

ENERGY SAVING GENERALITIES

- Turn off cooking and heating units that are not needed.
- Install twist-on timers or individual switches on food warming infrared heat lamps. Evaluate the necessity for infrared heat lamps.
- Install timers for all kitchen equipment to control cooking time automatically.
- Cluster heating equipment together and away from cooling equipment.
- Develop a schedule for equipment use. Equipment should be turned on at a specific time, to a specfic temperature and turned off at the designated time.
- Install an "in-the-meat" thermometer with gauge outside the oven to reduce heat loss from opening the oven to check roasting process. At the very least, however, an "in-the-meat" thermometer should be used so that the meat is not overcooked, thereby increasing energy expenditure and reducing the palatability of the product.
- Cook with lids in place on pots and kettles. This can reduce heat requirements by 50 percent.
- Use hot tap water, approximately 110°F. (44°C.) for cooking whenever possible because heated water requires less energy than most cook top equipment and kettles to heat the same amount of water.
- Thaw frozen foods in refrigerator compartments.
- If foods requiring different temperatures are to be baked in the same equipment in succession, the foods requiring the lowest temperatures should always be cooked first, when practical.
- Cook at the lowest temperature possible to maintain quality and sanitation standards.
- Check gas pressure to appliances to assure that adequate pressure is available from the supplier.

- Direct fans that cool workers so that they do not cool cooking equipment as well.
- Turn on food warmers and hot plates only if needed; do not let them run when not in use. Also, run at the lowest temperature permissible for safe food handling.
- Preheat ovens only for baked goods. Discourage preheating any sooner than necessary. Normally, insulated equipment requires 15 minutes to be preheated and noninsulated equipment requires approximately 30 minutes. The equipment should be preheated to the desired temperature before loading with food products.
- Keep cooking equipment clean so it will perform better and more efficiently. Spillage and splatters should be cleaned as they occur. This will prevent the foods from being burned on, which makes the equipment difficult to clean later. Burned on spillage and food particles will affect the performance of the equipment and can result in producing an inferior product and in some instances, "crippled" products. For example, large spillage on the hearth of a deck oven will act as insulation and cause uneven transfer of heat to the bottom of a bake pan.
- Schedule cleaning of equipment so as not to require the use of additional energy in the cleaning process. This means not permitting equipment to cool and thus require reheating for cleaning. Some types of equipment are easier to clean when hot, not necessarily at operating temperature but when cooled enough to handle. As an example, the surface of a griddle may be easy enough to clean even if it is allowed to cool to about 200°F. (94°C.). The grease chute and drip tray are easier to clean before the grease congeals.

ENERGY SAVING SPECIFICS

Ovens

Because of the time required to make and roast most food products, ovens are generally not used for cooked-to-order production and should be turned off during slack periods of the day.

Energy can be conserved by implementing the following procedures:

- Start the day with the lowest oven temperature.
- Load oven to capacity allowing a two inch clearance.
- Schedule oven use for full advantage of receding heat and discourage unnecessary opening of oven doors.

- When preheating ovens, set the thermostat at the desired temperature; it will preheat no faster and waste energy if you dial higher.
- Calibrate oven thermostats to assure that cooking temperature is appropriate to achieve the maximum energy efficiency. Use oven thermometer to monitor oven thermostat.
- Determine the cooking capacity of the oven. Use the small, more energy efficient oven when possible. Use only the size oven needed for the job; extra space heating results in wasted energy.
- Use correct size oven vent hood.
- Use proper blend of make up air in exhaust hoods. (See chapter on equipment selection.)
- Begin cooking food while oven is warming up (the exception being for food that will dry out or over cook, and in some instances, baked goods).
- Cook meat slowly at *low* temperatures. Cooking roast for five hours at 250°F. (122°C.) could save 25 to 50 percent of the energy that would be used in cooking for three hours at 350°F. (176°C.).
- Schedule baking or roasting so that oven capacity can be fully utilized, thereby reducing operating hours.
- Insert metal skewers lengthwise in potatoes to speed cooking. If foil is necessary, wrap the potato after it is baked.
- Place weight on bacon and sausage to quicken their cooking time and be aware that the characteristics of the product may be altered.
- Close open dampers on a deck oven to prevent heated air from escaping out the back, resulting in an excessive intake of cold air through the breather space at the front below the door. Open dampers will cause the product to be unfinished at the front and overdone at the back of the oven. Dampers on deck ovens should never be opened except when baking foods that contain an excessive amount of moisture, such as fruit pies and cobblers. A collection of moisture on the glass or at the top of the oven door indicates excessive moisture, and the damper should be opened enough to eliminate it.
- Do not place pans too close to the sides, back, or front of deck or convection ovens, since this results in poor circulation of hot air in the cavity and "crippled runs."
- Keep oven doors closed as much as possible because excessive opening to check the product wastes heat and may result in a poor quality finished product or "crippled runs." If the door is opened at scheduled times, the food will cook faster and lose less moisture. Slow loading

and unloading of ovens, especially convection ovens, as the cavity is so tall, causes not only a waste of heat but also may cool the oven down enough to result in a poor quality finished product. Every second the oven is open, it loses one percent of its heat. Careful attention to the time and temperature method of cooking should eliminate the necessity of opening doors to check the food.

- Oven cooking is more economical than surface cooking. Ovens require energy only periodically since insulation holds in the heat.

- Clean fans on convection ovens to provide maximum air delivery, to assure even heating throughout the oven capacity, and to prevent crippled runs. Regular cleaning and maintenance of filters is also necessary.

- Clean the breather space below the door on the deck frequently to permit proper closing of the doors.

Surface Units

- Check the fuel-air ratio on all gas burners and adjust to the most efficient mixture.

- Consult your local gas utility about using pilot lights. Adjustments made by persons not thoroughly familiar with the equipment could be dangerous.

- Huddle food on griddle close together whenever possible and heat only that portion of the griddle being used for cooking.

- Clean griddle every shift after use. Remove deposits, being careful to prevent loose deposits from falling on hot area and forming air pollution by formal degradation. Excessive buildup of burned-on food particles in spots on a griddle will cause uneven heat transfer and result in crippled food products. Unnecessary or excessive cleaning by "burning off" of the heating elements on fryers will waste energy and energy dollars.

- Cover pans with lids. Foods will cook faster when covered with lids. Flame tips need only to be touching utensil bottom, not engulfing it.

- Place foil under range burners and griddles to improve the operation efficiency and make equipment faster to clean. Electric range burners should always be smaller than the kettle or pot placed on them.

- Place kettles and pots close together on range tops to decrease heat loss. With preheat time of 10 to 15 minutes for electric ranges, only the section in use needs to be heated. Place pots in use specifically in this area. Gas open burners need no preheating.

- Turn off electric surface for a short period before the food is done as the food will continue to cook from stored energy.
- Choose the pot and pan carefully for the surface unit. To assure efficient heat transfer from hot plates, french plates of ranges, and hearths of deck ovens, only heavy, flat bottomed pots and pans should be used. Pans that are bent or warped not only waste energy because of inefficient heat transfer, but may also result in uneven finishing of the product. The bottom should cover the heating element while not extending more than one inch (2.5 centimeters) over the edge.

Steam Cookers

- Thaw frozen food in steam cookers instead of boiling.
- Maintain temperature control to avoid permitting clouds of steam from escaping.
- Clean steam cooker often to remove lime deposits.
- Check for steam leaks; this can be a significant source of wasted energy.
- Use only the amount of water required to make steam. Do not drown the vegetable!
- Reduce cooking to a simmer as soon as the steam point is reached and use a pan with a tight fitting cover. The vegetables will retain more vitamins and minerals as well as taste better.

Fryers

- Overloading baskets, insufficient fat levels and irregular replacement of fat often lead to less than quality cooking and wasteful energy. Proper loading and unloading of foods is important. One of the more common bad practices is overloading the fryer basket so that part of the food is not submerged, usually resulting in wasted food.
- Check for carbon buildup at least once a week as a carbon buildup will inhibit efficient heating.
- Keep cooking oil in fryers clean to prevent a poor quality finished product that would require cooking more food.
- Preheat fryers only 7 to 15 minutes and only to 325°-350°F. (162-176°C.).
- Maintain fryer at 200°F. (94°C.) rather than at an operating temperature of 350°F. (176°C.) as less than one-half of the energy is required. The time to recover from 200°F. (94°C.) to 350°F. (176°C.)

is only two minutes for the smaller, more popular fryers. Two minutes delay in frying is not going to result in any noticeable delay. If a food service operation has several fryers, during slack periods, one fryer may be set to idle at operating temperature, while another is set back to 200°F. (94°C.) and the other fryers are turned off. The same practice could apply to griddles, ranges, and broilers. Generally, this equipment is electrically divided into sections with separate controls for each section. In this case, only the number of sections required to meet slack period reduction requirements must be operating, and some of the sections could easily be set back to a lower temperature or turned off.

Hot Food Holding And Transporting Equipment

The equipment in this classification is generally used for "proofing" and for "holding" hot foods. Important considerations in the purchase and use of the equipment include the following.

- Be certain that the equipment is sized right for the job required and will not be expected to do more than it is designed to do.
- Be certain that adequate electric power, as specified by the manufacturer, is provided.
- Locate the equipment in areas that will result in an efficient operation.

Refrigeration and Storage

- Schedule times when refrigerator and freezer doors are open. Labeling stored items help, as does planning times when workers take several items out. This increases security as well.
- Cover all liquids stored in the refrigerator. Moisture is drawn into the air from the uncovered liquid making the refrigerator work even harder as moisture from the liquid raises the temperature of the refrigerator. Storing items improperly in front of coils may restrict air flow. Unrestricted air flow to the coils is essential to the cooling process.
- Do not refrigerate foods that do not require refrigeration, that is, unopened catsup, mustard, pickles, salad oils, etc.
- Place frequently used items near the front of the refrigeration unit.
- Close doors immediately after items have been removed from the refrigerator. Do not use cooler to store individual portions of products because that requires opening the door every time a portion is needed, i.e., salads, desserts, etc.

- Keep all gaskets and seals in good condition and the blower coil free of ice buildup. Replace worn or damaged compressor belts.
- Plan ahead so that a worker entering the walk-in cooler can fill many needs at one time. Prepare a schedule for use.
- Turn off lights in the walk-in when leaving. Unit should have pilot light or light switches to indicate that lights are on.
- Allow food to cool for a few minutes before placing in the refrigerator. However, do not permit food to remain at room temperature for too long a period of time to avoid the temperature danger zone (45° to 140°F.) (8°C. to 60°C.) in which bacteria grows the most readily.
- Check refrigerators for short cycling and loss of temperature control. Maintain a record of refrigeration temperature forms as indicated in Exhibit 11-1. Check refrigerant level if abnormal operation exists.
- Keep compressor coils free of dust and do not store anything within four feet of the compressor. Compressors need to have open space to give off the heat removed from the unit.
- Place compressors in cool areas rather than locating them near heating units.
- Clean freezer fan periodically and check compressor regularly. These procedures should be scheduled as a regular maintenance item.
- Consolidate refrigeration and freezer space where possible.
- Schedule food deliveries, whenever possible, to avoid overloading refrigeration facilities or using them below capacity.
- Expedite receiving and prompt refrigeration of frozen and perishable foods.
- Defrost freezers frequently. Ice should not be allowed to build up more than one-eight of an inch on the wall and shelves.

Dishwashers

- Reduce the amount of hot water used by monitoring the amount wasted. Consider cold chemical warewashing systems, which are detailed further in the chapter on energy-efficient equipment selection.
- Use the lowest temperature appropriate to the use intended.
- Keep distribution runs as short as possible. Hot water boosters should be located within 48 inches of dishwasher to avoid heat loss in the run.
- Use spring-operated valves on the hand levers and foot pedals to save water.

Exhibit 11-1 Record of Refrigeration Temperatures

Record of Refrigeration Temperatures

Equipment: _____

DATE	MONITOR	A. M. TEMPERATURE	MONITOR	P. M. TEMPERATURE

- Schedule the dishwasher for efficient use. Use the dish machine at specified times during the day as compared to running short loads all day long. Wash only full racks of dishes whenever possible.
- Keep use of the power dryer to a minimum.

- Consider wetting agents versus power drying.
- Operate dishwasher exhaust only when dishwasher is in use.
- Consider using sanitizing solutions that work at lower temperatures, that is, cold chemical warewashing systems.
- Check local sanitary codes to ensure that water is supplied at the lowest possible temperature.
- Install pressure regulators if not already present.
- Replace water jets that allow too much water to flow through the dishwasher.
- Insulate heating pipes and hot water lines.
- Stop leakage. Check pipes and faucets.
- Caution personnel to avoid letting faucets run unnecessarily.
- Keep heater coils free from lime accumulation.
- Turn off electric booster heaters on dishwashers when the kitchen is closed.
- Turn off the equipment heat boosters after most dishwashing is over and accumulate dishes until the next rush period.
- Obtain water pressure for the hot water line to dishwasher to reduce wasted hot water. Set regulator to the operating pressure required by the machine; make sure power rinse turns off automatically when a tray has gone through the machine.

SELECTED REFERENCES

Cook, Robert E. "Saving Energy with Hot Water." *Cooking for Profit,* 323:36-38.

Food Management. "Energy and Cooking."; "Energy and the Kitchen"; "Energy and Management." 12.

Food Service Marketing. "Efficient Energy Management: Cleaning Promotes Energy Savings." 37:12-15; "Energy Conservation of Warewashing System." 37:10; "Efficient Energy Management: Fitting New Equipment into Energy Savings Programs." 36:12-13.

Appendix A
Menus and Recipes

The menus given on the following pages are coordinated with the Georgia Dietetic Association Diet Manual. Note that at least one menu item per day is to be prepared with bran.

Soft/Bland Diet

The Soft Diet is a digestive soft diet. Due to the liberalization of the Bland Diet, the Bland Diet is coordinated with the Soft Diet. However, no black pepper, chili powder, chocolate, or caffeine should be served to Bland Diet patients.

Low Residue

The Low Residue Diet is a diet which restricts foods which are high in fiber.

2-3 gram Sodium

The "Low Salt" Diet permits foods cooked or canned in salt but no salt is added after the food is cooked. Foods with high sodium content are omitted.

Low Fat

The Low Fat Diet is a 40 gram Fat Diet.

Calorie Controlled Diets

The Calorie Controlled Diets are planned to provide 3 meals and bedtime snack. The 1976 Exchange Lists for Meal Planning are the basis of these diets.

171

DATE ___ Monday ___   WEEK NO. ___ One ___   MENU CYCLE ___ Fall/Winter

	REGULAR	SOFT/BLAND	2-3 gram sodium	LOW FAT	LOW RESIDUE
BREAKFAST	Orange juice Egg Cereal Toast milk coffee, tea	Orange juice Egg Cereal (no whole grain) Toast milk coffee, tea/sanka	Orange juice 1 Egg Cereal Toast milk coffee, tea	Orange juice 1 FF Egg FF Cereal Toast skim milk coffee, tea	Orange juice Egg Cereal (no whole grain) Toast milk coffee, tea
DINNER	Fresh roasted pork Sweet potato pattie Seasoned greens Cornbread Red fruited jello w/topping milk coffee, tea	Lean roast pork Sweet potato pattie Seasoned greens Cornbread Red fruited jello w/topping milk coffee, tea/sanka	Lean uncured pork Sweet potato pattie Seasoned greens Cornbread Red fruited jello w/topping coffee, tea	Lean roast pork FF Sweet potato FF Seasoned greens Loaf bread Red fruited jello skim milk coffee, tea	Roast pork Mashed potatoes Seasoned greens Loaf bread Red fruited jello w/topping coffee, tea
SUPPER	Hamburger Bun Mixed fresh vegetables Lettuce & sliced tomato Fruit w/topping milk coffee, tea	Hamburger Bun Buttered carrots Lettuce & sliced tomato Soft fruit/topping milk coffee, tea/sanka	Hamburger Bun Mixed fresh vegetables Lettuce & sliced tomato Fruit w/topping milk coffee, tea	Hamburger Bun FF mixed fresh vegetables Lettuce & sliced tomato Fruit skim milk coffee, tea	Hamburger Bun Buttered carrots Shredded lettuce Soft fruit/topping milk coffee, tea

DATE _____ Monday _____   WEEK NO. _____ One _____   MENU CYCLE _____ Fall/Winter

	1000 Calories	1200 Calories	1500 Calories	1800 Calories	2000 Calories
BREAKFAST	½ c. orange juice 1 FF egg ½ c. FF cooked cereal 1 oleo 1 c. skim milk coffee, tea	½ c. orange juice 1 FF egg ½ c. FF cooked cereal 1 oleo 1 c. skim milk coffee, tea	½ c. orange juice 1 FF egg ½ c. FF cooked cereal 1 oleo 1 c. skim milk coffee, tea	½ c. orange juice 1 FF egg ½ c. FF cooked cereal 1 toast 2 oleo 1 c. skim milk coffee, tea	½ c. orange juice 2 FF eggs ½ c. FF cooked cereal 1 toast 2 oleo 1 c. skim milk coffee, tea
DINNER	1 oz. pork 1 c. FF seasoned greens 1 oleo ½ c. diet applesauce coffee, tea	2 oz. pork 1 c. FF seasoned greens ¼ c. FF sweet potatoes 1 oleo ½ c. diet applesauce coffee, tea	2 oz. pork 1 c. FF seasoned greens ¼ c. FF sweet potatoes 2" square cornbread ½ c. diet applesauce coffee, tea	3 oz. pork 1 c. FF seasoned greens ¼ c. FF sweet potatoes 2" square cornbread 1 oleo ½ c. diet applesauce coffee, tea	3 oz. pork 1 c. FF seasoned greens ¼ c. FF sweet potatoes 2 2" squares cornbread ½ c. diet applesauce coffee, tea
SUPPER	2 oz. hamburger ½ c. FF mixed vegetables lettuce & sliced tomato 1 bread 1 oleo ½ c. diet fruit cocktail coffee, tea	2 oz. hamburger ½ c. FF mixed vegetables lettuce & sliced tomato 1 bread 1 oleo ½ c. diet fruit cocktail coffee, tea	3 oz. hamburger ½ c. FF mixed vegetables lettuce & sliced tomato 2 bread 2 oleo ½ c. diet fruit cocktail coffee, tea	3 oz. hamburger ½ c. FF mixed vegetables lettuce & sliced tomato 2 bread 2 oleo ½ c. diet fruit cocktail 5 vanilla wafers coffee, tea	3 oz. hamburger ½ c. FF mixed vegetables lettuce & sliced tomato 2 bread 2 oleo ½ c. diet fruit cocktail 5 vanilla wafers coffee, tea
SNACK	1 c. skim milk 2 sq. graham crackers	1 c. skim milk 2 sq. graham crackers	1 c. skim milk 2 sq. graham crackers	1 c. skim milk 2 sq. graham crackers	1 c. skim milk 4 sq. graham crackers

DATE _____ Tuesday _____   WEEK NO. _____ One _____   MENU CYCLE _____ Fall/Winter

	REGULAR	SOFT/BLAND	2-3 gram sodium	LOW FAT	LOW RESIDUE
BREAKFAST	Orange juice Egg Crisp Bacon Cereal Toast milk coffee, tea	Orange juice Egg Crisp Bacon Cereal (no whole grain) Toast milk coffee, tea/sanka	Orange juice 1 Egg Cereal Toast milk coffee, tea	Orange juice 1 FF Egg FF Cereal Toast skim milk coffee, tea	Orange juice Egg Crisp Bacon Cereal (no whole grain) Toast milk coffee, tea

DINNER	Crispy Fried chicken
	Hot potato salad
	Green peas with
	  red peppers
	Home-made biscuit
	Peach cobbler
	
	milk
	coffee, tea
		Baked chicken
		Hot potato salad
		  (no onion, pepper)
		Green peas
		Home-made biscuit
		Peach cobbler
		
		milk
		coffee, tea/sanka
			Crispy Fried chicken
			Hot potato salad
			  (no pickle)
			Green peas with
			  red peppers
			Home-made biscuit
			Peach cobbler
			
			coffee, tea
				Baked chicken-no skin
				Hot potato salad
				  (little mayonnaise)
				FF Green peas with
				  red peppers
				Loaf bread
				Peaches
				
				skim milk
				coffee, tea
					Baked chicken
					Hot potato salad
					  (no onion, pepper)
					Green peas
					Loaf bread
					Peaches
					
					coffee, tea

SUPPER	Fried fish fillet
	Buttered Rice
	Stewed tomatoes &
	  okra
	Roll
	Fruit mix w/topping
	
	milk
	coffee, tea
		Baked fish fillet
		Buttered Rice
		Stewed tomatoes &
		  okra
		Roll
		Canned fruit mix
		  w/topping
		
		milk
		coffee, tea/sanka
			Fried fish fillet
			Buttered Rice
			Stewed tomatoes &
			  okra
			Roll
			Fruit mix w/topping
			
			milk
			coffee, tea
				Baked fish fillet
				FF Rice
				FF Stewed tomatoes &
				  okra
				Roll
				Fruit mix
				
				skim milk
				coffee, tea
					Baked fish fillet
					Buttered Rice
					Tomato juice
					Roll
					Canned fruit mix
					  w/topping
					
					milk
					coffee, tea

DATE _____ Tuesday _____ WEEK NO. ____ One ____ MENU CYCLE ____ Fall/Winter

	1000 Calories	1200 Calories	1500 Calories	1800 Calories	2000 Calories
BREAKFAST	½ c. orange juice 1 FF egg 1 toast 1 bacon 1 c. skim milk coffee, tea	½ c. orange juice 1 FF egg 1 toast 1 bacon 1 c. skim milk coffee, tea	½ c. orange juice 1 FF egg 1 toast 1 bacon 1 c. skim milk coffee, tea	½ c. orange juice 1 FF egg ½ c. FF cooked cereal 1 toast 2 bacon 1 c. skim milk coffee, tea	½ c. orange juice 2 FF eggs ½ c. FF cooked cereal 1 toast 2 bacon 1 c. skim milk coffee, tea

DINNER	1 oz. baked chicken
	½ c. FF beets
	sliced tomato salad
	1 oleo
	½ c. diet peaches
	
	1 c. skim milk
	coffee, tea
		2 oz. baked chicken
		½ c. FF beets
		½ c. FF green peas/
		  pepper
		sliced tomato salad
		1 oleo
		½ c. diet peaches
		
		coffee, tea
			2 oz. baked chicken
			½ c. FF beets
			½ c. FF grn peas/
			  pepper
			sliced tomato salad
			1 2" biscuit
			½ c. diet peaches
			
			coffee, tea
				3 oz. baked chicken
				½ c. FF beets
				½ c. FF grn peas/
				  pepper
				sliced tomato salad
				2" biscuit
				1 oleo
				½ c. diet peaches
				coffee, tea
					3 oz. baked chicken
					½ c. FF beets
					½ c. FF grn peas/
					  pepper
					sliced tomato salad
					2 2" biscuits
					½ c. diet peaches
					
					coffee, tea

SUPPER	2 oz. broiled Fish
	½ c. FF stewed
	  tomatoes & okra
	½ c. FF rice
	1 oleo
	½ c. diet fruit mixed
	
	coffee, tea
		2 oz. broiled Fish
		½ c. FF stewed
		  tomatoes & okra
		½ c. FF rice
		tossed salad
		1 Tbsp. French
		  dressing
		½ c. diet fruit mixed
		coffee, tea
			3 oz. broiled Fish
			½ c. FF stewed
			  tomatoes & okra
			½ c. FF rice
			tossed salad
			1 Tbsp. French
			  dressing
			1 roll—1 oleo
			½ c. diet fruit mixed
			coffee, tea
				3 oz. broiled Fish
				½ c. FF stewed
				  tomatoes & okra
				½ c. FF rice
				tossed salad
				1 Tbsp. French
				  dressing
				2 rolls — 1 oleo
				½ c. diet fruit mixed
				coffee, tea
					3 oz. broiled Fish
					½ c. FF stewed
					  tomatoes & okra
					½ c. FF rice
					tossed salad
					1 Tbsp. French
					  dressing
					2 rolls—1 oleo
					½ c. diet fruit mixed
					coffee, tea

SNACK	1 c. skim milk 2 sq. graham crackers	1 c. skim milk 2 sq. graham crackers	1 c. skim milk 2 sq. graham crackers	1 c. skim milk 2 sq. graham crackers	1 c. skim milk 4 sq. graham crackers

DATE Wednesday   WEEK NO. One   MENU CYCLE Fall/Winter

	REGULAR	SOFT/BLAND	2-3 gram sodium	LOW FAT	LOW RESIDUE
BREAKFAST	Orange juice Egg Cereal Toast milk coffee, tea	Orange juice Egg Cereal (no whole grain) Toast milk coffee, tea/sanka	Orange juice 1 Egg Cereal Toast Milk Coffee, tea	Orange juice 1 FF Egg FF Cereal Toast milk coffee, tea	Orange juice Egg Cereal (no whole grain) Toast milk coffee, tea
DINNER	Broiled chicken livers Creamed potatoes Gravy Buttered Carrots Home-made biscuit Gingerbread/ lemon sauce milk coffee, tea	Broiled chicken livers Creamed potatoes Gravy Buttered Carrots Home-made biscuit Gingerbread/ lemon sauce milk coffee, tea/sanka	Broiled chicken livers Creamed potatoes SF Gravy Buttered Carrots Loaf bread Gingerbread/ lemon sauce coffee, tea	Broiled chicken livers FF Mashed potatoes FF Carrots Loaf bread Apricots skim milk coffee, tea	Broiled chicken livers Creamed potatoes Buttered Carrots Loaf bread Apricots coffee, tea
SUPPER	Baked ham Macaroni & Cheese Seasoned Green beans Cornbread Pear half w/topping milk coffee, tea	Baked ham Macaroni & Cheese Seasoned Green beans Cornbread Pear half w/topping milk coffee, tea/sanka	Beef pattie Buttered Macaroni Seasoned Green beans Cornbread Pear half w/topping milk coffee, tea	Beef pattie FF Macaroni FF Green beans Loaf bread Pear half skim milk coffee, tea	Beef pattie Buttered Macaroni Seasoned Green beans Loaf bread Pear half w/topping milk coffee, tea

DATE __Wednesday__   WEEK NO. __One__   MENU CYCLE __Fall/Winter__

	1000 Calories	1200 Calories	1500 Calories	1800 Calories	2000 Calories
BREAKFAST	½ c. orange juice 1 FF egg 1 toast 1 oleo 1 c. skim milk coffee, tea	½ c. orange juice 1 FF egg 1 toast 1 oleo 1 c. skim milk coffee, tea	½ c. orange juice 1 FF egg 1 toast 1 oleo 1 c. skim milk coffee, tea	½ c. orange juice 1 FF egg ¾ c. dry cereal 1 toast 2 oleo 1 c. skim milk coffee, tea	½ c. orange juice 2 FF eggs ¾ c. dry cereal 1 toast 2 oleo 1 c. skim milk coffee, tea
DINNER	1 oz. liver 1 c. FF carrots 1 oleo 2 diet pineapple rings 1 c. skim milk coffee, tea	2 oz. liver 1 c. FF carrots ½ c. FF mashed potatoes 1 oleo 2 diet pineapple rings coffee, tea	2 oz. liver 1 c. FF carrots ½ c. FF mashed potatoes 1 2" biscuit 2 diet pineapple rings coffee, tea	3 oz. liver 1 c. FF carrots ½ c. FF mashed potatoes 1 2" biscuit 2 diet pineapple rings coffee, tea	3 oz. liver 1 c. FF carrots ½ c. FF mashed potatoes 2 2" biscuits 2 diet pineapple rings coffee, tea
SUPPER	2 oz. ham ½ c. FF green beans 2" square cornbread 2 diet pear halves coffee, tea	2 oz. ham ½ c. FF green beans ½ c. tomato juice 2" square cornbread 2 diet pear halves coffee, tea	3 oz. ham ½ c. FF green beans ½ c. FF macaroni ½ c. tomato juice 2" square cornbread 1 oleo 2 diet pear halves coffee, tea	3 oz. ham ½ c. FF green beans ½ c. FF macaroni ½ c. tomato juice 2 2" squares cornbread 2 diet pear halves coffee, tea	3 oz. ham ½ c. FF green beans ½ c. FF macaroni ½ c. tomato juice 2 2" squares cornbread 2 diet pear halves coffee, tea
SNACK	1 c. skim milk 2 sq. graham crackers	1 c. skim milk 2 sq. graham crackers	1 c. skim milk 2 sq. graham crackers	1 c. skim milk 2 sq. graham crackers	1 c. skim milk 4 sq. graham crackers

DATE __Thursday__   WEEK NO. __One__   MENU CYCLE   __Fall/Winter__

	REGULAR	SOFT/BLAND	2-3 gram sodium	LOW FAT	LOW RESIDUE
BREAKFAST	Orange juice Egg Cereal Toast milk coffee, tea	Orange juice Egg Cereal (no whole grain) Toast milk coffee, tea/sanka	Orange juice 1 Egg Cereal Toast milk coffee, tea	Orange juice 1 FF Egg FF Cereal **Toast** skim milk coffee, tea	Orange juice Egg Cereal (no whole grain) Toast milk coffee, tea
DINNER	Meatloaf/tomato sauce Corn pudding Fried okra Home-made biscuit Banana pudding/ topping milk coffee, tea	Meatloaf/tomato sauce (no onion, pepper) Oven browned potatoes Boiled okra Home-made biscuit Banana pudding/ topping milk coffee, tea/sanka	Meatloaf Corn pudding Fried okra Home-made biscuit Banana pudding/ topping coffee, tea	Meatloaf/tomato sauce FF Corn FF Boiled okra Loaf bread Ripe banana skim milk coffee, tea	Meatloaf/tomato sauce (no onion, pepper) Oven browned potatoes Green peas Loaf bread Ripe banana coffee, tea
SUPPER	Cream of tomato soup Chix salad sandwich Cinnamon Applesauce Graham crackers Rainbow jello cubes w/topping milk coffee, tea	Cream of tomato soup Chix salad sandwich Cinnamon Applesauce Graham crackers Rainbow jello cubes w/topping milk coffee, tea/sanka	SF Cream of tomato soup Chix salad sandwich Cinnamon Applesauce Graham crackers Rainbow jello cubes w/topping ½ cup milk coffee, tea	FF Cream of tomato soup Chicken sandwich Cinnamon Applesauce Graham crackers Rainbow jello cubes skim milk coffee, tea	Cream of tomato soup Chix salad sandwich Cinnamon Applesauce Vanilla wafers Rainbow jello cubes w/topping milk coffee, tea

DATE ____ Thursday _____ WEEK NO. ___ One ___ MENU CYCLE ____ Fall/Winter

	1000 Calories	1200 Calories	1500 Calories	1800 Calories	2000 Calories
BREAKFAST	½ c. orange juice 1 FF egg ½ c. FF cooked cereal 1 oleo 1 c. skim milk coffee, tea	½ c. orange juice 1 FF egg ½ c. FF cooked cereal 1 oleo 1 c. skim milk coffee, tea	½ c. orange juice 1 FF egg ½ c. FF cooked cereal 1 oleo 1 c. skim milk coffee, tea	½ c. orange juice 1 FF egg ½ c. FF cooked cereal 1 toast 2 oleo 1 c. skim milk coffee, tea	½ c. orange juice 2 FF eggs ½ c. FF cooked cereal 1 toast 2 oleo 1 c. skim milk coffee, tea
DINNER	1 oz. meatloaf ½ c. FF okra ½ c. tomato juice 1 oleo ½ small banana 1 c. skim milk coffee, tea	2 oz. meatloaf ½ c. FF okra ½ c. tomato juice 1 2" biscuit ½ small banana coffee, tea	2 oz. meatloaf ½ c. FF okra ⅓ c. FF corn ½ c. tomato juice 1 2" biscuit ½ small banana coffee, tea	3 oz. meatloaf ½ c. FF okra ⅓ c. FF corn ½ c. tomato juice 1 2" biscuit 1 oleo ½ small banana coffee, tea	3 oz. meatloaf ½ c. FF okra ⅓ c. FF corn ½ c. tomato juice 2 2" biscuits ½ small banana coffee, tea
SUPPER	2 oz. chicken 1 slice bread 1 tsp. mayonnaise ½ c. FF mixed vegetables ½ c. diet applesauce diet jello cubes coffee, tea	2 oz. chicken 1 slice bread 1 tsp. mayonnaise 1 c. FF mix vegetables ½ c. diet applesauce diet jello cubes coffee, tea	3 oz. chicken 2 slices bread 2 tsp. mayonnaise 1 c. FF mix vegetables ½ c. diet applesauce diet jello cubes coffee, tea	3 oz. chicken 2 slices bread 2 tsp. mayonnaise 1 c. FF mix vegetables ½ c. diet applesauce 5 vanilla wafers diet jello cubes coffee, tea	3 oz. chicken 2 slices bread 2 tsp. mayonnaise 1 c. FF mix vegetables ½ c. diet applesauce 5 vanilla wafers diet jello cubes coffee, tea
SNACK	1 c. skim milk 2 sq. graham crackers	1 c. skim milk 2 sq. graham crackers	1 c. skim milk 2 sq. graham crackers	1 c. skim milk 2 sq. graham crackers	1 c. skim milk 4 sq. graham crackers

DATE ___ Friday ___   WEEK NO. ___ One ___   MENU CYCLE   Fall/Winter ___

	REGULAR	SOFT/BLAND	2-3 gram sodium	LOW FAT	LOW RESIDUE
BREAKFAST	Orange juice Egg Cereal Bacon Toast milk coffee, tea	Orange juice Egg Cereal (no whole grain) Bacon Toast milk coffee, tea/sanka	Orange juice 1 Egg Cereal Toast milk coffee, tea	Orange juice 1 FF Egg FF Cereal Toast skim milk coffee, tea	Orange juice Egg Cereal (no whole grain) Bacon Toast milk coffee, tea
DINNER	Paprika baked fish Steak fries Diced beets Cornbread Coleslaw Lemon pan pie milk coffee, tea	Paprika baked fish Oven browned steak fries Diced beets Cornbread Peach slices Lemon pan pie milk coffee, tea/sanka	Paprika baked fish Steak fries Diced beets Cornbread Coleslaw Lemon pan pie coffee, tea	Paprika baked fish Oven browned steak fries FF Diced beets Loaf bread Coleslaw-little mayo Peach slices skim milk coffee, tea	Paprika baked fish Oven browned steak fries Diced beets Loaf bread Peach slices Lemon pudding coffee, tea
SUPPER	Pancakes Syrup Sausage Pattie Fruit w/topping milk coffee, tea	Pancakes Syrup Bacon strips Scrambled eggs Fruit w/topping milk coffee, tea/sanka	Pancakes Syrup Beef pattie Fruit w/topping ½ cup milk coffee, tea	Chicken Bread FF Rice FF Green peas Fruit w/topping skim milk coffee, tea	Bacon Scrambled eggs Fruit w/topping Toast ½ cup milk coffee, tea

DATE ___Friday___   WEEK NO. ___One___   MENU CYCLE ___Fall/Winter___

	1000 Calories	1200 Calories	1500 Calories	1800 Calories	2000 Calories
BREAKFAST	½ c. orange juice 1 FF egg 1 toast 1 bacon 1 c. skim milk coffee, tea	½ c. orange juice 1 FF egg 1 toast 1 bacon 1 c. skim milk coffee, tea	½ c. orange juice 1 FF egg ½ c. FF cooked cereal 1 c. skim milk coffee, tea	½ c. orange juice 1 FF egg ½ c. FF cooked cereal 1 toast 2 bacon 1 c. skim milk coffee, tea	½ c. orange juice 2 FF eggs ½ c. FF cooked cereal 1 toast 2 bacon 1 c. skim milk coffee, tea
DINNER	1 oz. baked fish ½ c. FF beets ½ c. FF coleslaw 1 oleo 2 diet peach halves 1 c. skim milk coffee, tea	2 oz. baked fish ½ c. FF beets ½ c. FF potatoes ½ c. FF coleslaw 1 oleo 2 diet peach halves coffee, tea	2 oz. baked fish ½ c. FF beets ½ c. FF potatoes ½ c. FF coleslaw 1 slice bread 1 oleo 2 diet peach halves coffee, tea	3 oz. baked fish ½ c. FF beets ½ c. FF potatoes ½ c. FF coleslaw 1 slice bread 2 oleo 2 diet peach halves coffee, tea	3 oz. baked fish ½ c. FF beets ½ c. FF potatoes ½ c. FF coleslaw 2 slices bread 2 oleo 2 diet peach halves coffee, tea
SUPPER	2 oz. chicken ½ c. FF wax beans 1 bread 1 oleo ½ c. diet fruit mix coffee, tea	2 oz. chicken ½ c. FF wax beans ½ c. FF rice sliced tomato salad 1 oleo ½ c. diet fruit mix coffee, tea	3 oz. chicken ½ c. FF wax beans ½ c. FF rice sliced tomato salad 1 bread 2 oleo ½ c. diet fruit mix coffee, tea	3 oz. chicken ½ c. FF wax beans ½ c. FF rice sliced tomato salad 2 bread 2 oleo ½ c. diet fruit mix coffee, tea	3 oz. chicken ½ c. FF wax beans ½ c. FF rice sliced tomato salad 2 bread 2 oleo ½ c. diet fruit mix coffee, tea
SNACK	1 c. skim milk 2 sq. graham crackers	1 c. skim milk 2 sq. graham chickens	1 c. skim milk 2 sq. graham crackers	1 c. skim milk 2 sq. graham crackers	1 c. skim milk 4 sq. graham crackers

DATE Saturday WEEK NO. One MENU CYCLE Fall/Winter

	REGULAR	SOFT/BLAND	2-3 gram sodium	LOW FAT	LOW RESIDUE
B R E A K F A S T	Orange juice Egg Cereal Toast milk coffee, tea	Orange juice Egg Cereal (no whole grain) Toast milk coffee, tea/sanka	Orange juice 1 Egg Cereal Toast milk coffee, tea	Orange juice 1 FF Egg FF Cereal Toast skim milk coffee, tea	Orange juice Egg Cereal (no whole grain) Toast milk coffee, tea
D I N N E R	Beef & noodle casserole Seasoned Green beans Frosted fruit salad Toast triangles Ice cream milk coffee, tea	Beef & noodle casserole Seasoned Green beans Canned fruit salad Toast triangles Ice cream/no chocolate milk coffee, tea/sanka	Beef & noodle casserole Seasoned Green beans Frosted fruit salad Toast triangles Ice cream coffee, tea	Beef & noodle casserole FF Green beans Frosted fruit salad Toast triangles Sherbet skim milk coffee, tea	Beef & noodle casserole Seasoned Green beans Canned fruit salad Toast triangles ½ c. Ice cream coffee, tea
S U P P E R	Beef vegetable soup Pimento cheese sandwich Congealed fruit salad Cookies milk coffee, tea	Beef vegetable soup American cheese sandwich Congealed fruit salad Plain cookies/ no chocolate milk coffee, tea/sanka	SF Beef vegetable soup Sliced beef sandwich Congealed fruit salad Cookies milk coffee, tea	FF Beef vegetable soup Sliced beef sandwich Congealed fruit salad Vanilla wafers skim milk coffee, tea	Beef vegetable soup Sliced beef sandwich Congealed fruit salad Plain cookies ½ cup milk coffee, tea

DATE __Saturday__ WEEK NO. __One__ MENU CYCLE __Fall/Winter__

	1000 calories	1200 Calories	1500 Calories	1800 Calories	2000 Calories
BREAKFAST	½ c. orange juice 1 FF egg 1 toast 1 oleo 1 c. skim milk coffee, tea	½ c. orange juice 1 FF egg 1 toast 1 oleo 1 c. skim milk coffee, tea	½ c. orange juice 1 FF egg 1 toast 1 oleo 1 c. skim milk coffee, tea	½ c. orange juice 1 FF egg ¾ c. dry cereal 1 toast 2 oleo 1 c. skim milk coffee, tea	½ c. orange juice 2 FF eggs ¾ c. dry cereal 1 toast 2 oleo 1 c. skim milk coffee, tea
DINNER	1 oz. beef cubes 1 c. FF green beans 2 diet pear halves salad 1 oleo 1 c. skim milk coffee, tea	2 oz. beef cubes ½ c. FF noodles 1 c. FF green beans 2 diet pear halves salad 1 oleo coffee, tea	2 oz. beef cubes ½ c. FF noodles 1 c. FF green beans 2 diet pear halves salad ½ c. ice cream coffee, tea	3 oz. beef cubes ½ c. FF noodles 1 c. FF green beans 2 diet pear halves salad ½ c. ice cream coffee, tea	3 oz. beef cubes ½ c. FF noodles 1 c. FF green beans 2 diet pear halves salad 1 toast ½ c. ice cream coffee, tea
SUPPER	2 oz. cheese 1 slice bread 1 tsp. mayonnaise ½ c. FF mix vegetables ½ c. diet peach & pear diet jello cubes coffee, tea	2 oz. cheese 1 slice bread 1 tsp. mayonnaise ½ c. FF mix vegetables ½ c. diet peach & pear diet jello cubes coffee, tea	2 oz. cheese 1 oz. beef 2 slices bread 2 tsp. mayonnaise 1 c. FF mix vegetables ½ c. diet peach & pear diet jello cubes coffee, tea	2 oz. cheese 1 oz. beef 2 slices bread 2 tsp. mayonnaise 1 c. FF mix vegetables ½ c. diet peach & pear diet jello cubes 5 vanilla wafers coffee, tea	2 oz. cheese 1 oz. beef 2 slices bread 2 tsp. mayonnaise 1 c. FF mix vegetables ½ c. diet peach & pear diet jello cubes 5 vanilla wafers coffee, tea
SNACK	1 c. skim milk 2 sq. graham crackers	1 c. skim milk 2 sq. graham crackers	1 c. skim milk 2 sq. graham crackers	1 c. skim milk 2 sq. graham crackers	1 c. skim milk 4 sq. graham crackers

DATE ___ Sunday ___   WEEK NO. ___ One ___   MENU CYCLE ___ Fall/Winter

	REGULAR	SOFT/BLAND	2-3 gram sodium	LOW FAT	LOW RESIDUE
BREAKFAST	Orange juice Egg Cereal Toast milk coffee, tea	Orange juice Egg Cereal (no whole grain) Toast milk coffee, tea/sanka	Orange juice Egg Cereal Toast milk coffee, tea	Orange juice 1 FF Egg FF Cereal Toast skim milk coffee, tea	Orange juice Egg Cereal (no whole grain) Toast milk coffee, tea

DINNER	Baked chicken
	  w/paprika
	Dressing
	Gravy
	Cranberry sauce
	Green peas
	Home-made Biscuit
	White cake/choc icing
	
	milk
	coffee, tea
		Baked chicken
		  w/paprika
		Dressing
		Gravy
		Cranberry sauce
		Green peas
		Home-made Biscuit
		White cake/choc icing
		BLAND-no icing
		milk
		coffee, tea
			Baked chicken
			  w/paprika
			Dressing
			SF Gravy
			Cranberry sauce
			Green peas
			Home-made Biscuit
			White cake/choc icing
			
			coffee, tea
				Baked chicken
				  w/paprika
				FF Mashed potatoes
				Cranberry sauce
				FF Green peas
				Loaf bread
				White cake
				
				skim milk
				coffee, tea
					Baked chicken
					  w/paprika
					Mashed potatoes
					Cranberry sauce
					Green peas
					Loaf bread
					White cake
					
					coffee, tea

SUPPER	Beef cubes in gravy Buttered potatoes Parslied Carrots Roll Pineapple w/topping milk coffee, tea	Beef cubes in gravy Buttered potatoes Parslied Carrots Roll Fruit cocktail w/tpg milk coffee, tea/sanka	Beef cubes in SF gravy Buttered potatoes Parslied Carrots Roll Pineapple w/topping milk coffee, tea	Beef cubes au jus FF Potatoes FF Parslied Carrots Roll Pineapple skim milk coffee, tea	Beef cubes au jus Buttered potatoes Parslied Carrots Roll Fruit cocktail w/tpg milk coffee, tea

DATE ___Sunday___   WEEK NO. ___One___   MENU CYCLE   Fall/Winter

	1000 Calories	1200 Calories	1500 Calories	1800 Calories	2000 Calories
BREAKFAST	½ c. orange juice 1 FF egg ½ c. FF cooked cereal 1 oleo 1 c. skim milk coffee, tea	½ c. orange juice 1 FF egg ½ c. FF cooked cereal 1 oleo 1 c. skim milk coffee, tea	½ c. orange juice 1 FF egg ½ c. FF cooked cereal 1 oleo 1 c. skim milk coffee, tea	½ c. orange juice 1 FF egg ½ c. FF cooked cereal 1 toast 2 oleo 1 c. skim milk coffee, tea	½ c. orange juice 2 FF eggs ½ c. FF cooked cereal 1 toast 2 oleo 1 c. skim milk coffee, tea
DINNER	1 oz. baked chicken ½ c. FF squash shredded lettuce 1 oleo small fresh orange 1 c. skim milk coffee, tea	2 oz. baked chicken ½ c. FF squash ½ c. FF mashed potatoes shredded lettuce 1 oleo small fresh orange coffee, tea	2 oz. baked chicken ½ c. FF squash ½ c. FF mashed potatoes shredded lettuce 1 2" biscuit small fresh orange coffee, tea	3 oz. baked chicken ½ c. FF squash ½ c. FF mashed potatoes shredded lettuce 1 2" biscuit 1 oleo small fresh orange coffee, tea	3 oz. baked chicken ½ c. FF squash ½ c. FF mashed potatoes shredded lettuce 2 2" biscuits small fresh orange coffee, tea
SUPPER	2 oz. beef cubes ½ c. FF carrots ½ c. FF potatoes 1 oleo 2 diet pineapple rings coffee, tea	2 oz. beef cubes 1 c. FF carrots ½ c. FF potatoes 1 oleo 2 diet pineapple rings coffee, tea	3 oz. beef cubes ½ c. FF potatoes 1 c. FF carrots 1 roll 2 oleo 2 diet pineapple rings coffee, tea	3 oz. beef cubes 1 c. FF carrots ½ c. FF potatoes 2 rolls 2 oleo 2 diet pineapple rings coffee, tea	3 oz. beef cubes 1 c. FF carrots ½ c. FF potatoes 2 rolls 2 oleo 2 diet pineapple rings coffee, tea
SNACK	1 c. skim milk 2 sq. graham crackers	1 c. skim milk 2 sq. graham crackers	1 c. skim milk 2 sq. graham crackers	1 c. skim milk 2 sq. graham crackers	1 c. skim milk 4 sq. graham crackers

DATE ___ Monday ___ WEEK NO. ___ Two ___ MENU CYCLE ___ Fall/Winter

	REGULAR	SOFT/BLAND	2-3 gram sodium	LOW FAT	LOW RESIDUE
B R E A K F A S T	Orange juice Egg Cereal Toast milk coffee, tea	Orange juice Egg Cereal (no whole grain) Toast milk coffee, tea/sanka	Orange juice 1 Egg Cereal Toast milk coffee, tea	Orange juice 1 FF Egg FF Cereal Toast skim milk coffee, tea	Orange juice Egg Cereal (no whole grain) Toast milk coffee, tea
D I N N E R	Pork chop Blackeyed peas Seasoned Greens Cornbread Banana pudding/ topping milk coffee, tea	Pork chop Mashed potatoes Seasoned greens Cornbread Banana pudding/tpg milk coffee, tea/sanka	Pork chop Blackeyed peas Seasoned Greens Cornbread Banana pudding/tpg coffee, tea	Lean pork chop FF Blackeyed peas FF Seasoned greens Loaf bread Banana skim milk coffee, tea	Pork chop Mashed potatoes Seasoned greens Loaf bread Banana coffee, tea
S U P P E R	Crispy fried chicken Rice & Gravy Stewed okra Roll Fruited bread pudding milk coffee, tea	Broiled chicken Rice & Gravy Stewed okra Roll Fruited bread pudding milk coffee, tea/sanka	Crispy fried chicken Rice & SF Gravy Stewed okra Roll Fruited bread pudding ½ cup milk coffee, tea	Broiled chicken - no skin FF Rice FF Stewed okra Roll Fruit in season skim milk coffee, tea	Broiled chicken Buttered Rice Green peas Roll Soft fruit in season milk coffee, tea

DATE ___ Monday ___ WEEK NO. ___ Two ___ MENU CYCLE ___ Fall/Winter

	1000 Calories	1200 Calories	1500 Calories	1800 Calories	2000 Calories
BREAKFAST	½ c. orange juice 1 FF egg 1 toast 1 oleo 1 c. skim milk coffee, tea	½ c. orange juice 1 FF egg 1 toast 1 oleo 1 c. skim milk coffee, tea	½ c. orange juice 1 FF egg ½ c. FF cooked cereal 1 oleo 1 c. skim milk coffee, tea	½ c. orange juice 1 FF egg ½ c. FF cooked cereal 1 toast 2 oleo 1 c. skim milk coffee, tea	½ c. orange juice 2 FF eggs ½ c. FF cooked cereal 1 toast 2 oleo 1 c. skim milk coffee, tea
DINNER	1 oz. pork 1 c. FF greens 1 oleo ½ small banana 1 c. skim milk coffee, tea	2 oz. pork 1 c. FF greens ½ c. FF blackeyed peas 1 oleo ½ small banana coffee, tea	2 oz. pork 1 c. FF greens ½ c. FF blackeyed peas 2″ square cornbread ½ small banana coffee, tea	3 oz. pork 1 c. FF greens ½ c. FF blackeyed peas 2″ square cornbread 1 oleo ½ small banana coffee, tea	3 oz. pork 1 c. FF greens ½ c. FF blackeyed peas 2″ 2″ squares cornbread ½ small banana coffee, tea
SUPPER	2 oz. chicken ½ c. FF okra 1 roll 1 oleo ½ c. diet applesauce coffee, tea	2 oz. chicken ½ c. FF okra ½ c. FF rice ½ c. tomato juice 1 oleo ½ c. diet applesauce coffee, tea	3 oz. chicken ½ c. FF okra ½ c. FF rice ½ c. tomato juice 1 roll 2 oleo ½ c. diet applesauce coffee, tea	3 oz. chicken ½ c. FF okra ½ c. FF rice ½ c. tomato juice 2 rolls 2 oleo ½ c. diet applesauce coffee, tea	3 oz. chicken ½ c. FF okra ½ c. FF rice ½ c. tomato juice 2 rolls 2 oleo ½ c. diet applesauce coffee, tea
SNACK	1 c. skim milk 2 sq. graham crackers	1 c. skim milk 2 sq. graham crackers	1 c. skim milk 2 sq. graham crackers	1 c. skim milk 2 sq. graham crackers	1 c. skim milk 4 sq. graham crackers

DATE ___Tuesday___   WEEK NO. ___Two___   MENU CYCLE ___Fall/Winter___

	REGULAR	SOFT/BLAND	2-3 gram sodium	LOW FAT	LOW RESIDUE
B R E A K F A S T	Orange juice Egg Cereal Toast milk coffee, tea	Orange juice Egg Cereal (no whole grain) Toast milk coffee, tea/sanka	Orange juice 1 Egg Cereal Toast milk coffee, tea	Orange juice 1 FF Egg FF Cereal Toast skim milk coffee, tea	Orange juice Egg Cereal (no whole grain) Toast milk coffee, tea
D I N N E R	Beef patty w/ mushroom gravy Baby lima beans Squash casserole Cornbread Red jello cake w/tpg milk coffee, tea	Beef patty w/mushroom gravy Baby lima beans Squash casserole (no onion) Cornbread Red jello cake w/tpg milk coffee, tea/sanka	Beef patty Baby lima beans Squash casserole Cornbread Red jello cake w/tpg coffee, tea	Beef patty FF Baby lima beans FF Squash Loaf bread Red jello cubes skim milk coffee, tea	Beef patty Baby lima beans Squash casserole (no onion) Loaf bread Red jello cake w/tpg coffee, tea
S U P P E R	Vegetable soup Toasted cheese sandwich Deviled Egg Fruit mix Chopped lettuce Cookies milk coffee, tea	Vegetable soup Toasted cheese sandwich Deviled Egg Canned fruit mix Chopped lettuce Plain cookies/ no chocolate milk coffee, tea/sanka	SF Vegetable soup Sliced chicken sandwich Fruit mix Chopped lettuce Cookies milk coffee, tea	Vegetable soup FF Sliced chicken sandwich Fruit mix Chopped lettuce Vanilla wafers skim milk coffee, tea	Vegetable soup Sliced chicken sandwich Canned fruit mix Chopped lettuce Plain cookies milk coffee, tea

DATE Tuesday   WEEK NO. Two   MENU CYCLE   Fall/Winter

	1000 Calories	1200 Calories	1500 Calories	1800 Calories	2000 Calories
BREAKFAST	½ c. orange juice 1 FF egg ½ c. FF cooked cereal 1 oleo coffee, tea	½ c. orange juice 1 FF egg ½ c. FF cooked cereal 1 oleo 1 c. skim milk coffee, tea	½ c. orange juice 1 FF egg 1 toast 1 oleo 1 c. skim milk coffee, tea	½ c. orange juice 1 FF egg ½ c. FF cooked cereal 1 toast 2 oleo 1 c. skim milk coffee, tea	½ c. orange juice 2 FF eggs ½ c. FF cooked cereal 1 toast 2 oleo 1 c. skim milk coffee, tea
DINNER	1 oz. beef patty ½ c. FF squash shredded lettuce 1 oleo ½ c. diet peaches 1 c. skim milk coffee, tea	2 oz. beef patty ½ c. FF squash ½ c. FF lima beans shredded lettuce 1 oleo ½ c. diet peaches coffee, tea	2 oz. beef patty ½ c. FF squash ½ c. FF lima beans shredded lettuce 2" square cornbread ½ c. diet peaches coffee, tea	3 oz. beef patty ½ c. FF squash ½ c. FF lima beans shredded lettuce 2" square cornbread 1 oleo ½ c. diet peaches coffee, tea	3 oz. beef patty ½ c. FF squash ½ c. FF lima beans shredded lettuce 2 2" squares cornbread ½ c. diet peaches
SUPPER	2 oz. cheese 1 slice bread 1 tsp. mayonnaise ½ c. FF mix vegetables ½ c. diet frt cocktail coffee, tea	2 oz. cheese 1 slice bread 1 tsp. mayonnaise ½ c. FF mix vegetables ½ c. hot tomato juice ½ c. diet frt cocktail coffee, tea	1 oz. cheese 2 oz. chicken 2 slices bread 2 tsp. mayonnaise ½ c. FF mix vegetables ½ c. hot tomato juice ½ c. diet frt cocktail coffee, tea	1 oz. cheese 2 oz. chicken 2 slices bread 2 tsp. mayonnaise ½ c. FF mix vegetables ½ c. hot tomato juice ½ c. diet frt cocktail 5 vanilla wafers coffee, tea	1 oz. cheese 2 oz. chicken 2 slices bread 2 tsp. mayonnaise ½ c. FF mix vegetables ½ c. hot tomato juice ½ c. diet frt cocktail 5 vanilla wafers coffee, tea
SNACK	1 c. skim milk 2 sq. graham crackers	1 c. skim milk 2 sq. graham crackers	1 c. skim milk 2 sq. graham crackers	1 c. skim milk 2 sq. graham crackers	1 c. skim milk 4 sq. graham crackers

DATE Wednesday   WEEK NO. Two   MENU CYCLE Fall/Winter

	REGULAR	SOFT/BLAND	2-3 gram sodium	LOW FAT	LOW RESIDUE
BREAKFAST	Orange juice Egg Cereal Bacon Toast milk coffee, tea	Orange juice Egg Cereal (no whole grain) Bacon Toast milk coffee, tea/sanka	Orange juice 1 Egg Cereal Toast milk coffee, tea	Orange juice 1 FF Egg FF Cereal Toast skim milk coffee, tea	Orange juice Egg Cereal (no whole grain) Bacon Toast milk coffee, tea
DINNER	Baked ham Scalloped potatoes Seasoned Green beans Home-made Biscuit Chocolate pan pie milk coffee	Baked Ham Scalloped potatoes (no onion) Seasoned Green beans Home-made Biscuit Chocolate pan pie BLAND-vanilla ice cream milk coffee, tea/sanka	Beef cubes au jus Sliced potatoes Seasoned Green beans Home-made Biscuit Chocolate pan pie coffee, tea	Beef cubes au jus FF Sliced potatoes FF Green beans Roll Pineapple skim milk coffee, tea	Beef cubes au jus Sliced potatoes Seasoned Green beans Roll Chocolate pudding coffee, tea
SUPPER	Meat hash Whole kernel corn Okra & tomatoes Cornbread Pear half milk coffee	Meat hash - no onion Creamed potatoes Okra & tomatoes Cornbread Pear half milk coffee, tea/sanka	Meat hash Whole kernel corn Okra & tomatoes Cornbread Pear half ½ cup milk coffee, tea	Meat hash FF Whole kernel corn FF Okra & tomatoes Loaf bread Pear half skim milk coffee, tea	Meat hash - no onion Creamed potatoes Tomato juice Loaf bread Pear half ½ cup milk coffee, tea

DATE ___Wednesday___ WEEK NO. ___Two___ MENU CYCLE ___Fall/Winter___

	1000 Calories	1200 Calories	1500 Calories	1800 Calories	2000 Calories
BREAKFAST	½ c. orange juice 1 FF egg 1 toast 1 bacon 1 c. skim milk coffee, tea	½ c. orange juice 1 FF egg 1 toast 1 bacon 1 c. skim milk coffee, tea	½ c. orange juice 1 FF egg 1 toast 1 bacon 1 c. skim milk coffee, tea	½ c. orange juice 1 FF egg ½ c. FF cooked cereal 1 toast 2 bacon 1 c. skim milk coffee, tea	½ c. orange juice 2 FF eggs ½ c. FF cooked cereal 1 toast 2 bacon 1 c. skim milk coffee, tea
DINNER	1 oz. ham 1 c. FF green beans 1 oleo 2 diet pineapple rings 1 c. skim milk coffee, tea	2 oz. ham 1 c. FF green beans ½ c. FF sliced potatoes 1 oleo 2 diet pineapple rings coffee, tea	2 oz. ham 1 c. FF green beans ½ c. FF sliced potatoes 1 2" home-made biscuit 2 diet pineapple rings coffee, tea	3 oz. ham 1 c. FF green beans ½ c. FF sliced potatoes 2" home-made biscuit 1 oleo 2 diet pineapple rings coffee, tea	3 oz. ham 1 c. FF green beans ½ c. FF sliced potatoes 2 2" home-made biscuits 2 diet pineapple rings coffee, tea
SUPPER	2 oz. ground beef ½ c. FF okra ⅓ c. FF corn 1 oleo 2 diet pear halves coffee, tea	2 oz. ground beef ½ c. FF okra ½ c. FF tomatoes 2" square cornbread 2 diet pear halves coffee, tea	3 oz. ground beef ½ c. FF okra ½ c. FF tomatoes ⅓ c. FF corn 2" square cornbread 1 oleo 2 diet pear halves coffee, tea	3 oz. ground beef ½ c. FF okra ½ c. FF tomatoes ⅓ c. FF corn 2 2" squares cornbread 2 diet pear halves coffee, tea	3 oz. ground beef ½ c. FF okra ½ c. FF tomatoes ⅓ c. FF corn 2 2" squares cornbread 2 diet pear halves coffee, tea
SNACK	1 c. skim milk 2 sq. graham crackers	1 c. skim milk 2 sq. graham crackers	1 c. skim milk 2 sq. graham crackers	1 c. skim milk 2 sq. graham crackers	1 c. skim milk 4 sq. graham crackers

DATE ___Thursday___   WEEK NO. __Two__   MENU CYCLE ___Fall/Winter___

	REGULAR	SOFT/BLAND	2-3 gram sodium	LOW FAT	LOW RESIDUE
BREAKFAST	Orange juice Egg Cereal Toast milk coffee, tea	Orange juice Egg Cereal (no whole grain) Toast milk coffee, tea/sanka	Orange juice 1 Egg Cereal Toast milk coffee, tea	Orange juice 1 FF Egg FF Cereal Toast skim milk coffee, tea	Orange juice Egg Cereal (no whole grain) Toast milk coffee, tea
DINNER	Chicken & Dumplings Green peas Home-made Biscuit Apple crisp milk coffee, tea	Chicken & Dumplings Green peas Home-made Biscuit Apple crisp milk coffee, tea/sanka	Chicken & Dumplings Green peas Home-made Biscuit Apple crisp coffee, tea	Baked Chicken - no skin FF Rice FF Green peas Loaf bread FF Stewed apples skim milk coffee, tea	Baked chicken Buttered rice Green peas Loaf bread Stewed apples coffee, tea
SUPPER	Scrambled egg Sausage pattie Cheese grits Home-made Biscuit Cinnamon fruit mix milk coffee, tea	Scrambled egg Crisp bacon Cheese grits Home-made Biscuit Cinnamon fruit mix milk coffee, tea/sanka	Beef pattie Grits Home-made Biscuit Cinnamon fruit mix milk coffee, tea	Beef pattie FF Grits Toast triangles Cinnamon fruit mix skim milk coffee, tea	Scrambled egg Crisp bacon Cheese grits Toast triangles Cinnamon fruit mix milk coffee, tea

DATE ___Thursday___   MENU CYCLE ___Fall/Winter___

WEEK NO. ___Two___

	1000 Calories	1200 Calories	1500 Calories	1800 Calories	2000 Calories
B R E A K F A S T	½ c. orange juice 1 FF egg 1 toast 1 oleo 1 c. skim milk coffee, tea	½ c. orange juice 1 FF egg 1 toast 1 oleo 1 c. skim milk coffee, tea	½ c. orange juice 1 FF egg 1 toast 1 oleo 1 c. skim milk coffee, tea	½ c. orange juice 1 FF egg ¾ c. dry cereal 1 toast 2 oleo 1 c. skim milk coffee, tea	½ c. orange juice 2 FF eggs ¾ c. dry cereal 1 toast 2 oleo 1 c. skim milk coffee, tea
D I N N E R	1 oz. chicken ½ c. FF cabbage ½ c. tomato juice 1 oleo ½ c. FF stewed apples (no sugar added) 1 c. skim milk coffee, tea	2 oz. chicken ½ c. FF cabbage ½ c. FF rice ½ c. tomato juice 1 oleo ½ c. FF stewed apples (no sugar added) coffee, tea	2 oz. chicken ½ c. FF cabbage ½ c. FF rice ½ c. tomato juice 1 2″ biscuit ½ c. FF stewed apples (no sugar added) coffee, tea	3 oz. chicken ½ c. FF cabbage ½ c. FF rice ½ c. tomato juice 1 2″ biscuit 1 oleo ½ c. FF stewed apples (no sugar added) coffee, tea	3 oz. chicken ½ c. FF cabbage ½ c. FF rice ½ c. tomato juice 2 2″ biscuits ½ c. FF stewed apples (no sugar added) coffee, tea
S U P P E R	2 oz. beef pattie ½ c. FF mix vegetables ½ c. FF mashed potatoes 1 oleo ½ c. diet frt cocktail with cinnamon coffee, tea	2 oz. beef pattie 1 c. FF mix vegetables 1 2″ home-made biscuit ½ c. diet frt cocktail with cinnamon coffee, tea	3 oz. beef pattie 1 c. FF mix vegetables ½ c. FF mashed potatoes 1 2″ home-made biscuit 1 oleo ½ c. diet frt cocktail with cinnamon coffee, tea	3 oz. beef pattie 1 c. FF vegetables ½ c. FF mashed potatoes 2 2″ home-made biscuits ½ c. diet frt cocktail with cinnamon coffee, tea	3 oz. beef pattie 1 c. FF mix vegetables ½ c. FF mashed potatoes 2 2″ home-made biscuits ½ c. diet frt cocktail with cinnamon coffee, tea
S N A C K	1 c. skim milk 2 sq. graham crackers	1 c. skim milk 2 sq. graham crackers	1 c. skim milk 2 sq. graham crackers	1 c. skim milk 2 sq. graham crackers	1 c. skim milk 4 sq. graham crackers

DATE ___Friday___   WEEK NO. ___Two___   MENU CYCLE ___Fall/Winter___

	REGULAR	SOFT/BLAND	2-3 gram sodium	LOW FAT	LOW RESIDUE
BREAKFAST	Orange juice Egg Cereal Toast milk coffee, tea	Orange juice Egg Cereal (no whole grain) Toast milk coffee, tea/ sanka	Orange juice 1 Egg Cereal Toast milk coffee, tea	Orange juice 1 FF Egg FF Cereal Toast skim milk coffee, tea	Orange juice Egg Cereal (no whole grain) Toast milk coffee, tea
DINNER	Baked Chicken Field peas Stewed tomatoes Roll Peaches w/topping milk coffee, tea	Baked Chicken Buttered rice Stewed tomatoes Roll Peaches w/topping milk coffee, tea/sanka	Baked Chicken Field peas Stewed tomatoes Roll Peaches w/topping coffee, tea	Baked Chicken—no skin FF Field peas FF Stewed tomatoes Roll Peaches skim milk coffee, tea	Baked Chicken Buttered rice Tomato juice Roll Peaches w/topping coffee, tea
SUPPER	Beef cubes in gravy Mashed potatoes Glazed Carrots Cornbread Vanilla pudding w/ Grapes jubilee milk coffee, tea	Beef cubes in gravy Mashed potatoes Glazed Carrots Cornbread Vanilla pudding w/ Grapes jubilee milk coffee, tea/sanka	Beef cubes in SF gravy Mashed potatoes Glazed Carrots Cornbread Vanilla pudding w/ Grapes jubilee ½ cup milk coffee, tea	Beef cubes au jus FF Mashed potatoes FF Carrots Loaf bread Grapes jubilee skim milk coffee, tea	Beef cubes au jus Mashed potatoes Glazed Carrots Loaf bread Vanilla pudding w/ Grapes jubilee ½ cup milk coffee, tea

DATE ___Friday___   WEEK NO. ___Two___   MENU CYCLE ___Fall/Winter___

	1000 Calories	1200 Calories	1500 Calories	1800 Calories	2000 Calories
BREAKFAST	½ c. orange juice 1 FF egg 1 toast 1 oleo coffee, tea	½ c. orange juice 1 FF egg 1 toast 1 oleo 1 c. skim milk coffee, tea	½ c. orange juice 1 FF egg 1 toast 1 oleo 1 c. skim milk coffee, tea	½ c. orange juice 1 FF egg ½ c. FF cooked cereal 1 toast 2 oleo 1 c. skim milk coffee, tea	½ c. orange juice 2 FF eggs ½ c. FF cooked cereal 1 toast 2 oleo 1 c. skim milk coffee, tea
DINNER	1 oz. chicken ½ c. FF stewed tomatoes shredded lettuce 1 oleo ½ c. diet peaches 1 c. skim milk coffee, tea	2 oz. chicken ½ c. FF stewed tomatoes ½ c. FF field peas shredded lettuce 1 oleo ½ c. diet peaches coffee, tea	2 oz. chicken ½ c. FF stewed tomatoes ½ c. FF field peas shredded lettuce 1 roll 1 oleo ½ c. diet peaches coffee, tea	3 oz. chicken ½ c. FF stewed tomatoes ½ c. FF field peas shredded lettuce 1 roll 2 oleo ½ c. diet peaches coffee, tea	3 oz. chicken ½ c. FF stewed tomatoes ½ c. FF field peas shredded lettuce 2 rolls 2 oleo ½ c. diet peaches coffee, tea
SUPPER	2 oz. beef cubes ½ c. FF carrots ½ c. FF mashed potatoes 1 oleo 2 tinted diet pear halves coffee, tea	2 oz. beef cubes 1 c. FF carrots 2" sq. cornbread 2 tinted diet pear halves coffee, tea	3 oz. beef cubes 1 c. FF carrots ½ c. FF mashed potatoes 2" sq. cornbread 1 oleo 2 tinted diet pear halves coffee, tea	3 oz. beef cubes 1 c. FF carrots ½ c. FF mashed potatoes 2" sq. cornbread 2 tinted diet pear halves coffee, tea	3 oz. beef cubes 1 c. FF carrots ½ c. FF mashed potatoes 2" sq. cornbread 2 tinted diet pears halves coffee, tea
SNACK	1 c. skim milk 2 sq. graham crackers	1 c. skim milk 2 sq. graham crackers	1 c. skim milk 2 sq. graham crackers	1 c. skim milk 2 sq. graham crackers	1 c. skim milk 4 sq. graham crackers

DATE ___Saturday___   WEEK NO. ___Two___   MENU CYCLE ___Fall/Winter___

	REGULAR	SOFT/BLAND	2-3 gram sodium	LOW FAT	LOW RESIDUE
BREAKFAST	Orange juice Egg Cereal Toast Bacon milk coffee, tea	Orange juice Egg Cereal (no whole grain) Toast Bacon milk coffee, tea/sanka	Orange juice 1 Egg Cereal Toast milk coffee, tea	Orange juice Dry Cereal Toast skim milk coffee, tea	Orange juice Egg Cereal (no whole grain) Toast Bacon milk coffee, tea

DINNER	Vegetable soup
	Egg salad on white &
	  whole wheat bread
	Macaroni salad
	Slice of cheese
	Coleslaw w/tomato
	Rice Krispie square
	
	milk
	coffee, tea
		Vegetable soup
		Egg salad on white &
		  whole wheat bread
		Macaroni salad
		  (no onion, pepper)
		Slice of cheese
		Shredded lettuce
		Rice Krispie square
		
		milk
		coffee, tea/sanka
			SF Vegetable soup
			Egg salad on white &
			  whole wheat bread
			Macaroni salad
			Coleslaw w/tomato
			Rice Krispie square
			
			coffee, tea
				FF Vegetable soup
				Scrambled egg on
				  white & ww bread
				Macaroni salad
				  (little mayonnaise)
				Coleslaw w/tomato
				  (NO mayonnaise)
				Fruit cup
				
				skim milk
				coffee, tea
					Vegetable soup
					Egg salad on white
					  bread
					Macaroni salad
					  (no onion, pepper)
					Shredded lettuce
					Rice Krispie square
					
					coffee, tea

SUPPER	Mock swiss steak Home-made Biscuit Tater Tots Seasoned green beans Tinted applesauce milk coffee, tea	Mock swiss steak Home-made Biscuit Tater Tots Seasoned green beans Tinted applesauce milk coffee, tea/sanka	Mock swiss steak Home-made Biscuit Baked French fries Seasoned green beans Tinted applesauce milk coffee, tea	Mock swiss steak Roll Baked French fries FF green beans Tinted applesauce skim milk coffee, tea	Mock swiss steak Roll Tater Tots Seasoned green beans Tinted applesauce milk coffee, tea

DATE ___Saturday___   WEEK NO. ___Two___   MENU CYCLE ___Fall/Winter___

	1000 Calories	1200 Calories	1500 Calories	1800 Calories	2000 Calories
B R E A K F A S T	½ c. orange juice 1 FF egg ½ c. FF cooked cereal 1 bacon coffee, tea	½ c. orange juice 1 FF egg ½ c. FF cooked cereal 1 bacon 1 c. skim milk coffee, tea	½ c. orange juice 1 FF egg 1 toast 1 bacon 1 c. skim milk coffee, tea	½ c. orange juice 1 FF egg ½ c. FF cooked cereal 1 toast 2 bacon 1 c. skim milk coffee, tea	½ c. orange juice 2 FF eggs ½ c. FF cooked cereal 1 toast 2 bacon 1 c. skim milk coffee, tea
D I N N E R	1 FF egg 1 oleo or mayonnaise ½ c. FF mix vegetables ½ c. FF coleslaw ½ c. diet fruit mix 1 c. skim milk coffee, tea	2 FF eggs 1 whole wheat bread 1 oleo or mayonnaise ½ c. FF mix vegetables ½ c. FF coleslaw ½ c. diet fruit mix coffee, tea	2 FF eggs 2 whole wheat bread 1 oleo or mayonnaise ½ c. FF mix vegetables ½ c. FF coleslaw ½ c. diet fruit mix coffee, tea	2 FF eggs 1 oz. cheese 1 whole wheat bread 2 oleo or mayonnaise ½ c. FF mix vegetables ½ c. FF coleslaw 5 vanilla wafers ½ c. diet fruit mix coffee, tea	2 FF eggs 1 oz. cheese 2 whole wheat bread 2 oleo or mayonnaise ½ c. FF mix vegetables ½ c. FF coleslaw 5 vanilla wafers ½ c. diet fruit mix coffee, tea
S U P P E R	2 oz. beef pattie ½ c. FF green beans 8 baked French fries 1 oleo ½ c. diet pink applesauce coffee, tea	2 oz. beef pattie 1 c. FF green beans 8 baked French fries 1 oleo ½ c. diet pink applesauce coffee, tea	3 oz. beef pattie 1 c. FF green beans 8 baked French fries 1 bread 2 oleo ½ c. diet pink applesauce coffee, tea	3 oz. beef pattie 1 c. FF green beans 16 baked French fries 1 bread 2 oleo ½ c. diet pink applesauce coffee, tea	3 oz. beef pattie 1 c. FF green beans 16 baked French fries 1 bread 2 oleo ½ c. diet pink applesauce coffee, tea
S N A C K	1 c. skim milk 2 sq. graham crackers	1 c. skim milk 2 sq. graham crackers	1 c. skim milk 2 sq. graham crackers	1 c. skim milk 2 sq. graham crackers	1 c. skim milk 4 sq. graham crackers

DATE _____ Sunday _____   WEEK NO. _____ Two _____   MENU CYCLE _____ Fall/Winter

	REGULAR	SOFT/BLAND	2-3 gram sodium	LOW FAT	LOW RESIDUE
B R E A K F A S T	Orange juice Egg Cereal Toast milk coffee, tea	Orange juice Egg Cereal (no whole grain) Toast milk coffee, tea/sanka	Orange juice 1 Egg Cereal Toast milk coffee, tea	Orange juice 1 FF egg FF cereal Toast skim milk coffee, tea	Orange juice Egg Cereal (no whole grain) Toast milk coffee, tea
D I N N E R	Baked ham slice Sweet potato fluff Steamed cabbage Cornbread Pineapple upside-down cake milk coffee, tea	Baked ham slice Sweet potato fluff Spinach/egg slice Cornbread Yellow cake w/ applesauce milk coffee, tea/sanka	Baked fish fillet Sweet potato fluff Steamed cabbage Cornbread Pineapple upside-down cake coffee, tea	FF Baked fish fillet FF Sweet potato fluff FF Steamed cabbage Roll Pineapple rings skim milk coffee, tea	Baked fish fillet Buttered rice Spinach/egg slice Roll Yellow cake w/applesauce coffee, tea
S U P P E R	Chicken fillet Creamed potatoes Sliced beets Loaf bread (white or whole wheat) Green fruited jello w/ topping milk coffee, tea	Chicken fillet Creamed potatoes Sliced Beets Loaf bread (white or whole wheat) Green fruited jello w/ topping milk coffee, tea/sanka	Chicken fillet Creamed potatoes Sliced beets Loaf bread (white or whole wheat) Green fruited jello w/topping milk coffee, tea	Chicken fillet—no skin FF Creamed potatoes FF Sliced beets Loaf bread (white or whole wheat) Green fruited jello w/topping skim milk coffee, tea	Chicken fillet Creamed potatoes Sliced beets Loaf bread (white) Green fruited jello w/topping milk coffee, tea

DATE ___Sunday___   WEEK NO. ___Two___   MENU CYCLE ___Fall/Winter___

	1000 Calories	1200 Calories	1500 Calories	1800 Calories	2000 Calories
B R E A K F A S T	½ c. orange juice 1 FF egg 1 toast 1 oleo 1 c. skim milk coffee, tea	½ c. orange juice 1 FF egg 1 toast 1 oleo 1 c. skim milk coffee, tea	½ c. orange juice 1 FF egg ½ c. FF cooked cereal 1 oleo 1 c. skim milk coffee, tea	½ c. orange juice 1 FF egg ½ c. FF cooked cereal 1 toast 2 oleo 1 c. skim milk coffee, tea	½ c. orange juice 2 FF eggs ½ c. FF cooked cereal 1 toast 2 oleo 1 c. skim milk coffee, tea
D I N N E R	1 oz. ham ½ c. FF cabbage ½ c. FF spinach 1 oleo 2 diet pineapple rings 1 c. skim milk coffee, tea	2 oz. ham ½ c. FF cabbage ½ c. FF spinach ¼ c. FF sweet potato 1 oleo 2 diet pineapple rings coffee, tea	2 oz. ham ½ c. FF cabbage ½ c. FF spinach ¼ c. FF sweet potato 2" square cornbread 2 diet pineapple rings coffee, tea	3 oz. ham ½ c. FF cabbage ½ c. FF spinach ¼ c. FF sweet potato 2" square cornbread 1 oleo 2 diet pineapple rings coffee, tea	3 oz. ham ½ c. FF cabbage ½ c. FF spinach ½ c. FF sweet potato 2" square cornbread 1 oleo 2 diet pineapple rings coffee, tea
S U P P E R	2 oz. chicken ½ c. FF beets ½ c. FF creamed potatoes 1 oleo 1 diet peach half 1 diet pear half coffee, tea	2 oz. chicken ½ c. FF beets ½ c. FF creamed potatoes lettuce salad 1 oleo 1 diet peach half 1 diet pear half coffee, tea	3 oz. chicken ½ c. FF beets ½ c. FF creamed potatoes lettuce salad 1 bread 2 oleo 1 diet peach half 1 diet pear half coffee, tea	3 oz. chicken ½ c. FF beets ½ c. FF creamed potatoes lettuce salad 2 bread 2 oleo 1 diet peach half 1 diet pear half coffee, tea	3 oz. chicken ½ c. FF beets ½ c. FF creamed potatoes lettuce salad 2 breads 2 oleo 1 diet peach half 1 diet pear half coffee, tea
S N A C K	1 c. skim milk 2 sq. graham crackers	1 c. skim milk 2 sq. graham crackers	1 c. skim milk 2 sq. graham crackers	1 c. skim milk 2 sq. graham crackers	1 c. skim milk 4 sq. graham crackers

DATE ___ Monday   WEEK NO. ___ Three   MENU CYCLE ___ Fall/Winter

	REGULAR	SOFT/BLAND	2-3 gram sodium	LOW FAT	LOW RESIDUE
BREAKFAST	Orange juice Egg Cereal Toast milk coffee, tea	Orange juice Egg Cereal (no whole grain) Toast milk coffee, tea/sanka	Orange juice 1 Egg Cereal Toast milk coffee, tea	Orange juice 1 FF Egg FF Cereal Toast skim milk coffee, tea	Orange juice Egg Cereal (no whole grain) Toast milk coffee, tea
DINNER	BBQ Beef Buttered potatoes Seasoned Green beans Cornbread Mock Pecan pie milk coffee, tea	Mild BBQ Beef Buttered potatoes Seasoned Green beans Cornbread Lemon pudding milk coffee, tea/sanka	Plain Beef Buttered potatoes Seasoned Green beans Cornbread Mock Pecan pie coffee, tea	Plain Beef FF Potatoes FF Green beans Loaf bread Fruit in season skim milk coffee, tea	Plain Beef Buttered potatoes Seasoned Green beans Loaf bread Lemon pudding coffee, tea
SUPPER	Salmon pattie Baked grits Breaded tomatoes Whole Wheat bread Pear w/prune milk coffee, tea	Salmon pattie Baked grits Breaded tomatoes Whole Wheat bread Pear halves milk coffee, tea/sanka	Fish fillet Baked grits Breaded tomatoes Whole Wheat bread Pear w/prune milk coffee, tea	Salmon pattie FF Baked grits FF Breaded tomatoes Whole Wheat bread Pear w/prune skim milk coffee, tea	Salmon pattie Baked grits Tomato juice White bread Pear halves ½ cup milk coffee, tea

DATE ___Monday___   WEEK NO. ___Three___   MENU CYCLE ___Fall/Winter___

	1000 Calories	1200 Calories	1500 Calories	1800 Calories	2000 Calories
BREAKFAST	½ c. orange juice 1 FF egg 1 toast 1 oleo coffee, tea	½ c. orange juice 1 FF egg 1 toast 1 oleo 1 c. skim milk coffee, tea	½ c. orange juice 1 FF egg 1 toast 1 oleo 1 c. skim milk coffee, tea	½ c. orange juice 1 FF egg ½ c. FF cooked cereal 1 toast 2 oleo 1 c. skim milk coffee, tea	½ c. orange juice 2 FF eggs ½ c. FF cooked cereal 1 toast 2 oleo 1 c. skim milk coffee, tea
DINNER	1 oz. beef 1 c. FF green beans 1 oleo ½ c. diet fruit 1 c. skim milk coffee, tea	2 oz. beef 1 c. FF green beans 2" sq. cornbread ½ c. diet fruit coffee, tea	2 oz. beef 1 c. FF green beans ½ c. FF potatoes 2" sq. cornbread ½ c. diet fruit coffee, tea	3 oz. beef 1 c. FF green beans ½ c. FF potatoes 2" sq. cornbread 1 oleo ½ c. diet fruit coffee, tea	3 oz. beef 1 c. FF green beans ½ c. FF potatoes 2 2" sq. cornbread ½ c. diet fruit coffee, tea
SUPPER	2 oz. baked salmon ½ c. FF tomatoes ½ c. FF grits 1 oleo 1 diet pear half 1 prune coffee, tea	2 oz. baked salmon ½ c. FF tomatoes ½ c. FF grits shredded lettuce 1 oleo 1 diet pear half 1 prune coffee, tea	3 oz. baked salmon ½ c. FF tomatoes ½ c. FF grits shredded lettuce 1 slice bread 2 oleo 1 diet pear half 1 prune coffee, tea	3 oz. baked salmon ½ c. FF tomatoes ½ c. FF grits shredded lettuce 2 slices bread 2 oleo 1 diet pear half 1 prune coffee, tea	3 oz. baked salmon ½ c. FF tomatoes ½ c. FF grits shredded lettuce 2 slices bread 2 oleo 1 diet pear half 1 prune coffee, tea
SNACK	1 c. skim milk 2 sq. graham crackers	1 c. skim milk 2 sq. graham crackers	1 c. skim milk 2 sq. graham crackers	1 c. skim milk 2 sq. graham crackers	1 c. skim milk 4 sq. graham crackers

DATE Tuesday WEEK NO. Three MENU CYCLE Fall/Winter

	REGULAR	SOFT/BLAND	2-3 gram sodium	LOW FAT	LOW RESIDUE
BREAKFAST	Orange juice Egg Cereal Toast milk coffee, tea	Orange juice Egg Cereal (no whole grain) Toast milk coffee, tea/sanka	Orange juice 1 Egg Cereal Toast milk coffee, tea	Orange juice 1 FF Egg FF Cereal Toast skim milk coffee, tea	Orange juice Egg Cereal (**no** whole grain) Toast milk coffee, tea

DINNER	Roast pork
	Pinto beans
	Seasoned greens
	Cornbread
	White cake/
	  peanut butter icing
	
	milk
	coffee, tea
		Roast pork
		Buttered rice
		Seasoned greens
		Cornbread
		White cake/
		  peanut butter icing
		
		milk
		coffee, tea/sanka
			Fresh roast pork
			Pinto beans
			Seasoned greens
			Cornbread
			White cake/
			  peanut butter icing
			
			coffee, tea
				Lean roast pork
				FF Pinto beans
				FF Greens
				Loaf bread
				Cherries
				
				skim milk
				coffee, tea
					Roast pork
					Buttered rice
					Seasoned greens
					Loaf bread
					White cake/
					  peanut butter icing
					
					coffee, tea

SUPPER	Chicken paprika
	Cheese scalloped
	  potatoes
	Green peas
	Roll
	Fruit mix w/topping
	
	milk
	coffee, tea
		Chicken paprika
		Cheese scalloped
		  potatoes (no onion)
		Green peas
		Roll
		Canned fruit mix
		  w/topping
		
		milk
		coffee, tea/sanka
			Chicken paprika
			Sliced potatoes
			Green peas
			Roll
			Fruit mix w/topping
			
			milk
			coffee, tea
				Chicken paprika—
				  no skin
				FF Sliced potatoes
				FF Green peas
				Roll
				Fruit mix
				
				skim milk
				coffee, tea
					Chicken paprika
					Sliced potatoes
					Green peas
					Roll
					Canned fruit mix
					  w/topping
					
					milk
					coffee, tea

DATE _____ Tuesday _____   WEEK NO. _____ Three _____   MENU CYCLE _____ Fall/Winter

	1000 Calories	1200 Calories	1500 Calories	1800 Calories	2000 Calories
BREAKFAST	½ c. orange juice 1 FF egg 1 toast 1 oleo	½ c. orange juice 1 FF egg 1 toast 1 oleo	½ c. orange juice 1 FF egg 1 toast 1 oleo	½ c. orange juice 1 FF egg ¾ c. dry cereal 1 toast 2 oleo	½ c. orange juice 2 FF eggs ¾ c. dry cereal 1 toast 2 oleo
	1 c. skim milk coffee, tea	1 c. skim milk coffee, tea	1 c. skim milk coffee, tea	1 c. skim milk coffee, tea	1 c. skim milk coffee, tea
DINNER	1 oz. pork ½ c. FF greens ½ c. FF carrots 1 oleo 2 diet pineapple rings	2 oz. pork ½ c. FF greens ½ c. FF carrots ½ c. FF pinto beans 1 oleo 2 diet pineapple rings	2 oz. pork ½ c. FF greens ½ c. FF carrots ½ c. FF pinto beans 2" square cornbread 2 diet pineapple rings	3 oz. pork ½ c. FF greens ½ c. FF carrots ½ c. FF pinto beans 2" square cornbread 1 oleo 2 diet pineapple rings	3 oz. pork ½ c. FF greens ½ c. FF carrots ½ c. FF pinto beans 2 2" squares cornbread 2 diet pineapple rings
	1 c. skim milk coffee, tea	coffee, tea	coffee, tea	coffee, tea	coffee, tea
SUPPER	2 oz. chicken ½ c. FF spinach ½ c. FF sliced potatoes 1 oleo ½ c. diet fruit mixed	2 oz. chicken ½ c. FF spinach ½ c. FF squash ½ c. FF sliced potatoes 1 oleo ½ c. diet fruit mixed	3 oz. chicken ½ c. FF spinach ½ c. FF squash ½ c. FF sliced potatoes 1 roll 2 oleo ½ c. diet fruit mixed	3 oz. chicken ½ c. FF spinach ½ c. FF squash ½ c. FF sliced potatoes 2 rolls 2 oleo ½ c. diet fruit mixed	3 oz. chicken ½ c. FF spinach ½ c. FF squash ½ c. FF sliced potatoes 2 rolls 2 oleo ½ c. diet fruit mixed
	coffee, tea	coffee, tea	coffee, tea	coffee, tea	coffee, tea
SNACK	1 c. skim milk 2 sq. graham crackers	1 c. skim milk 2 sq. graham crackers	1 c. skim milk 2 sq. graham crackers	1 c. skim milk 2 sq. graham crackers	1 c. skim milk 4 sq. graham crackers

DATE Wednesday   WEEK NO. Three   MENU CYCLE   Fall/Winter

	REGULAR	SOFT/BLAND	2-3 gram sodium	LOW FAT	LOW RESIDUE
BREAKFAST	Orange juice Egg Cereal Toast milk coffee, tea	Orange juice Egg Cereal (no whole grain) Toast milk coffee, tea/sanka	Orange juice 1 Egg Cereal Toast milk coffee, tea	Orange juice 1 FF Egg FF Cereal Toast skim milk coffee, tea	Orange juice Egg Cereal (no whole grain) Toast milk coffee, tea
DINNER	Fried fish fillet Creamed corn Stewed okra Cornbread Red fruited jello w/topping milk coffee, tea	Baked fish fillet Buttered rice Stewed okra Cornbread Red fruited jello w/topping milk coffee, tea/sanka	Fried fish fillet Creamed corn Stewed okra Cornbread Red fruited jello w/topping coffee, tea	Baked fish fillet FF Creamed corn FF stewed okra Roll Red fruited jello skim milk coffee, tea	Baked fish fillet Buttered rice Tomato juice Roll Red fruited jello w/topping coffee, tea
SUPPER	Pancakes Syrup Eggs w/cheese Crisp bacon Cinnamon applesauce milk coffee, tea	Pancakes Syrup Egg w/cheese Crisp bacon Cinnamon applesauce milk coffee, tea/sanka	Pancakes Syrup Beef pattie Cinnamon applesauce milk coffee, tea	Rinsed cottage cheese Asst. fruits FF Chicken broth Toast triangles Cinnamon applesauce skim milk coffee, tea	Egg w/cheese Crisp bacon Cinnamon applesauce Toast triangles milk coffee, tea

DATE Wednesday WEEK NO. Three MENU CYCLE Fall/Winter

	1000 Calories	1200 Calories	1500 Calories	1800 Calories	2000 Calories
BREAKFAST	½ c. orange juice 1 FF egg ½ c. FF cooked cereal 1 oleo coffee, tea	½ c. orange juice 1 FF egg ½ c. FF cooked cereal 1 oleo 1 c. skim milk coffee, tea	½ c. orange juice 1 FF egg ½ c. FF cooked cereal 1 oleo 1 c. skim milk coffee, tea	½ c. orange juice 1 FF egg ½ c. FF cooked cereal 1 toast 2 oleo 1 c. skim milk coffee, tea	½ c. orange juice 2 FF eggs ½ c. FF cooked cereal 1 toast 2 oleo 1 c. skim milk coffee, tea
DINNER	2 oz. baked fish ½ c. FF okra shredded lettuce 1 oleo ½ small banana 1 c. skim milk coffee, tea	2 oz. baked fish ½ c. FF okra ⅓ c. FF corn shredded lettuce 1 oleo ½ small banana coffee, tea	2 oz. baked fish ½ c. FF okra ⅓ c. FF corn shredded lettuce 2" square cornbread ½ small banana coffee, tea	3 oz. baked fish ½ c. FF okra ⅓ c. FF corn shredded lettuce 2" square cornbread 1 oleo ½ small banana coffee, tea	3 oz. baked fish ½ c. FF okra ⅔ c. FF corn shredded lettuce 2" square cornbread 1 oleo ½ small banana coffee, tea
SUPPER	2 FF eggs 1 5" pancake ½ c. tomato juice ½ c. diet applesauce coffee, tea	2 FF eggs 1 5" pancake 1 c. tomato juice ½ c. diet applesauce coffee, tea	2 FF eggs 1 oz. cheese 2 5" pancakes ½ c. tomato juice ½ c. diet applesauce coffee, tea	2 FF eggs 1 oz. cheese 2 5" pancakes 1 c. tomato juice 5 vanilla wafers ½ c. diet applesauce coffee, tea	2 FF eggs 1 oz. cheese 2 5" pancakes 1 c. tomato juice 5 vanilla wafers ½ c. diet applesauce coffee, tea
SNACK	1 c. skim milk 2 sq. graham crackers	1 c. skim milk 2 sq. graham crackers	1 c. skim milk 2 sq. graham crackers	1 c. skim milk 2 sq. graham crackers	1 c. skim milk 4 sq. graham crackers

DATE Thursday WEEK NO. Three MENU CYCLE Fall/Winter

	REGULAR	SOFT/BLAND	2-3 gram sodium	LOW FAT	LOW RESIDUE
BREAKFAST	Orange juice Egg Cereal Toast Crisp bacon milk coffee, tea	Orange juice Egg Cereal (no whole grain) Toast Crisp bacon milk coffee, tea/sanka	Orange juice 1 Egg Cereal Toast milk coffee, tea	Orange juice 1 FF Egg FF Cereal Toast skim milk coffee, tea	Orange juice Egg Cereal (no whole grain) Toast Crisp bacon milk coffee, tea
DINNER	Crispy fried chicken Creamed potatoes Seasoned green beans Home-made biscuit Peach cobbler milk coffee, tea	Crispy baked chicken Creamed potatoes Seasoned green beans Home-made biscuit Peach cobbler milk coffee, tea/sanka	Crispy fried chicken Creamed potatoes Seasoned green beans Home-made biscuit Peach cobbler coffee, tea	Baked chicken— no skin FF Creamed potatoes FF Green beans Roll Peaches skim milk coffee, tea	Baked chicken Creamed potatoes Green beans Roll Peaches coffee, tea
SUPPER	Vegetable plate: Macaroni & cheese Sliced beets Green peas Deviled egg Slice of bread Peanut butter "Smore" milk coffee, tea	Vegetable plate: Macaroni & cheese Sliced beets Green peas Deviled egg Slice of bread Peanut butter "Smore" milk coffee, tea/sanka	Vegetable plate: Buttered macaroni Sliced beets Green peas Beef pattie Slice of bread Graham crackers milk coffee, tea	Vegetable plate: FF Macaroni FF Sliced beets FF Green peas Beef pattie Slice of bread Graham crackers skim milk coffee, tea	Vegetable plate: Macaroni & cheese Sliced beets Green peas Deviled egg Bread Peanut butter "Smore" milk coffee, tea

DATE ___Thursday___   WEEK NO. ___Three___   MENU CYCLE ___Fall/Winter___

	1000 Calories	1200 Calories	1500 Calories	1800 Calories	2000 Calories
BREAKFAST	½ c. orange juice 1 FF egg 1 toast 1 bacon 1 c. skim milk coffee, tea	½ c. orange juice 1 FF egg 1 toast 1 bacon 1 c. skim milk coffee, tea	½ c. orange juice 1 FF egg ½ c. FF cooked cereal 1 bacon 1 c. skim milk coffee, tea	½ c. orange juice 1 FF egg ½ c. FF cooked cereal 1 toast 2 bacon 1 c. skim milk coffee, tea	½ c. orange juice 2 FF eggs ½ c. FF cooked cereal 1 toast 2 bacon 1 c. skim milk coffee, tea
DINNER	1 oz. baked chicken 1 c. FF green beans 1 oleo ½ c. diet peaches 1 c. skim milk coffee, tea	2 oz. baked chicken 1 c. FF green beans ½ c. FF crm potatoes 1 oleo ½ c. diet peaches coffee, tea	2 oz. baked chicken 1 c. FF green beans ½ c. FF crm potatoes 1 2" biscuit ½ c. diet peaches coffee, tea	3 oz. baked chicken 1 c. FF green beans ½ c. FF crm potatoes 2" biscuit 1 oleo ½ c. diet peaches coffee, tea	3 oz. baked chicken 1 c. FF green beans ½ c. FF crm potatoes 2 2" biscuits ½ c. diet peaches coffee, tea
SUPPER	2 oz. beef patty ½ c. FF beets 1 bread 1 oleo 2 diet pear halves coffee, tea	2 oz. beef patty ½ c. FF beets ¼ c. FF green peas 1 bread 1 oleo 2 diet pear halves coffee, tea	2 oz. beef patty 1 hard cooked egg ½ c. FF beets ¼ c. FF green peas 1 bread 2 oleo 5 vanilla wafers 2 diet pear halves coffee, tea	2 oz. beef patty 1 hard cooked egg ½ c. FF beets ¼ c. FF green peas 2 bread 2 oleo 5 vanilla wafers 2 diet pear halves coffee, tea	2 oz. beef patty 1 hard cooked egg ½ c. FF beets ¼ c. FF green peas 2 bread 2 oleo 5 vanilla wafers 2 diet pear halves coffee, tea
SNACK	1 c. skim milk 2 sq. graham crackers	1 c. skim milk 2 sq. graham crackers	1 c. skim milk 2 sq. graham crackers	1 c. skim milk 2 sq. graham crackers	1 c. skim milk 4 sq. graham crackers

DATE ___Friday___   WEEK NO. ___Three___   MENU CYCLE ___Fall/Winter___

	REGULAR	SOFT/BLAND	2-3 gram sodium	LOW FAT	LOW RESIDUE
BREAKFAST	Orange juice Egg Cereal Toast milk coffee, tea	Orange juice Egg Cereal (no whole grain) Toast milk coffee, tea/sanka	Orange juice 1 Egg Cereal Toast milk coffee, tea	Orange juice 1 FF Egg FF Cereal Toast skim milk coffee, tea	Orange juice Egg Cereal (no whole grain) Toast milk coffee, tea

DINNER	Pork chop
	Blackeyed peas
	Seasoned greens
	Cornbread
	White cake w/2-3 oz.
	  fruit topping
	
	milk
	coffee, tea
		Pork chop
		Buttered rice
		Seasoned greens
		Cornbread
		White cake w/2-3 oz.
		  fruit topping
		
		milk
		coffee, tea/sanka
			Pork chop
			Blackeyed peas
			Seasoned greens
			Cornbread
			White cake w/2-3 oz.
			  fruit topping
			
			coffee, tea
				Lean pork chop
				FF Blackeyed peas
				FF Greens
				Roll
				Fruit in season
				
				skim milk
				coffee, tea
					Pork chop
					Buttered rice
					Seasoned greens
					Roll
					White cake w/2-3 oz.
					  fruit topping
					
					coffee, tea

SUPPER	Sloppy Joe on bun
	Potato salad w/paprika
	Sliced tomatoes
	Dill pickle strips
	Fruit mix w/topping
	
	milk
	coffee, tea
		Sloppy Joe on bun
		  (no onion, pepper)
		Potato salad w/paprika
		  (no onion, pepper)
		Sliced tomatoes
		Canned fruit mix
		  w/topping
		
		milk
		coffee, tea/sanka
			Scrambled beef on bun
			Potato salad w/paprika
			Sliced tomatoes
			Fruit mix w/topping
			
			milk
			coffee, tea
				Sloppy Joe on bun
				Potato salad w/paprika
				  (little mayonnaise)
				Sliced tomatoes
				Fruit mix
				
				skim milk
				coffee, tea
					Sloppy Joe on bun
					  (no onion, pepper)
					Potato salad w/paprika
					  (no onion, pepper)
					Tomato juice
					Canned fruit mix
					  w/topping
					
					milk
					coffee, tea

DATE Friday WEEK NO. Three MENU CYCLE Fall/Winter

	1000 Calories	1200 Calories	1500 Calories	1800 Calories	2000 Calories
BREAKFAST	½ c. orange juice	½ c. orange juice	½ c. orange juice	½ c. orange juice	½ c. orange juice
	1 FF egg	1 FF egg	1 FF egg	1 FF egg	2 FF eggs
	½ c. FF cooked cereal	½ c. FF cooked cereal	½ c. FF cooked cereal	½ c. FF cooked cereal	½ c. FF cooked cereal
	1 oleo	1 oleo	1 oleo	1 toast	1 toast
				2 oleo	2 oleo
	1 c. skim milk	1 c. skim milk	1 c. skim milk	1 c. skim milk	1 c. skim milk
	coffee, tea	coffee, tea	coffee, tea	coffee, tea	coffee, tea
DINNER	1 oz. pork	2 oz. pork	2 oz. pork	3 oz. pork	3 oz. pork
	1 c. FF greens	1 c. FF greens	1 c. FF greens	1 c. FF greens	1 c. FF greens
	1 oleo	2" square cornbread	½ c. FF blackeyed peas	½ c. FF blackeyed peas	½ c. FF blackeyed peas
	½ c. diet frt cocktail	½ c. diet frt cocktail	2" square cornbread	2" square cornbread	2 2" squares cornbread
			½ c. diet frt cocktail	1 oleo	½ c. diet frt cocktail
	1 c. skim milk			½ c. diet frt cocktail	
	coffee, tea	coffee, tea	coffee, tea	coffee, tea	coffee, tea
SUPPER	2 oz. ground beef	2 oz. ground beef	3 oz. ground beef	3 oz. ground beef	3 oz. ground beef
	½ c. FF mix vegetables	½ c. FF mix vegetables	½ c. FF mix vegetables	1 bun	1 bun
	½ c. FF potatoes	sliced tomatoes	sliced tomatoes	½ c. FF mix vegetables	½ c. FF mix vegetables
	1 oleo	½ c. FF potatoes	½ c. FF potatoes	sliced tomatoes	sliced tomatoes
	1 diet pineapple ring	1 oleo	1 bread	½ c. FF potatoes	½ c. FF potatoes
	1 diet peach half	1 diet pineapple ring	2 oleo or mayonnaise	2 oleo or mayonnaise	2 oleo or mayonnaise
		1 diet peach half	1 diet pineapple ring	1 diet pineapple ring	1 diet pineapple ring
			1 diet peach half	1 diet peach half	1 diet peach half
	coffee, tea	coffee, tea	coffee, tea	coffee, tea	coffee, tea
SNACK	1 c. skim milk	1 c. skim milk	1 c. skim milk	1 c. skim milk	1 c. skim milk
	2 sq. graham crackers	2 sq. graham crackers	2 sq. graham crackers	2 sq. graham crackers	4 sq. graham crackers

DATE __Saturday__   WEEK NO. __Three__   MENU CYCLE   __Fall/Winter__

	REGULAR	SOFT/BLAND	2-3 gram sodium	LOW FAT	LOW RESIDUE
BREAKFAST	Orange juice Egg Cereal Toast milk coffee, tea	Orange juice Egg Cereal (no whole grain) Toast milk coffee, tea/sanka	Orange juice 1 Egg Cereal Toast milk coffee, tea	Orange juice 1 FF Egg FF Cereal Toast skim milk coffee, tea	Orange juice Egg Cereal (no whole grain) Toast milk coffee, tea
DINNER	Baked calves liver Field peas Steamed cabbage Cornbread Baked apple milk coffee, tea	Baked calves liver Buttered potatoes Wax beans Cornbread Baked apple—no skin milk coffee, tea/sanka	Baked calves liver Field peas Steamed cabbage Cornbread Baked apple coffee, tea	Baked calves liver FF field peas FF steamed cabbage Loaf bread Baked apple skim milk coffee, tea	Baked calves liver Buttered potatoes Wax beans Loaf bread Baked apple—no skin coffee, tea
SUPPER	Chicken supreme Buttered rice Broccoli/cheese sauce Roll Citrus sections milk coffee, tea	Chicken supreme Buttered rice Stewed squash Roll Citrus sections milk coffee, tea/sanka	Chicken/SF mushroom soup Buttered rice Broccoli/lemon wedge Roll Citrus sections milk coffee, tea	Chicken supreme— no skin FF rice Broccoli/lemon wedge Roll Citrus sections skim milk coffee, tea	Chicken supreme Buttered rice Stewed squash Roll Citrus sections milk coffee, tea

DATE _____   Saturday _____   WEEK NO. _____   Three _____   MENU CYCLE _____   Fall/Winter

	1000 Calories	1200 Calories	1500 Calories	1800 Calories	2000 Calories
BREAKFAST	½ c. orange juice 1 FF egg 1 toast 1 oleo coffee, tea	½ c. orange juice 1 FF egg 1 toast 1 oleo 1 c. skim milk coffee, tea	½ c. orange juice 1 FF egg 1 toast 1 oleo 1 c. skim milk coffee, tea	½ c. orange juice 1 FF egg ¾ c. dry cereal 1 toast 2 oleo 1 c. skim milk coffee, tea	½ c. orange juice 2 FF eggs ¾ c. dry cereal 1 toast 2 oleo 1 c. skim milk coffee, tea
DINNER	1 oz. liver ½ c. FF cabbage ½ c. FF wax beans 1 oleo small baked apple FF (no sugar added) 1 c. skim milk coffee, tea	2 oz. liver ½ c. FF cabbage ½ c. FF wax beans ½ c. FF field peas 1 oleo small baked apple FF (no sugar added) coffee, tea	2 oz. liver ½ c. FF cabbage ½ c. FF wax beans ½ c. FF field peas 2" square cornbread small baked apple FF (no sugar added) coffee, tea	3 oz. liver ½ c. FF cabbage ½ c. FF wax beans ½ c. FF field peas 2" square cornbread 1 oleo small baked apple FF (no sugar added) coffee, tea	3 oz. liver ½ c. FF cabbage ½ c. FF wax beans ½ c. FF field peas 2 2" squares cornbread small baked apple FF (no sugar added) coffee, tea
SUPPER	2 oz. chicken ½ c. FF broccoli ½ c. FF rice 1 oleo 1 small orange coffee, tea	2 oz. chicken ½ c. FF broccoli ½ c. FF squash ½ c. FF rice 1 oleo 1 small orange coffee, tea	3 oz. chicken ½ c. FF broccoli ½ c. FF squash ½ c. FF rice 1 roll 2 oleo 1 small orange coffee, tea	3 oz. chicken ½ c. FF broccoli ½ c. FF squash ½ c. FF rice 2 rolls 2 oleo 1 small orange coffee, tea	3 oz. chicken ½ c. FF broccoli ½ c. FF squash ½ c. FF rice 2 rolls 2 oleo 1 small orange coffee, tea
SNACK	1 c. skim milk 2 sq. graham crackers	1 c. skim milk 2 sq. graham crackers	1 c. skim milk 2 sq. graham crackers	1 c. skim milk 2 sq. graham crackers	1 c. skim milk 4 sq. graham crackers

DATE ___Sunday___ WEEK NO. ___Three___ MENU CYCLE ___Fall/Winter___

	REGULAR	SOFT/BLAND	2-3 gram sodium	LOW FAT	LOW RESIDUE
BREAKFAST	Orange juice Egg Bacon Cereal Toast milk coffee, tea	Orange juice Egg Bacon Cereal (no whole grain) Toast milk coffee, tea/sanka	Orange juice 1 Egg Cereal Toast milk coffee, tea	Orange juice 1 FF Egg FF Cereal Toast skim milk coffee, tea	Orange juice Egg Bacon Cereal (no whole grain) Toast milk coffee, tea
DINNER	Country fried steak Baked potato Glazed Carrots Home-made Biscuit Strawberry shortcake milk coffee, tea	Country baked steak Baked potato - no skin Glazed Carrots Home-made Biscuit Cake w/applesauce milk coffee, tea/sanka	Country fried steak Baked potato Glazed Carrots Home-made Biscuit Strawberry shortcake coffee, tea	Country baked steak Baked potato FF Carrots Loaf bread Strawberries skim milk coffee, tea	Country baked steak Baked potato - no skin Glazed carrots Loaf bread Cake w/applesauce coffee, tea
SUPPER	Vegetable soup Egg salad sandwich Slice of cheese Fruited jello square Ice cream milk coffee, tea	Vegetable soup Egg salad sandwich Slice of cheese Fruited jello square Ice cream/no chocolate milk coffee, tea/sanka	SF Vegetable soup Sliced chicken sandwich Fruited jello square Ice cream milk coffee, tea	Vegetable soup Sliced chicken sandwich Fruited jello square Sherbet skim milk coffee, tea	Vegetable soup Egg salad sandwich Fruited jello square Ice cream ½ cup milk coffee, tea

DATE _____ Sunday   WEEK NO. _____ Three   MENU CYCLE   Fall/Winter

	1000 Calories	1200 Calories	1500 Calories	1800 Calories	2000 Calories
BREAKFAST	½ c. orange juice 1 FF egg 1 toast 1 bacon 1 c. skim milk coffee, tea	½ c. orange juice 1 FF egg 1 toast 1 bacon 1 c. skim milk coffee, tea	½ c. orange juice 1 FF egg ½ c. FF cooked cereal 1 bacon 1 c. skim milk coffee, tea	½ c. orange juice 1 FF egg ½ c. FF cooked cereal 1 toast 2 bacon 1 c. skim milk coffee, tea	½ c. orange juice 2 FF eggs ½ c. FF cooked cereal 1 toast 2 bacon 1 c. skim milk coffee, tea
DINNER	1 oz. baked steak 1 c. FF carrots 1 oleo ½ c. diet fruit mixed 1 c. skim milk coffee, tea	2 oz. baked steak 1 c. FF carrots ½ c. FF potato 1 oleo ½ c. diet fruit mixed coffee, tea	2 oz. baked steak 1 c. FF carrots ½ c. FF potato 1 2" biscuit ½ c. diet fruit mixed coffee, tea	3 oz. baked steak 1 c. FF carrots ½ c. FF potato 1 2" biscuit 1 oleo ½ c. diet fruit mixed coffee, tea	3 oz. baked steak 1 c. FF carrots ½ c. FF potato 2 2" biscuits ½ c. diet fruit mixed coffee, tea
SUPPER	1 oz. chicken 1 bread 1 tsp. mayonnaise 1 FF egg ½ c. FF mix vegetables ½ c. tomato juice ½ c. diet tinted applesauce coffee, tea	1 oz. chicken 1 bread 1 tsp. mayonnaise 1 FF egg ½ c. FF mix vegetables ½ c. tomato juice ½ c. diet tinted applesauce coffee, tea	2 oz. chicken 2 bread 2 tsp. mayonnaise 1 FF egg ½ c. FF mix vegetables ½ c. tomato juice ½ c. diet tinted applesauce coffee, tea	2 oz. chicken 2 bread 2 tsp. mayonnaise 1 FF egg ½ c. FF mix vegetables ½ c. tomato juice ½ c. diet tinted applesauce 5 vanilla wafers coffee, tea	2 oz. chicken 2 bread 2 tsp. mayonnaise 1 FF egg ½ c. FF mix vegetables ½ c. tomato juice ½ c. diet tinted applesauce 5 vanilla wafers coffee, tea
SNACK	1 c. skim milk 2 sq. graham crackers	1 c. skim milk 2 sq. graham crackers	1 c. skim milk 2 sq. graham crackers	1 c. skim milk 2 sq. graham crackers	1 c. skim milk 4 sq. graham crackers

DATE   Monday   WEEK NO.   One   MENU CYCLE   Spring/Summer

	REGULAR	SOFT/BLAND	2-3 gram sodium	LOW FAT	LOW RESIDUE
B R E A K F A S T	Orange juice Egg Cereal Toast Milk Coffee, tea	Orange juice Egg Cereal (no whole grain) Toast Milk Coffee, tea/Sanka	Orange juice 1 Egg Cereal Toast Milk Coffee, tea	Orange juice 1 FF Egg FF Cereal Toast Skim milk Coffee, tea	Orange juice Egg Cereal (no whole grain) Toast Milk Coffee, tea
D I N N E R	Country fried steak Snowflake Potatoes Seasoned Greens Cornbread Sunshine gingerbread (w/peaches) Milk Coffee, tea	Country baked steak Snowflake Potatoes Seasoned Greens Cornbread Sunshine gingerbread (w/peaches) Milk Coffee, tea/Sanka	Country fried steak Snowflake Potatoes Seasoned Greens Cornbread Peaches Coffee, tea	Country baked steak FF Snowflake Potatoes FF Greens Loaf bread Peaches Skim milk Coffee, tea	Country baked steak Snowflake Potatoes Greens Loaf bread Peaches Coffee, tea
S U P P E R	Frankfurter Baked beans Slice of cheese Coleslaw Lime jello/fruit mix Bun Butterscotch pudding/topping Milk Coffee, tea	Hamburger Potatoes Sliced tomatoes Lime jello/fruit mix Bun Butterscotch pudding/topping Milk Coffee, tea/Sanka	Hamburger Potatoes Coleslaw Lime jello/fruit mix Bun Butterscotch pudding/topping ½ cup Milk Coffee, tea	Hamburger Potatoes Tomato juice Coleslaw Lime jello/fruit mix Bun Graham crackers Skim milk Coffee, tea	Hamburger Potatoes Tomato juice Lime jello/fruit mix Bun Butterscotch pudding/topping ½ cup Milk Coffee, tea

At least one menu per day is to be prepared with bran.

DATE ___Monday___   WEEK NO. ___One___   MENU CYCLE   Spring/Summer

	1000 Calories	1200 Calories	1500 Calories	1800 Calories	2000 Calories
BREAKFAST	½ c. orange juice 1 FF egg 1 toast	½ c. orange juice 1 FF egg 1 toast 1 oleo	½ c. orange juice 1 FF egg 1 toast 1 oleo	½ c. orange juice 1 FF egg 1 toast ½ c. FF cooked cereal 2 oleo	½ c. orange juice 2 FF eggs 1 toast ½ c. FF cooked cereal 2 oleo
	1 c. skim milk coffee, tea	1 c. skim milk coffee, tea	1 c. skim milk coffee, tea	1 c. skim milk coffee, tea	1 c. skim milk coffee, tea
DINNER	1 oz. baked steak 1 c. FF greens 2 diet peach halves 1 oleo	2 oz. baked steak 1 c. FF greens ½ c. FF potatoes 2 diet peach halves 1 oleo	2 oz. baked steak 1 c. FF greens ½ c. FF potatoes 2" sq. cornbread 2 diet peach halves	3 oz. baked steak 1 c. FF greens ½ c. FF potatoes 2" sq. cornbread 2 diet peach halves 1 oleo	3 oz. baked steak 1 c. FF greens ½ c. FF potatoes 2 2" sq. cornbread 2 diet peach halves
	1 c. skim milk coffee, tea	coffee, tea	coffee, tea	coffee, tea	coffee, tea
SUPPER	2 frankfurters ½ c. FF coleslaw 1 bread 1 tsp. mayonnaise ½ c. diet fruit cocktail	2 frankfurters ½ c. sliced tomatoes ½ c. FF coleslaw 1 bread 1 tsp. mayonnaise ½ c. diet fruit cocktail	2 frankfurters ½ c. sliced tomatoes 1 oz. cheese ½ c. FF coleslaw 2 bread 2 tsp. mayonnaise ½ c. diet fruit cocktail	2 frankfurters ½ c. sliced tomatoes 1 oz. cheese ½ c. FF coleslaw 2 bread 2 tsp. mayonnaise ½ c. diet fruit cocktail 5 vanilla wafers	2 frankfurters ½ c. sliced tomatoes 1 oz. cheese ½ c. FF coleslaw 2 bread 2 tsp. mayonnaise ½ c. diet fruit cocktail 5 vanilla wafers
	coffee, tea	coffee, tea	coffee, tea	coffee, tea	coffee, tea
SNACK	1 c. skim milk 2 sq. graham crackers	1 c. skim milk 2 sq. graham crackers	1 c. skim milk 2 sq. graham crackers	1 c. skim milk 2 sq. graham crackers	1 c. skim milk 4 sq. graham crackers

At least one menu per day is to be prepared with bran.

DATE _____ Tuesday   WEEK NO. _____ One   MENU CYCLE   Spring/Summer

	REGULAR	SOFT/BLAND	2-3 gram sodium	LOW FAT	LOW RESIDUE
B R E A K F A S T	Orange juice Cereal Toast Milk Coffee, tea	Orange juice Egg Cereal (no whole grain) Toast Milk Coffee, tea/Sanka	Orange juice 1 Egg Cereal Toast Milk Coffee, tea	Orange juice 1 FF Egg FF Cereal Toast Skim milk Coffee, tea	Orange juice Egg Cereal (no whole grain) Toast Milk Coffee, tea
D I N N E R	Southern fried chicken Whole kernel corn Seasoned Green beans Roll Pineapple upside down cake/grape jubilee Milk Coffee, tea	Baked chicken Mashed potatoes Seasoned Green beans Roll Cake/applesauce Milk Coffee, tea/Sanka	Southern fried chicken Whole kernel corn Seasoned Green beans Roll Pineapple upside down cake/grape jubilee Coffee, tea	Baked chicken - no skin FF Whole kernel corn FF Green beans Roll Applesauce Skim milk Coffee, tea	Baked chicken Mashed potatoes Green beans Roll Cake/applesauce Coffee, tea
S U P P E R	Ham/macaroni & cheese casserole Pear/prune salad on lettuce leaf Bread Mock pecan pie Milk Coffee, tea	Beef pattie Macaroni & cheese Pear halves salad on lettuce Bread Pudding/no chocolate Milk Coffee, tea/Sanka	Beef pattie Mashed potatoes Pear/prune salad on lettuce leaf Bread Pudding ½ cup Milk Coffee, tea	Beef pattie FF Mashed potatoes Pear/prune salad on lettuce leaf Bread Vanilla wafers Skim milk Coffee, tea	Beef pattie Macaroni & cheese Pear halves salad on lettuce leaf Bread Pudding ½ cup Milk Coffee, tea

At least one menu per day is to be prepared with bran.

DATE __Tuesday__   WEEK NO. __One__   MENU CYCLE   Spring/Summer

	1000 Calories	1200 Calories	1500 Calories	1800 Calories	2000 Calories
B R E A K F A S T	½ c. orange juice 1 FF egg ½ c. FF cooked cereal 1 oleo 1 c. skim milk coffee, tea	½ c. orange juice 1 FF egg ½ c. FF cooked cereal 1 oleo 1 c. skim milk coffee, tea	½ c. orange juice 1 FF egg ½ c. FF cooked cereal 1 oleo 1 c. skim milk coffee, tea	½ c. orange juice 1 FF egg ½ c. FF cooked cereal 1 toast 2 oleo 1 c. skim milk coffee, tea	½ c. orange juice 2 FF eggs ½ c. FF cooked cereal 1 toast 2 oleo 1 c. skim milk coffee, tea
D I N N E R	1 oz. baked chicken 1 c. FF green beans 1 oleo ½ c. diet pineapple 1 c. skim milk coffee, tea	2 oz. baked chicken 1 c. FF green beans ⅓ c. FF w.k. corn 1 Oleo ½ c. diet pineapple coffee, tea	2 oz. baked chicken 1 c. FF green beans ⅓ c. FF w.k. corn 1 roll 1 oleo ½ c. diet pineapple coffee, tea	3 oz. baked chicken 1 c. FF green beans ⅓ c. FF w.k. corn 1 roll 2 oleo ½ c. diet pineapple coffee, tea	3 oz. baked chicken 1 c. FF green beans ⅔ c. FF w.k. corn 1 roll 2 oleo ½ c. diet pineapple coffee, tea
S U P P E R	2 oz. baked ham ½ c. FF squash 1 slice bread 1 oleo 1 diet pear half 1 prune coffee, tea	2 oz. baked ham ½ c. FF squash ½ c. baked noodles# 1 oleo 1 diet pear half 1 prune coffee, tea	3 oz. baked ham ½ c. FF squash ½ c. baked noodles# 1 slice bread 2 oleo 1 diet pear half 1 prune coffee, tea	3 oz. baked ham ½ c. FF squash ½ c. baked noodles# 2 slice bread 1 oleo 1 diet pear half 1 prune coffee, tea	3 oz. baked ham ½ c. FF squash ½ c. baked noodles# 2 slice bread 2 oleo 1 diet pear half 1 prune coffee, tea
S N A C K	1 c. skim milk 2 sq. graham crackers	1 c. skim milk 2 sq. graham crackers	1 c. skim milk 2 sq. graham crackers	1 c. skim milk 2 sq. graham crackers	1 c. skim milk 4 sq. graham crackers

At least one menu per day is to be prepared with bran.   # see recipe (1 bread, 1 vegetable)

DATE __Wednesday__   WEEK NO. __One__   MENU CYCLE Spring/Summer

	REGULAR	SOFT/BLAND	2-3 gram sodium	LOW FAT	LOW RESIDUE
B R E A K F A S T	Orange juice Egg Cereal Toast Bacon Milk Coffee, tea	Orange juice Egg Cereal (no whole grain) Toast Crisp bacon Milk Coffee, tea/Sanka	Orange juice 1 Egg Cereal Toast Milk Coffee, tea	Orange juice 1 FF Egg FF Cereal Toast Skim milk Coffee, tea	Orange juice Egg Cereal (no whole grain) Toast Crisp bacon Milk Coffee, tea
D I N N E R	Meatloaf Baby lima beans Sliced beets Roll Fruit cocktail scallop Milk Coffee, tea	Meatloaf (no onion, pepper) Baby lima beans Sliced beets Roll Fruit cocktail scallop Milk Coffee, tea/Sanka	Meatloaf Baby lima beans Sliced beets Roll Fruit cocktail scallop Coffee, tea	Meatloaf FF Baby lima beans FF Sliced beets Roll Fruit cocktail Skim milk Coffee, tea	Meatloaf (no onion, pepper) Baby lima beans Sliced beets Roll Fruit cocktail scallop Coffee, tea

S U P P E R	Sliced meats
	Slice of cheese
	Fresh sliced tomatoes
	Jellied applesauce
	Whole wheat bread
	Fruit in season
	  with topping
	Milk
	Coffee, tea
		Sliced turkey
		Slice of cheese
		Fresh sliced tomatoes
		Jellied applesauce
		Bread
		Soft fruit in season
		  with topping
		Milk
		Coffee, tea/Sanka
			Sliced turkey
			Fresh sliced tomatoes
			Jellied applesauce
			Whole wheat bread
			Fruit in season
			  with topping
			Milk
			Coffee, tea
				Sliced turkey
				Fresh sliced tomatoes
				Jellied applesauce
				Whole wheat bread
				Fruit cup in season
				
				Skim Milk
				Coffee, tea
					Sliced turkey
					Tomato juice
					Jellied applesauce
					Bread
					Canned fruit with
					  topping
					Milk
					Coffee, tea

At least one menu per day is to be prepared with bran.

DATE ____ Wednesday   WEEK NO. ____ One   MENU CYCLE   Spring/Summer

Meal	1000 Calories	1200 Calories	1500 Calories	1800 Calories	2000 Calories
BREAKFAST	½ c. orange juice 1 FF egg 1 toast 1 crisp bacon coffee, tea	½ c. orange juice 1 FF egg 1 toast 1 crisp bacon 1 c. skim milk coffee, tea	½ c. orange juice 1 FF egg 1 toast 1 crisp bacon 1 c. skim milk coffee, tea	½ c. orange juice 1 FF egg 1 toast ½ c. FF cooked cereal 2 crisp bacon 1 c. skim milk coffee, tea	½ c. orange juice 2 FF eggs 1 toast ½ c. FF cooked cereal 2 crisp bacon 1 c. skim milk coffee, tea
DINNER	1 oz. meatloaf ½ c. FF beets lettuce salad zero dressing 1 oleo ½ c. diet fruit cocktail 1 c. skim milk coffee, tea	2 oz. meatloaf ½ c. FF beets ½ c. FF baby lima beans lettuce salad zero dressing 1 oleo ½ c. diet fruit cocktail	2 oz. meatloaf ½ c. FF beets ½ c. FF baby lima beans lettuce salad zero dressing 1 roll 1 oleo ½ c. diet fruit cocktail	3 oz. meatloaf ½ c. FF beets ½ c. FF baby lima beans lettuce salad zero dressing 1 roll 2 oleo ½ c. diet fruit cocktail	3 oz. meatloaf ½ c. FF beets ½ c. FF baby lima beans lettuce salad zero dressing 2 rolls 2 oleo ½ c. diet fruit cocktail
SUPPER	2 oz. cold cuts marinated green bean salad# 1 bread 1 tsp. mayonnaise 1 exchange fresh fruit coffee, tea	2 oz. cold cuts marinated green bean salad# ½ c. tomatoes 1 bread 1 tsp. mayonnaise 1 exchange fresh fruit coffee, tea	2 oz. cold cuts 1 oz. cheese marinated green bean salad# ½ c. tomatoes 2 bread 2 tsp. mayonnaise 1 exchange fresh fruit coffee, tea	2 oz. cold cuts 1 oz. cheese marinated green bean salad# ½ c. tomatoes 2 bread 2 tsp. mayonnaise 1 exchange fresh fruit 5 vanilla wafers coffee, tea	2 oz. cold cuts 1 oz. cheese marinated green bean salad# ½ c. tomatoes 2 bread 2 tsp. mayonnaise 1 exchange fresh fruit 5 vanilla wafers coffee, tea
SNACK	1 c. skim milk 2 sq. graham crackers	1 c. skim milk 2 sq. graham crackers	1 c. skim milk 2 sq. graham crackers	1 c. skim milk 2 sq. graham crackers	1 c. skim milk 4 sq. graham crackers

At least one menu per day is to be prepared with bran.   # see recipe (1 vegetable)

DATE ___Thursday___   WEEK NO. ___One___   MENU CYCLE ___Spring/Summer___

	REGULAR	SOFT/BLAND	2-3 gram sodium	LOW FAT	LOW RESIDUE
BREAKFAST	Orange juice Egg Cereal Toast Milk Coffee, tea	Orange juice Egg Cereal (no whole grain) Toast Milk Coffee, tea/Sanka	Orange juice 1 Egg Cereal Toast Milk Coffee, tea	Orange juice 1 FF Egg FF Cereal Toast Skim milk Coffee, tea	Orange juice Egg Cereal (no whole grain) Toast Milk Coffee, tea
DINNER	Glazed Roast pork Sweet potato fluff Seasoned Greens Cornbread Apple cobbler Milk Coffee, tea	Lean roast pork Sweet potato fluff Seasoned Greens Cornbread Apple cobbler Milk Coffee, tea/Sanka	Fresh Roast uncured pork Sweet potato fluff Seasoned Greens Cornbread Apple cobbler Coffee, tea	Lean roast pork FF Sweet potato fluff FF Greens Roll FF Stewed apples Skim Milk Coffee, tea	Glazed Roast pork Sweet potato fluff Seasoned Greens Roll Stewed apples Coffee, tea
SUPPER	Chicken supreme Stewed Okra/tomatoes Cape cod fruit salad Home-made Biscuit Graham crackers Milk Coffee, tea	Chicken supreme Stewed Okra/tomatoes Cape cod fruit salad Home-made Biscuit Graham crackers Milk Coffee, tea/Sanka	Baked chicken Stewed Okra/tomatoes Cape cod fruit salad Home-made Biscuit Graham crackers Milk Coffee, tea	Baked chicken - no skin FF Okra/tomatoes Cape cod fruit salad Bread Graham crackers Skim milk Coffee, tea	Baked chicken Tomato juice Cape cod fruit salad Bread Vanilla wafers Milk Coffee, tea

At least one menu per day is to be prepared with bran.

DATE _____   Thursday _____   WEEK NO. _____   One _____   MENU CYCLE _____   Spring/Summer

	1000 Calories	1200 Calories	1500 Calories	1800 Calories	2000 Calories
BREAKFAST	½ c. orange juice 1 FF egg ½ c. FF cooked cereal 1 oleo 1 c. skim milk coffee, tea	½ c. orange juice 1 FF egg ½ c. FF cooked cereal 1 oleo 1 c. skim milk coffee, tea	½ c. orange juice 1 FF egg ½ c. FF cooked cereal 1 oleo 1 c. skim milk coffee, tea	½ c. orange juice 1 FF egg ½ c. FF cooked cereal 1 toast 2 oleo 1 c. skim milk coffee, tea	½ c. orange juice 2 FF eggs ½ c. FF cooked cereal 1 toast 2 oleo 1 c. skim milk coffee, tea
DINNER	1 oz. roast pork 1 c. FF greens ½ c. FF stewed apples (no sugar added) 1 oleo 1 c. skim milk coffee, tea	2 oz. roast pork 1 c. FF greens ¼ c. FF sweet potatoes ½ c. FF stewed apples (no sugar added) 1 oleo coffee, tea	2 oz. roast pork 1 c. FF greens ¼ c. FF sweet potatoes 2" square cornbread ½ c. FF stewed apples (no sugar added) coffee, tea	3 oz. roast pork 1 c. FF greens ¼ c. FF sweet potatoes 2" square cornbread ½ c. FF stewed apples (no sugar added) 1 oleo coffee, tea	3 oz. roast pork 1 c. FF greens ¼ c. FF sweet potatoes 2 2" squares cornbread ½ c. FF stewed apples (no sugar added) coffee, tea
SUPPER	2 oz. baked chicken ½ c. FF okra ½ c. FF rice 2 diet pineapple rings 1 oleo coffee, tea	2 oz. baked chicken ½ c. FF okra ½ c. FF tomatoes ½ c. FF rice 2 diet pineapple rings 1 oleo coffee, tea	3 oz. baked chicken ½ c. FF okra ½ c. FF tomatoes ½ c. FF rice 2 2" home-made biscuits 2 diet pineapple rings 1 oleo coffee, tea	3 oz. baked chicken ½ c. FF okra ½ c. FF tomatoes ½ c. FF rice 2 2" home-made biscuits 2 diet pineapple rings coffee, tea	3 oz. baked chicken ½ c. FF okra ½ c. FF tomatoes ½ c. FF rice 2 2" home-made biscuits 2 diet pineapple rings coffee, tea
SNACK	1 c. skim milk 2 sq. graham crackers	1 c. skim milk 2 sq. graham crackers	1 c. skim milk 2 sq. graham crackers	1 c. skim milk 2 sq. graham crackers	1 c. skim milk 4 sq. graham crackers

At least one menu per day is to be prepared with bran.

DATE ___Friday___   WEEK NO. ___One___   MENU CYCLE ___Spring/Summer___

	REGULAR	SOFT/BLAND	2-3 gram sodium	LOW FAT	LOW RESIDUE
BREAKFAST	Orange juice Egg Cereal Toast Milk Coffee, tea	Orange juice Egg Cereal (no whole grain) Toast Milk Coffee, tea/Sanka	Orange juice 1 Egg Cereal Toast Milk Coffee, tea	Orange juice FF Egg FF Cereal Toast Skim milk Coffee, tea	Orange juice Egg Cereal (no whole grain) Toast Milk Coffee, tea
DINNER	Old-fashioned Beef stew with carrots, potatoes Lemon jello/pear salad on lettuce Home-made Biscuit Ice cream Milk Coffee, tea	Old-fashioned Beef stew with carrots, potatoes (no onion) Lemon jello/pear salad on lettuce Roll Ice cream/no choc. Milk Coffee, tea/Sanka	Old-fashioned Beef stew with carrots, potatoes Lemon jello/pear salad on lettuce Home-made Biscuit Ice cream Coffee, tea	Old-fashioned Beef stew with FF carrots, potatoes Lemon jello/pear salad on lettuce Roll Sherbet Skim milk Coffee, tea	Old-fashioned Beef stew with carrots, potatoes (no onion) Lemon jello/pear salad on lettuce Roll Ice cream Coffee, tea
SUPPER	Broiled fish fillet French fried potatoes Sliced tomatoes Cornbread Spiced Peach half with topping Milk Coffee, tea	Baked fish Baked potato Sliced tomatoes Loaf bread Peach half with topping Milk Coffee, tea/Sanka	Broiled fish fillet Baked potato Sliced tomatoes Cornbread Spiced Peach half with topping Milk Coffee, tea	Broiled fish fillet FF Baked potato Sliced tomatoes Loaf bread Spiced Peach half Skim milk Coffee, tea	Broiled fish fillet Baked potato Tomato juice Loaf bread Peach half with topping ½ cup Milk Coffee, tea

At least one menu per day is to be prepared with bran.

DATE _____ Friday _____ WEEK NO. _____ One _____ MENU CYCLE _____ Spring/Summer

	1000 Calories	1200 Calories	1500 Calories	1800 Calories	2000 Calories
B R E A K F A S T	½ c. orange juice 1 FF egg 1 toast 1 oleo coffee, tea	½ c. orange juice 1 FF egg 1 toast 1 oleo 1 c. skim milk coffee, tea	½ c. orange juice 1 FF egg 1 toast 1 oleo 1 c. skim milk coffee, tea	½ c. orange juice 1 FF egg 1 toast ½ c. FF cooked cereal 2 oleo 1 c. skim milk coffee, tea	½ c. orange juice 2 FF eggs 1 toast ½ c. FF cooked cereal 2 oleo 1 c. skim milk coffee, tea
D I N N E R	1 oz. beef cubes 1 c. FF carrots 2 diet pear halves diet jello cubes 1 oleo 1 c. skim milk coffee, tea	2 oz. beef cubes 1 c. FF carrots ½ c. FF potatoes 2 diet pear halves diet jello cubes 1 oleo	2 oz. beef cubes 1 c. FF carrots ½ c. FF potatoes 2 diet pear halves diet jello cubes 1 2" home-made biscuit	3 oz. beef cubes 1 c. FF carrots ½ c. FF potatoes 2 diet pear halves diet jello cubes 1 2" home-made biscuit 1 oleo	3 oz. beef cubes 1 c. FF carrots ½ c. FF potatoes 2 diet pear halves diet jello cubes 2 2" home-made biscuits
	coffee, tea	coffee, tea	coffee, tea	coffee, tea	coffee, tea
S U P P E R	2 oz. baked fish ½ c. FF cabbage ½ c. FF potatoes 1 oleo 2 diet peach halves coffee, tea	2 oz. baked fish ½ c. FF cabbage ½ c. sliced tomatoes ½ c. FF potatoes 1 oleo 2 diet peach halves coffee, tea	3 oz. baked fish ½ c. FF cabbage ½ c. sliced tomatoes ½ c. FF potatoes 2 2" square cornbread 1 oleo 2 diet peach halves coffee, tea	3 oz. baked fish ½ c. FF cabbage ½ c. sliced tomatoes ½ c. FF potatoes 2 2" sq. cornbread 2 diet peach halves coffee, tea	3 oz. baked fish ½ c. FF cabbage ½ c. sliced tomatoes ½ c. FF potatoes 2 2" sq. cornbread 2 diet peach halves coffee, tea
S N A C K	1 c. skim milk 2 sq. graham crackers	1 c. skim milk 2 sq. graham crackers	1 c. skim milk 2 sq. graham crackers	1 c. skim milk 2 sq. graham crackers	1 c. skim milk 4 sq. graham crackers

At least one menu per day is to be prepared with bran.

DATE ___Saturday___ WEEK NO. ___One___ MENU CYCLE ___Spring/Summer___

	REGULAR	SOFT/BLAND	2-3 gram sodium	LOW FAT	LOW RESIDUE
BREAKFAST	Orange juice Egg Cereal Toast Milk Coffee, tea	Orange juice Egg Cereal (no whole grain) Toast Milk Coffee, tea/Sanka	Orange juice 1 Egg Cereal Toast Milk Coffee, tea	Orange juice 1 FF Egg FF Cereal Toast Skim milk Coffee, tea	Orange juice Egg Cereal (no whole grain) Toast Milk Coffee, tea

DINNER	Chicken & dumplings
	Asparagus spears
	Roll
	Fruited bread
	  pudding/tpg
	
	Milk
	Coffee, tea
		Chicken & dumplings
		Asparagus spears
		Roll
		Fruited bread
		  pudding/tpg
		
		Milk
		Coffee, tea/Sanka
			Chicken & dumplings
			Asparagus spears
			Roll
			Fruited bread
			  pudding/tpg
			
			Coffee, tea
				Bkd chicken - no skin
				FF Mashed potatoes
				FF Asparagus spears
				Roll
				Fruit cocktail
				
				Skim milk
				Coffee, tea
					Baked chicken
					Mashed potatoes
					Asparagus spears
					Roll
					Fruit cocktail/topping
					
					Coffee, tea

SUPPER	Beef vegetable soup
	Crackers
	Grilled cheese
	  sandwich
	Hard cooked egg
	Cookies
	Purple plum/
	  pineapple ring
	
	Milk
	Coffee, tea
		Beef vegetable soup
		Crackers
		Grilled cheese
		  sandwich
		Hard cooked egg
		Plain cookies/no choc.
		Purple plums
		
		Milk
		Coffee, tea/Sanka
			SF Beef vegetable
			  soup
			Bread
			Sliced beef sandwich
			Cookies
			Purple plum/
			  pineapple ring
			
			Milk
			Coffee, tea
				FF Beef vegetable soup
				Crackers
				Sliced beef sandwich
				Graham crackers
				Purple plum/
				  pineapple ring
				
				Skim milk
				Coffee, tea
					Beef vegetable soup
					Crackers
					Sliced beef sandwich
					Plain cookies
					Purple plums
					
					Milk
					Coffee, tea

At least one menu per day is to be prepared with bran.

DATE Saturday   WEEK NO. One   MENU CYCLE Spring/Summer

	1000 Calories	1200 Calories	1500 Calories	1800 Calories	2000 Calories
BREAKFAST	½ c. orange juice 1 FF egg ½ c. FF cooked cereal 1 oleo coffee, tea	½ c. orange juice 1 FF egg ½ c. FF cooked cereal 1 oleo 1 c. skim milk coffee, tea	½ c. orange juice 1 FF egg ½ c. FF cooked cereal 1 oleo 1 c. skim milk coffee, tea	½ c. orange juice 1 FF egg ½ c. FF cooked cereal 1 toast 2 oleo 1 c. skim milk coffee, tea	½ c. orange juice 2 FF eggs ½ c. FF cooked cereal 1 toast 2 oleo 1 c. skim milk coffee, tea
DINNER	1 oz. baked chicken ½ c. FF broccoli or asparagus ½ c. FF beets 1 oleo 1 exchange fresh fruit 1 c. skim milk coffee, tea	2 oz. baked chicken ½ c. FF broccoli or asparagus ½ c. FF mashed potato ½ c. FF beets 1 oleo 1 exchange fresh fruit coffee, tea	2 oz. baked chicken ½ c. FF broccoli or asparagus ½ c. FF mashed potato ½ c. FF beets 1 roll - 1 oleo 1 exchange fresh fruit coffee, tea	3 oz. baked chicken ½ c. FF broccoli or asparagus ½ c. FF mashed potato ½ c. FF beets 1 roll - 2 oleo 1 exchange fresh fruit coffee, tea	3 oz. baked chicken ½ c. FF broccoli or asparagus ½ c. FF mashed potato ½ c. FF beets 2 rolls - 2 oleo 1 exchange fresh fruit coffee, tea
SUPPER	2 oz. beef 1 slice bread 1 tsp. mayonnaise ½ c. hot tomato juice 2 diet pineapple rings coffee, tea	2 oz. beef 1 slice bread 1 tsp. mayonnaise ½ c. hot tomato juice ½ c. FF vegetables 2 diet pineapple rings coffee, tea	2 oz. beef 2 slices bread 2 tsp. mayonnaise 1 oz. cheese ½ c. hot tomato juice ½ c. FF vegetables 2 diet pineapple rings coffee, tea	2 oz. beef 2 slices bread 2 tsp. mayonnaise 1 oz. cheese ½ c. hot tomato juice ½ c. FF vegetables 5 vanilla wafers 2 diet pineapple rings coffee, tea	2 oz. beef 2 slices bread 2 tsp. mayonnaise 1 oz. cheese ½ c. hot tomato juice ½ c. FF vegetables 2 diet pineapple rings 5 vanilla wafers coffee, tea
SNACK	1 c. skim milk 2 sq. graham crackers	1 c. skim milk 2 sq. graham crackers	1 c. skim milk 2 sq. graham crackers	1 c. skim milk 2 sq. graham crackers	1 c. skim milk 4 sq. graham crackers

At least one menu per day is to be prepared with bran.

DATE ___ Sunday ___ WEEK NO. ___ One ___ MENU CYCLE ___ Spring/Summer

	REGULAR	SOFT/BLAND	2-3 gram sodium	LOW FAT	LOW RESIDUE
B R E A K F A S T	Orange juice Egg Cereal Toast Bacon Milk Coffee, tea	Orange juice Egg Cereal (no whole grain) Toast Crisp bacon Milk Coffee, tea/Sanka	Orange juice 1 Egg Cereal Toast Milk Coffee, tea	Orange juice 1 FF Egg FF Cereal Toast Skim milk Coffee, tea	Orange juice Egg Cereal (no whole grain) Toast Crisp bacon Milk Coffee, tea
D I N N E R	Roast beef au jus Scalloped potatoes Seasoned Green beans Roll Strawberry shortcake Milk Coffee, tea	Roast beef au jus Scalloped potatoes (no onion, pepper) Seasoned Green beans Roll Cake/fruit mix Milk Coffee, tea/Sanka	Roast beef au jus Sliced potatoes Seasoned Green beans Roll Strawberry shortcake Coffee, tea	Roast beef au jus FF Sliced potatoes FF Green beans Roll Strawberries Skim Milk Coffee, tea	Roast beef au jus Scalloped potatoes (no onion, pepper) Green beans Roll Cake/fruit mix Coffee, tea
S U P P E R	Scrambled egg Cheese grits Sausage pattie Toast triangles Cinnamon Applesauce Milk Coffee, tea	Scrambled egg Cheese grits Bacon strips Toast triangles Cinnamon Applesauce Milk Coffee, tea/Sanka	Beef pattie Fluffy rice Green peas Bread Cinnamon Applesauce Milk Coffee, tea	Beef pattie FF Fluffy rice FF Green peas Bread Cinnamon Applesauce Skim milk Coffee, tea	Scrambled egg Cheese grits Bacon strips Toast triangles Cinnamon Applesauce ½ c. Milk Coffee, tea

At least one menu per day is to be prepared with bran.

DATE ___Sunday___   WEEK NO. ___One___   MENU CYCLE ___Spring/Summer___

	1000 Calories	1200 Calories	1500 Calories	1800 Calories	2000 Calories
BREAKFAST	½ c. orange juice 1 FF egg 1 toast 1 crisp bacon coffee, tea	½ c. orange juice 1 FF egg 1 toast 1 crisp bacon 1 c. skim milk coffee, tea	½ c. orange juice 1 FF egg 1 toast 1 crisp bacon 1 c. skim milk coffee, tea	½ c. orange juice 1 FF egg 1 toast ½ c. FF cooked cereal 2 crisp bacon 1 c. skim milk coffee, tea	½ c. orange juice 2 FF eggs 1 toast ½ c. FF cooked cereal 2 crisp bacon 1 c. skim milk coffee, tea
DINNER	1 oz. roast beef 1 c. FF green beans 1 oleo ¾ c. strawberries 1 c. skim milk coffee, tea	2 oz. roast beef 1 c. FF green beans ½ c. FF potatoes 1 oleo ¾ c. strawberries coffee, tea	2 oz. roast beef 1 c. FF green beans ½ c. FF potatoes ¾ c. strawberries over 1 2" biscuit opened coffee, tea	3 oz. roast beef 1 c. FF green beans ½ c. FF potatoes 1 oleo ¾ c. strawberries over 1 2" biscuit opened coffee, tea	3 oz. roast beef 1 c. FF green beans ½ c. FF potatoes 1 roll 1 oleo ¾ c. strawberries over 1 2" biscuit opened coffee, tea
SUPPER	2 FF eggs ½ c. FF grits ½ c. tomato juice ½ c. diet applesauce 1 crisp bacon coffee, tea	2 FF eggs ½ c. FF grits ¼ c. FF green peas ½ c. tomato juice ½ c. diet applesauce 1 crisp bacon coffee, tea	2 FF eggs 1 oz. cheese ½ c. FF grits 1 toast triangle ¼ c. FF green peas ½ c. tomato juice ½ c. diet applesauce 2 crisp bacon coffee, tea	2 FF eggs 1 oz. cheese ½ c. FF grits 2 toast triangles ¼ c. FF green peas ½ c. tomato juice ½ c. diet applesauce 2 crisp bacon coffee, tea	2 FF eggs 1 oz. cheese ½ c. FF grits 2 toast triangles ¼ c. FF green peas ½ c. tomato juice ½ c. diet applesauce 2 crisp bacon coffee, tea
SNACK	1 c. skim milk 2 sq. graham crackers	1 c. skim milk 2 sq. graham crackers	1 c. skim milk 2 sq. graham crackers	1 c. skim milk 2 sq. graham crackers	1 c. skim milk 4 sq. graham crackers

At least one menu per day is to be prepared with bran.

DATE   Monday   WEEK NO.   Two   MENU CYCLE   Spring/Summer

	REGULAR	SOFT/BLAND	2-3 gram sodium	LOW FAT	LOW RESIDUE
B R E A K F A S T	Orange juice Egg Cereal Toast Milk Coffee, tea	Orange juice Egg Cereal (no whole grain) Toast Milk Coffee, tea/Sanka	Orange juice 1 Egg Cereal Toast Milk Coffee, tea	Orange juice 1 FF Egg FF Cereal Toast Skim milk Coffee, tea	Orange juice Egg Cereal (no whole grain) Toast Milk Coffee, tea
D I N N E R	BBQ Chicken Cream corn Seasoned steamed cabbage Roll Ice cream Milk Coffee, tea	Mild BBQ Chicken Mashed potatoes Seasoned spinach Roll Ice cream/no choc. Milk Coffee, tea/Sanka	Baked Chicken Cream corn Seasoned steamed cabbage Roll Ice cream Coffee, tea	BBQ Chicken-no skin FF Corn FF Steamed cabbage Roll Sherbet Skim milk Coffee, tea	Mild BBQ Chicken Mashed potatoes Seasoned spinach Roll Ice cream Coffee, tea
S U P P E R	Mock swiss steak Whipped Potatoes Mixed Fresh Vegetables Roll Fruit Heavenly Hash Milk Coffee, tea	Mock swiss steak Whipped Potatoes Carrots Roll Fruit Heavenly Hash Milk Coffee, tea/Sanka	Mock swiss steak Whipped Potatoes Mixed Fresh Vegetables Roll Fruit Heavenly Hash Milk Coffee, tea	Mock swiss steak FF Whipped Potatoes FF Mixed Fresh Vegetables Roll Plain fruit cup Skim milk Coffee, tea	Mock swiss steak Whipped Potatoes Carrots Roll Plain fruit cup ½ cup Milk Coffee, tea

At least one menu per day is to be prepared with bran.

DATE _____ Monday _____   WEEK NO. _____ Two _____   MENU CYCLE _____ Spring/Summer

	1000 Calories	1200 Calories	1500 Calories	1800 Calories	2000 Calories
BREAKFAST	½ c. orange juice 1 FF egg 1 toast 1 oleo coffee, tea	½ c. orange juice 1 FF egg 1 toast 1 oleo 1 c. skim milk coffee, tea	½ c. orange juice 1 FF egg 1 toast 1 oleo 1 c. skim milk coffee, tea	½ c. orange juice 1 FF egg ¾ c. cold cereal 1 toast 2 oleo 1 c. skim milk coffee, tea	½ c. orange juice 2 FF egg ¾ c. cold cereal 1 toast 2 oleo 1 c. skim milk coffee, tea
DINNER	1 oz. baked chicken 1 c. FF cabbage 2 diet pineapple rings 1 oleo 1 c. skim milk coffee, tea	2 oz. baked chicken 1 c. FF cabbage ⅓ c. FF corn 2 diet pineapple rings 1 oleo coffee, tea	2 oz. baked chicken 1 c. FF cabbage ⅓ c. FF corn 2 diet pineapple rings ½ c. ice cream** coffee, tea	3 oz. baked chicken 1 c. FF cabbage ⅓ c. FF corn 2 diet pineapple rings ½ c. ice cream** coffee, tea	3 oz. baked chicken 1 c. FF cabbage ⅓ c. FF corn 1 roll 2 diet pineapple rings ½ c. ice cream** coffee, tea
SUPPER	2 oz. beef cake ½ c. FF tomatoes ½ c. FF potatoes 1 oleo ½ c. diet fruit cocktail coffee, tea	2 oz. beef cake ½ c. FF tomatoes ½ c. FF carrots ½ c. FF potatoes 1 oleo ½ c. diet fruit cocktail coffee, tea	3 oz. beef cake ½ c. FF tomatoes ½ c. FF carrots ½ c. FF potatoes 1 roll 1 oleo ½ c. diet fruit cocktail coffee, tea	3 oz. beef cake ½ c. FF tomatoes ½ c. FF carrots ½ c. FF potatoes 2 rolls 2 oleo ½ c. diet fruit cocktail coffee, tea	3 oz. beef cake ½ c. FF tomatoes ½ c. FF carrots ½ c. FF potatoes 2 rolls 2 oleo ½ c. diet fruit cocktail coffee, tea
SNACK	1 c. skim milk 2 sq. graham crackers	1 c. skim milk 2 sq. graham crackers	1 c. skim milk 2 sq. graham crackers	1 c. skim milk 2 sq. graham crackers	1 c. skim milk 4 sq. graham crackers

At least one menu per day is to be prepared with bran.   **½ c. ice cream = 1 bread, 2 fat

DATE ___ Tuesday ___   WEEK NO. ___ Two ___   MENU CYCLE ___ Spring/Summer

	REGULAR	SOFT/BLAND	2-3 gram sodium	LOW FAT	LOW RESIDUE
BREAKFAST	Orange juice Egg Cereal Toast Milk Coffee, tea	Orange juice Egg Cereal - no whole grain Toast Milk Coffee, tea/Sanka	Orange juice 1 Egg Cereal Toast Milk Coffee, tea	Orange juice 1 FF Egg FF Cereal Toast Skim milk Coffee, tea	Orange juice Egg Cereal - no whole grain Toast Milk Coffee, tea
DINNER	Salmon croquette Buttered potatoes with parsley Seasoned Green beans Cornbread Banana split cake Milk Coffee, tea	Baked fish fillet Buttered potatoes with parsley Seasoned Green beans Cornbread Banana split cake (no nuts) Milk Coffee, tea/Sanka	Salmon croquette Buttered potatoes with parsley Seasoned Green beans Cornbread Banana Coffee, tea	Bkd salmon croquette FF Potatoes with parsley FF Green beans Loaf bread Banana Skim milk Coffee, tea	Bkd salmon croquette Buttered potatoes with parsley Seasoned Green beans Loaf bread Ripe banana Coffee, tea
SUPPER	Chicken salad plate Sliced fresh tomatoes Fruits in season Bread Chocolate pie Milk Coffee, tea	Chicken salad plate Sliced fresh tomatoes Soft fruits in season Bread Chocolate pie BLAND-vanilla ice crm Milk Coffee, tea/Sanka	Chicken salad plate Sliced fresh tomatoes Fruits in season Bread Chocolate pie Milk Coffee, tea	Chicken salad plate (little mayonnaise) Sliced tomatoes Fruits in season Bread Sherbet Skim Milk Coffee, tea	Chicken salad plate Tomato juice Soft fruits in season Bread Vanilla ice cream ½ cup Milk Coffee, tea

At least one menu per day is to be prepared with bran.

DATE ___Tuesday___   WEEK NO. ___Two___   MENU CYCLE ___Spring/Summer___

	1000 Calories	1200 Calories	1500 Calories	1800 Calories	2000 Calories
BREAKFAST	½ c. orange juice 1 FF egg 1 toast 1 oleo coffee, tea	½ c. orange juice 1 FF egg 1 toast 1 oleo 1 c. skim milk coffee, tea	½ c. orange juice 1 FF egg 1 toast 1 oleo 1 c. skim milk coffee, tea	½ c. orange juice 1 FF egg 1 toast ½ c. FF cooked cereal 2 oleo 1 c. skim milk coffee, tea	½ c. orange juice 2 FF eggs 1 toast ½ c. FF cooked cereal 2 oleo 1 c. skim milk coffee, tea
DINNER	1 oz. salmon croquette 1 c. FF green beans ½ small banana 1 oleo 1 c. skim milk coffee, tea	2 oz. salmon croquette 1 c. FF green beans ½ c. FF potatoes ½ small banana 1 oleo coffee, tea	2 oz. salmon croquette 1 c. FF green beans ½ c. FF potatoes 2" square cornbread ½ small banana coffee, tea	3 oz. salmon croquette 1 c. FF green beans ½ c. FF potatoes 2" sq. cornbread ½ small banana 1 oleo coffee, tea	3 oz. salmon croquette 1 c. green beans ½ c. FF potatoes 2 2" sq. cornbread ½ small banana coffee, tea
SUPPER	2 oz. chicken ½ c. sliced tomatoes 1 bread 1 tsp. mayonnaise 1 exchange fresh fruit coffee, tea	2 oz. chicken ½ c. sliced tomatoes lettuce salad zero dressing 1 bread 1 tsp. mayonnaise 1 exchange fresh fruit coffee, tea	3 oz. chicken ½ c. sliced tomatoes lettuce salad zero dressing 2 bread 2 tsp. mayonnaise 1 exchange fresh fruit coffee, tea	3 oz. chicken ½ c. sliced tomatoes lettuce salad zero dressing 2 bread 2 tsp. mayonnaise 1 exchange fresh fruit 5 vanilla wafers coffee, tea	3 oz. chicken ½ c. sliced tomatoes lettuce salad zero dressing 2 bread 2 tsp. mayonnaise 1 exchange fresh fruit 5 vanilla wafers coffee, tea
SNACK	1 c. skim milk 2 sq. graham crackers	1 c. skim milk 2 sq. graham crackers	1 c. skim milk 2 sq. graham crackers	1 c. skim milk 2 sq. graham crackers	1 c. skim milk 4 sq. graham crackers

At least one menu per day is to be prepared with bran.

DATE ___Wednesday___   WEEK NO. ___Two___   MENU CYCLE   Spring/Summer

	REGULAR	SOFT/BLAND	2-3 gram sodium	LOW FAT	LOW RESIDUE
B R E A K F	Orange juice Egg Cereal Toast Bacon	Orange juice Egg Cereal (no whole grain) Toast Crisp bacon	Orange juice 1 Egg Cereal Toast	Orange juice 1 FF Egg FF Cereal Toast	Orange juice Egg Cereal (no whole grain) Toast Crisp bacon
A S T	Milk Coffee, tea	Milk Coffee, tea/Sanka	Milk Coffee, tea	Skim milk Coffee, tea	Milk Coffee, tea
D I N N E R	Ham slice Orange-glazed Sweet potatoes Seasoned Greens Cornbread Baked apple slices	Ham slice Orange-glazed Sweet potatoes Seasoned Greens Cornbread Baked apple slices	Uncured pork Orange-glazed Sweet potatoes Seasoned Greens Cornbread Baked apple slices	Uncured lean pork FF Sweet potatoes FF Greens Roll FF Bkd apple slices	Uncured pork Whipped potatoes Seasoned Greens Roll Baked apple slices
	Milk Coffee, tea	Milk Coffee, tea/Sanka	Coffee, tea	Skim milk Coffee, tea	Coffee, tea
S U P P E R	Melon in season Eggs Cheese grits Crisp bacon Home-made Biscuit	Melon in season Eggs Cheese grits Crisp bacon Home-made Biscuit	Melon in season Beef pattie Grits Home-made Biscuit	Melon in season Beef pattie FF Grits Toast triangles	Melon in season Eggs Grits Crisp bacon Toast triangles
	Milk Coffee, tea	Milk Coffee, tea/Sanka	Milk Coffee, tea	Skim milk Coffee, tea	Milk Coffee, tea

At least one menu per day is to be prepared with bran.

DATE ___Wednesday___   WEEK NO. ___Two___   MENU CYCLE ___Spring/Summer___

	1000 Calories	1200 Calories	1500 Calories	1800 Calories	2000 Calories
BREAKFAST	½ c. orange juice 1 FF egg ½ c. FF cooked cereal 1 crisp bacon 1 c. skim milk coffee, tea	½ c. orange juice 1 FF egg ½ c. FF cooked cereal 1 crisp bacon 1 c. skim milk coffee, tea	½ c. orange juice 1 FF egg ½ c. FF cooked cereal 1 crisp bacon 1 c. skim milk coffee, tea	½ c. orange juice 1 FF egg ½ c. FF cooked cereal 1 toast 2 crisp bacon 1 c. skim milk coffee, tea	½ c. orange juice 2 FF eggs ½ c. FF cooked cereal 1 toast 2 crisp bacon 1 c. skim milk coffee, tea
DINNER	1 oz. baked ham 1 c. FF greens ½ c. baked cinnamon apples# 1 oleo 1 c. skim milk coffee, tea	2 oz. baked ham 1 c. FF greens ¼ c. FF swt potatoes ½ c. baked cinnamon apples# 1 oleo coffee, tea	2 oz. baked ham 1 c. FF greens ¼ c. FF swt potatoes 2" square cornbread ½ c. baked cinnamon apples# coffee, tea	3 oz. baked ham 1 c. FF greens ¼ c. FF swt potatoes 2" sq. cornbread ½ c. baked cinnamon apples# 1 oleo coffee, tea	3 oz. baked ham 1 c. FF greens ¼ c. FF swt potatoes 2" sq. cornbread ½ c. baked cinnamon apples# coffee, tea
SUPPER	2 oz. beef pattie ½ c. FF carrots 1 home-made 2" biscuit ½ c. diet fruit cocktail coffee, tea	2 oz. beef pattie ½ c. FF carrots ½ c. tomato juice 1 home-made 2" biscuit ½ c. diet fruit cocktail coffee, tea	2 oz. beef pattie 1 FF egg ½ c. FF carrots ½ c. tomato juice 2 home-made 2" biscuits ½ c. diet fruit cocktail coffee, tea	2 oz. beef pattie 1 FF egg ½ c. FF carrots ½ c. tomato juice 2 home-made 2" biscuits 5 vanilla wafers ½ c. diet fruit cocktail coffee, tea	2 oz. beef pattie 1 FF egg ½ c. FF carrots ½ c. tomato juice 2 home-made 2" biscuits 5 vanilla wafers ½ c. diet fruit cocktail coffee, tea
SNACK	1 c. skim milk 2 sq. graham crackers	1 c. skim milk 2 sq. graham crackers	1 c. skim milk 2 sq. graham crackers	1 c. skim milk 2 sq. graham crackers	1 c. skim milk 4 sq. graham crackers

At least one menu per day is to be prepared with bran.   # see recipe (1 fruit)

DATE __Thursday__   WEEK NO. __Two__   MENU CYCLE __Spring/Summer__

	REGULAR	SOFT/BLAND	2-3 gram sodium	LOW FAT	LOW RESIDUE
BREAKFAST	Orange juice Egg Cereal Toast Milk Coffee, tea	Orange juice Egg Cereal (no whole grain) Toast Milk Coffee, tea/Sanka	Orange juice 1 Egg Cereal Toast Milk Coffee, tea	Orange juice 1 FF Egg FF Cereal Toast Skim milk Coffee, tea	Orange juice Egg Cereal (no whole grain) Toast Milk Coffee, tea
DINNER	Salisbury steak Hash browned potatoes Green peas/red pepper Home-made Biscuit Peach cobbler Milk Coffee, tea	Salisbury steak no onion Hash browned potatoes Green peas Home-made Biscuit Peach cobbler Milk Coffee, tea/Sanka	Salisbury steak Hash browned potatoes Green peas/red pepper Home-made Biscuit Peach cobbler Coffee, tea	Salisbury steak FF Potatoes FF Grn peas/red pepper Roll Peaches with topping Skim milk Coffee, tea	Salisbury steak no onion Potatoes Green peas Roll Peaches with topping Coffee, tea
SUPPER	Macaroni & cheese Deviled egg Harvard beets Bread Fruited jello fluff Milk Coffee, tea	Macaroni & cheese Deviled egg Harvard beets Bread Fruited jello fluff Milk Coffee, tea/Sanka	Beef cubes Steamed rice Harvard beets Bread Fruited jello fluff Milk Coffee, tea	Beef cubes FF Steamed rice FF Beets Bread Fruited jello fluff Skim Milk Coffee, tea	Macaroni & cheese Deviled egg Harvard beets Bread Fruited jello fluff ½ cup Milk Coffee, tea

At least one menu per day is to be prepared with bran.

DATE _____ Thursday   WEEK NO. _____ Two   MENU CYCLE   Spring/Summer

	1000 Calories	1200 Calories	1500 Calories	1800 Calories	2000 Calories
BREAKFAST	½ c. orange juice 1 FF egg 1 toast 1 oleo coffee, tea	½ c. orange juice 1 FF egg 1 toast 1 oleo 1 c. skim milk coffee, tea	½ c. orange juice 1 FF egg 1 toast 1 oleo 1 c. skim milk coffee, tea	½ c. orange juice 1 FF egg 1 toast ½ c. FF cooked cereal 2 Oleo 1 c. skim milk coffee, tea	½ c. orange juice 2 FF eggs 1 toast ½ c. FF cooked cereal 2 Oleo 1 c. skim milk coffee, tea
DINNER	1 oz. steak ½ c. FF tomatoes ¼ c. FF peas/pepper ½ c. diet peaches 1 oleo 1 c. skim milk coffee, tea	2 oz. steak ½ c. FF tomatoes ¼ c. FF peas/pepper ½ c. FF potatoes ½ c. diet peaches 1 oleo coffee, tea	2 oz. steak ½ c. FF tomatoes ¼ c. FF peas/pepper ½ c. FF potatoes 1 2" biscuit ½ c. diet peaches coffee, tea	3 oz. steak ½ c. FF tomatoes ¼ c. FF peas/pepper ½ c. FF potatoes 1 2" biscuit ½ c. diet peaches 1 oleo coffee, tea	3 oz. steak ½ c. FF tomatoes ¼ c. FF peas/pepper ½ c. FF potatoes 2 2" biscuits ½ c. diet peaches coffee, tea
SUPPER	2 oz. beef cubes ½ c. FF beets 1 bread - 1 oleo ½ c. apple fluff## coffee, tea	2 oz. beef cubes ½ c. FF beets ½ c. baked noodles# 1 oleo ½ c. apple fluff## coffee, tea	3 oz. beef cubes ½ c. FF beets ½ c. baked noodles# 1 bread - 2 oleo ½ c. apple fluff## coffee, tea	3 oz. beef cubes ½ c. FF beets ½ c. baked noodles# 2 bread - 2 oleo ½ c. apple fluff## coffee, tea	3 oz. beef cubes ½ c. FF beets ½ c. baked noodles# 2 bread - 2 oleo ½ c. apple fluff## coffee, tea
SNACK	1 c. skim milk 2 sq. graham crackers	1 c. skim milk 2 sq. graham crackers	1 c. skim milk 2 sq. graham crackers	1 c. skim milk 2 sq. graham crackers	1 c. skim milk 4 sq. graham crackers

At least one menu per day is to be prepared with bran.
see recipe (1 bread, 1 vegetable)
see recipe (1 fruit)

DATE ___Friday___   WEEK NO. ___Two___   MENU CYCLE ___Spring/Summer___

	REGULAR	SOFT/BLAND	2-3 gram sodium	LOW FAT	LOW RESIDUE
B R E A K F A S T	Orange juice Egg Cereal Toast Milk Coffee, tea	Orange juice Egg Cereal (no whole grain) Toast Milk Coffee, tea/Sanka	Orange juice 1 Egg Cereal Toast Milk Coffee, tea	Orange juice 1 FF Egg FF Cereal Toast Skim milk Coffee, tea	Orange juice Egg Cereal (no whole grain) Toast Milk Coffee, tea
D I N N E R	Crispy fried chicken Rice/gravy Squash casserole Roll Red jello cake/tpg Milk Coffee, tea	Baked chicken Rice/gravy Squash casserole Roll Red jello cake/tpg Milk Coffee, tea/Sanka	Crispy fried chicken Rice Squash casserole Roll Red jello cake/tpg Coffee, tea	Bkd chicken - no skin FF Rice FF Squash Roll Red jello cubes Skim milk Coffee, tea	Baked chicken Rice Squash casserole Roll Red jello cake Coffee, tea

S U P P E R	Vegetable soup
	Crackers
	Ham salad sandwich
	Cottage cheese/
	  pineapple salad
	Cookies
	
	Milk
	Coffee, tea
		Vegetable soup
		Crackers
		Ham salad sandwich
		Cottage cheese/sliced
		  peaches salad
		Plain cookies/no choc
		
		Milk
		Coffee, tea/Sanka
			SF Vegetable soup
			Beef sandwich
			with lettuce & tomato
			Cottage cheese/
			  pineapple salad
			Cookies
			
			Milk
			Coffee, tea
				FF Vegetable soup
				Crackers
				Beef sandwich
				with lettuce & tomato
				Cottage cheese/
				  pineapple salad
				Plain cookies
				
				Skim Milk
				Coffee, tea
					Vegetable soup
					Crackers
					Ham salad sandwich
					Cottage cheese/sliced
					  peaches salad
					Plain cookies
					
					Coffee, tea

At least one menu per day is to be prepared with bran.

DATE ___Friday___ WEEK NO. ___Two___ MENU CYCLE ___Spring/Summer

	1000 Calories	1200 Calories	1500 Calories	1800 Calories	2000 Calories
BREAKFAST	½ c. orange juice 1 FF egg ½ c. FF cooked cereal 1 oleo 1 c. skim milk coffee, tea	½ c. orange juice 1 FF egg ½ c. FF cooked cereal 1 oleo 1 c. skim milk coffee, tea	½ c. orange juice 1 FF egg ½ c. FF cooked cereal 1 oleo 1 c. skim milk coffee, tea	½ c. orange juice 1 FF egg ½ c. FF cooked cereal 1 toast 2 Oleo 1 c. skim milk coffee, tea	½ c. orange juice 2 FF eggs ½ c. FF cooked cereal 1 toast 2 Oleo 1 c. skim milk coffee, tea
DINNER	1 oz. baked chicken ½ c. FF squash lettuce salad zero dressing 1 oleo 2 diet pear halves 1 c. skim milk coffee, tea	2 oz. baked chicken ½ c. FF squash lettuce salad zero dressing ½ c. FF rice 1 Oleo 2 diet pear halves coffee, tea	2 oz. baked chicken ½ c. FF squash lettuce salad zero dressing ½ c. FF rice 1 roll 1 Oleo 2 diet pear halves coffee, tea	3 oz. baked chicken ½ c. FF squash lettuce salad zero dressing ½ c. FF rice 1 roll 2 Oleo 2 diet pear halves coffee, tea	3 oz. baked chicken ½ c. FF squash lettuce salad zero dressing ½ c. FF rice 2 rolls 2 Oleo 2 diet pear halves coffee, tea
SUPPER	2 oz. ham 1 bread 1 tsp. mayonnaise ½ c. FF mixed vegetables 2 diet pineapple rings coffee, tea	2 oz. ham 1 bread 1 tsp. mayonnaise ½ c. FF mixed vegetables ½ c. hot tomato juice 2 diet pineapple rings coffee, tea	2 oz. ham 2 bread 2 tsp. mayonnaise ½ c. FF mixed vegetables ½ c. hot tomato juice ¼ c. cottage cheese 2 diet pineapple rings coffee, tea	2 oz. ham 2 bread 2 tsp. mayonnaise ½ c. FF mixed vegetables ½ c. hot tomato juice ¼ c. cottage cheese 2 diet pineapple rings 5 vanilla wafers coffee, tea	2 oz. ham 2 bread 2 tsp. mayonnaise ½ c. FF mixed vegetables ½ c. hot tomato juice ¼ c. cottage cheese 2 diet pineapple rings 5 vanilla wafers coffee, tea
SNACK	1 c. skim milk 2 sq. graham crackers	1 c. skim milk 2 sq. graham crackers	1 c. skim milk 2 sq. graham crackers	1 c. skim milk 2 sq. graham crackers	1 c. skim milk 4 sq. graham crackers

At least one menu per day is to be prepared with bran.

DATE ___Saturday___ WEEK NO. ___Two___ MENU CYCLE ___Spring/Summer___

	REGULAR	SOFT/BLAND	2-3 gram sodium	LOW FAT	LOW RESIDUE
B R E A K F A S T	Orange juice Egg Cereal Toast Milk Coffee, tea	Orange juice Egg Cereal (no whole grain) Toast Milk Coffee, tea/Sanka	Orange juice 1 Egg Cereal Toast Milk Coffee, tea	Orange juice 1 FF Egg FF Cereal Toast Skim milk Coffee, tea	Orange juice Egg Cereal (no whole grain) Toast Milk Coffee, tea
D I N N E R	Roast pork Black eye peas Seasoned Cabbage Cornbread Peach shortcake Milk Coffee, tea	Roast lean pork Mashed potatoes Seasoned Spinach Cornbread Peach shortcake Milk Coffee, tea/Sanka	Roast uncured pork Black eye peas Seasoned Cabbage Cornbread Peach shortcake Coffee, tea	Roast lean pork FF Black eye peas FF Cabbage Roll Peaches Skim milk Coffee, tea	Roast pork Mashed potatoes Seasoned Spinach Roll Peach shortcake Coffee, tea
S U P P E R	Sloppy Joe Potato salad Pickle/lettuce Purple plums Ice cream Milk Coffee, tea	Sloppy Joe (no onion, pepper) Potato salad (no onion, pepper) Slice tomato/lettuce Purple plums Ice cream - no choc Milk Coffee, tea/Sanka	Sloppy Joe Potato salad Slice tomato/lettuce Purple plums Ice cream Milk Coffee, tea	Sloppy Joe Plain potatoes FF Pickle/lettuce Purple plums Sherbet Skim milk Coffee, tea	Sloppy Joe (no onion, pepper) Potato salad (no onion, pepper) Tomato juice Purple plums Ice cream ½ cup Milk Coffee, tea

At least one menu per day is to be prepared with bran.

DATE   Saturday   WEEK NO.   Two   MENU CYCLE   Spring/Summer

	1000 Calories	1200 Calories	1500 Calories	1800 Calories	2000 Calories
B R E A K F A S T	½ c. orange juice 1 FF egg 1 toast 1 oleo 1 c. skim milk coffee, tea	½ c. orange juice 1 FF egg 1 toast 1 oleo 1 c. skim milk coffee, tea	½ c. orange juice 1 FF egg 1 toast 1 oleo 1 c. skim milk coffee, tea	½ c. orange juice 1 FF egg 1 toast ½ c. FF cooked cereal 2 Oleo 1 c. skim milk coffee, tea	½ c. orange juice 2 FF eggs 1 toast ½ c. FF cooked cereal 2 Oleo 1 c. skim milk coffee, tea
D I N N E R	1 oz. pork 1 c. FF cabbage 2 diet peach halves 1 oleo 1 c. skim milk coffee, tea	2 oz. pork 1 c. FF cabbage ½ c. FF black eye peas 2 diet peach halves 1 oleo coffee, tea	2 oz. pork 1 c. FF cabbage ½ c. FF black eye peas 2" square cornbread 2 diet peach halves coffee, tea	3 oz. pork 1 c. FF cabbage ½ c. FF black eye peas 2" square cornbread 2 diet peach halves 1 oleo coffee, tea	3 oz. pork 1 c. FF cabbage ½ c. FF black eye peas 2 2" squares cornbread 2 diet peach halves coffee, tea
S U P P E R	2 oz. scrambled beef ½ c. FF spinach ½ c. FF potatoes 1 oleo 2 diet purple plums coffee, tea	2 oz. scrambled beef ½ c. FF spinach pickle/lettuce/ sliced tomato ½ c. FF potatoes 1 oleo 2 diet purple plums coffee, tea	3 oz. scrambled beef ½ c. FF spinach pickle/lettuce/ sliced tomato ½ c. FF potatoes 2 diet purple plums ½ c. ice cream coffee, tea	3 oz. scrambled beef ½ c. FF spinach pickle/lettuce/ sliced tomato ½ c. FF potatoes 1 slice bread 2 diet purple plums ½ c. ice cream coffee, tea	3 oz. scrambled beef ½ c. FF spinach pickle/lettuce/ sliced tomato ½ c. FF potatoes 1 slice bread 2 diet purple plums ½ c. ice cream coffee, tea
S N A C K	1 c. skim milk 2 sq. graham crackers	1 c. skim milk 2 sq. graham crackers	1 c. skim milk 2 sq. graham crackers	1 c. skim milk 2 sq. graham crackers	1 c. skim milk 4 sq. graham crackers

At least one menu per day is to be prepared with bran.

DATE _____ Sunday   WEEK NO. _____ Two   MENU CYCLE   Spring/Summer

	REGULAR	SOFT/BLAND	2-3 gram sodium	LOW FAT	LOW RESIDUE
B R E A K F A S T	Orange juice Egg Cereal Toast Bacon Milk Coffee, tea	Orange juice Egg Cereal (no whole grain) Toast Crisp bacon Milk Coffee, tea/Sanka	Orange juice 1 Egg Cereal Toast Milk Coffee, tea	Orange juice 1 FF Egg FF Cereal Toast Skim milk Coffee, tea	Orange juice Egg Cereal (no whole grain) Toast Crisp bacon Milk Coffee, tea
D I N N E R	Chicken & dressing Cranberry sauce Green peas Roll Vanilla pudding/ Fruit mix Milk Coffee, tea	Chicken & dressing (no onion) Cranberry sauce Green peas Roll Vanilla pudding/ Fruit mix Milk Coffee, tea/Sanka	Chicken & dressing Cranberry sauce Green peas Roll Vanilla pudding/ Fruit mix Coffee, tea	Bkd chicken - no skin FF Mashed potatoes Cranberry sauce FF Green peas Roll Fruit mix Skim milk Coffee, tea	Baked chicken Mashed potatoes Cranberry sauce Green peas Roll Vanilla pudding/ Fruit mix Coffee, tea
S U P P E R	Frankfurter Pork & beans Slice of cheese Fruited jello Bread Rice Krispie square Milk Coffee, tea	Hamburger Buttered rice Carrots Fruited jello Bread Rice Krispie square Milk Coffee, tea/Sanka	Hamburger Buttered rice Carrots Fruited jello Bread Rice Krispie square Milk Coffee, tea	Hamburger FF Rice FF Carrots Fruited jello Bread Vanilla wafers Skim milk Coffee, tea	Hamburger Buttered rice Carrots Fruited jello Bread Vanilla wafers Milk Coffee, tea

At least one menu per day is to be prepared with bran.

DATE _____ Sunday _____ WEEK NO. _____ Two _____ MENU CYCLE _____ Spring/Summer

	1000 Calories	1200 Calories	1500 Calories	1800 Calories	2000 Calories
BREAKFAST	½ c. orange juice 1 FF egg ½ c. FF cooked cereal 1 crisp bacon coffee, tea	½ c. orange juice 1 FF egg ½ c. FF cooked cereal 1 crisp bacon 1 c. skim milk coffee, tea	½ c. orange juice 1 FF egg ½ c. FF cooked cereal 1 crisp bacon 1 c. skim milk coffee, tea	½ c. orange juice 1 FF egg ½ c. FF cooked cereal 1 toast 2 crisp bacon 1 c. skim milk coffee, tea	½ c. orange juice 2 FF eggs ½ c. FF cooked cereal 1 toast 2 crisp bacon 1 c. skim milk coffee, tea
DINNER	1 oz. chicken ½ c. FF squash ¼ c. FF green peas 1 oleo ½ c. diet fruit cocktail 1 c. skim milk coffee, tea	2 oz. chicken ½ c. FF squash ¼ c. FF green peas ½ c. mashed potatoes 1 oleo ½ c. diet fruit cocktail coffee, tea	2 oz. chicken ½ c. FF squash ¼ c. FF green peas ½ c. FF mashed potatoes 1 roll 1 oleo ½ c. diet fruit cocktail coffee, tea	3 oz. chicken ½ c. FF squash ¼ c. FF green peas ½ c. FF mashed potatoes 1 roll 2 oleo ½ c. diet fruit cocktail coffee, tea	3 oz. chicken ½ c. FF squash ¼ c. FF green peas ½ c. FF mashed potatoes 2 rolls 2 oleo ½ c. diet fruit cocktail coffee, tea
SUPPER	2 frankfurters ½ c. FF carrots 1 bread - 1 oleo ½ c. diet pineapple coffee, tea	2 frankfurters ½ c. FF carrots ½ c. FF coleslaw 1 bread - 1 oleo ½ c. diet pineapple coffee, tea	2 frankfurters 1 oz. cheese ½ c. FF carrots ½ c. FF coleslaw 2 bread - 2 oleo ½ c. diet pineapple coffee, tea	2 frankfurters 1 oz. cheese ½ c. FF carrots ½ c. FF coleslaw 2 bread - 2 oleo ½ c. diet pineapple 5 vanilla wafers coffee, tea	2 frankfurters 1 oz. cheese ½ c. FF carrots ½ c. FF coleslaw 2 bread - 2 oleo ½ c. diet pineapple 5 vanilla wafers coffee, tea
SNACK	1 c. skim milk 2 sq. graham crackers	1 c. skim milk 2 sq. graham crackers	1 c. skim milk 2 sq. graham crackers	1 c. skim milk 2 sq. graham crackers	1 c. skim milk 4 sq. graham crackers

At least one menu per day is to be prepared with bran.

DATE _Monday_   WEEK NO. _Three_   MENU CYCLE   Spring/Summer

	REGULAR	SOFT/BLAND	2-3 gram sodium	LOW FAT	LOW RESIDUE
BREAKFAST	Orange juice Egg Cereal Toast Milk Coffee, tea	Orange juice Egg Cereal (no whole grain) Toast Milk Coffee, tea/Sanka	Orange juice 1 Egg Cereal Toast Milk Coffee, tea	Orange juice 1 FF Egg FF Cereal Toast Skim milk Coffee, tea	Orange juice Egg Cereal (no whole grain) Toast Milk Coffee, tea
DINNER	Braised beef cubes over buttered noodles Seasoned Green beans Roll Cake/sparkling fruit sauce Milk Coffee, tea	Braised beef cubes over buttered noodles Seasoned Green beans Roll Cake/sparkling fruit sauce Milk Coffee, tea/Sanka	Braised beef cubes over buttered noodles Seasoned Green beans Roll Cake/sparkling fruit sauce Coffee, tea	Braised beef cubes over FF Noodles FF Green beans Roll Fruit cocktail Skim milk Coffee, tea	Braised beef cubes over buttered noodles Seasoned Green beans Roll Cake/sparkling fruit sauce Coffee, tea
SUPPER	Pancakes Egg w/cheese Sausage pattie Cinn. applesauce Milk Coffee, tea	Pancakes Egg w/cheese Bacon strips Cinn. applesauce Milk Coffee, tea/Sanka	Pancakes Beef pattie Fruit salad with cottage cheese Cinn. applesauce ½ cup Milk Coffee, tea	Chicken - no skin FF Mashed potatoes FF Tomatoes Cinn. applesauce Toast Skim milk Coffee, tea	Eggs Crisp bacon Cinn. applesauce Toast ½ cup Milk Coffee, tea

At least one menu per day is to be prepared with bran.

DATE ___Monday___ WEEK NO. ___Three___ MENU CYCLE Spring/Summer

Meal	1000 Calories	1200 Calories	1500 Calories	1800 Calories	2000 Calories
BREAKFAST	½ c. orange juice 1 FF egg ½ c. FF cereal 1 oleo 1 c. skim milk coffee, tea	½ c. orange juice 1 FF egg ½ c. FF cereal 1 oleo 1 c. skim milk coffee, tea	½ c. orange juice 1 FF egg ½ c. FF cooked cereal 1 oleo 1 c. skim milk coffee, tea	½ c. orange juice 1 FF egg ½ c. FF cooked cereal 1 toast 2 oleo 1 c. skim milk coffee, tea	½ c. orange juice 2 FF eggs ½ c. FF cooked cereal 1 toast 2 oleo 1 c. skim milk coffee, tea
DINNER	1 oz. braised beef 1 c. FF green beans 1 oleo 1 diet pear half 1 diet peach half 1 c. skim milk coffee, tea	2 oz. braised beef 1 c. FF green beans ½ c. FF noodles 1 oleo 1 diet pear half 1 diet peach half coffee, tea	2 oz. braised beef 1 c. FF green beans ½ c. FF noodles 1 roll 1 oleo 1 diet pear half 1 diet peach half coffee, tea	3 oz. braised beef 1 c. FF green beans ½ c. FF noodles 1 roll 2 oleo 1 diet pear half 1 diet peach half coffee, tea	3 oz. braised beef 1 c. FF green beans ½ c. FF noodles 2 rolls 2 oleo 1 diet pear half 1 diet peach half coffee, tea
SUPPER	2 FF eggs ½ c. tomato juice 1 5" pancake or waffle ½ c. diet cinn. applesauce coffee, tea	2 FF eggs 1 c. tomato juice 1 5" pancake or waffle ½ c. diet cinn. applesauce coffee, tea	1 FF egg 2 oz. beef pattie 1 c. tomato juice 2 5" pancakes or waffles ½ c. diet cinn. applesauce coffee, tea	1 FF egg 2 oz. beef pattie 1 c. tomato juice 2 5" pancakes or waffles ½ c. diet cinn. applesauce 5 vanilla wafers coffee, tea	1 FF egg 2 oz. beef pattie 1 c. tomato juice 2 5" pancakes or waffles ½ c. diet cinn. applesauce 5 vanilla wafers coffee, tea
SNACK	1 c. skim milk 2 sq. graham crackers	1 c. skim milk 2 sq. graham crackers	1 c. skim milk 2 sq. graham crackers	1 c. skim milk 2 sq. graham crackers	1 c. skim milk 4 sq. graham crackers

At least one menu per day is to be prepared with bran.

DATE ___ Tuesday ___ WEEK NO. ___ Three ___ MENU CYCLE Spring/Summer

	REGULAR	SOFT/BLAND	2-3 gram sodium	LOW FAT	LOW RESIDUE
BREAKFAST	Orange juice Egg Cereal Toast Milk Coffee, tea	Orange juice Egg Cereal (no whole grain) Toast Milk Coffee, tea/Sanka	Orange juice 1 Egg Cereal Toast Milk Coffee, tea	Orange juice 1 FF Egg FF Cereal Toast Skim milk Coffee, tea	Orange juice Egg Cereal (no whole grain) Toast Milk Coffee, tea
DINNER	Tender baked liver Scalloped potatoes Beets Apple crisp Roll Milk Coffee, tea	Tender baked liver Scalloped potatoes (no onion) Beets Roll Apple crisp Milk Coffee, tea/Sanka	Tender baked liver Sliced potatoes Beets Roll Apple crisp Coffee, tea	Tender baked liver FF Sliced potatoes FF Beets Roll Applesauce Skim milk Coffee, tea	Tender baked liver Scalloped potatoes (no onion) Beets Roll Applesauce Coffee, tea
SUPPER	Chicken pan pie w/ mixed vegetables Homemade Biscuit Peach jello/peaches/ topping Milk Coffee, tea	Chicken pan pie w/ mixed vegetables Homemade Biscuit Peach jello/peaches/ topping Milk Coffee, tea/Sanka	Chicken pan pie w/ mixed vegetables Homemade Biscuit Peach jello/peaches/ topping Milk Coffee, tea	Bkd chicken - no skin FF Mixed vegetables Roll Peach jello/peaches Skim milk Coffee, tea	Baked chicken Mixed vegetables Roll Peach jello/peaches/ topping Milk Coffee, tea

At least one menu per day is to be prepared with bran.

DATE _____   Tuesday _____   WEEK NO. _____   Three _____   MENU CYCLE _____   Spring/Summer

	1000 Calories	1200 Calories	1500 Calories	1800 Calories	2000 Calories
BREAKFAST	½ c. orange juice 1 FF egg ½ c. FF cooked cereal 1 oleo 1 c. skim milk coffee, tea	½ c. orange juice 1 FF egg ½ c. FF cooked cereal 1 oleo 1 c. skim milk coffee, tea	½ c. orange juice 1 FF egg ½ c. FF cooked cereal 1 oleo 1 c. skim milk coffee, tea	½ c. orange juice 1 FF egg ½ c. FF cooked cereal 1 toast 2 oleo 1 c. skim milk coffee, tea	½ c. orange juice 2 FF eggs ½ c. FF cooked cereal 1 toast 2 oleo 1 c. skim milk coffee, tea
DINNER	1 oz. liver ½ c. FF beets ½ c. FF okra ½ c. diet applesauce 1 oleo 1 c. skim milk coffee, tea	2 oz. liver ½ c. FF beets ½ c. FF okra ½ c. FF potatoes ½ c. diet applesauce 1 oleo coffee, tea	2 oz. liver ½ c. FF beets ½ c. FF okra ½ c. FF potatoes 1 home-made 2" biscuit ½ c. diet applesauce coffee, tea	3 oz. liver ½ c. FF beets ½ c. FF okra ½ c. FF potatoes 1 home-made 2" biscuit ½ c. diet applesauce 1 oleo coffee, tea	3 oz. liver ½ c. FF beets ½ c. FF okra ½ c. FF potatoes 2 2" home-made biscuits ½ c. diet applesauce coffee, tea
SUPPER	2 oz. chicken ½ c. FF mix vegetables ½ c. FF potatoes 1 oleo ½ c. diet peaches coffee, tea	2 oz. chicken ½ c. FF mix vegetables ½ c. FF cabbage ½ c. FF potatoes 1 oleo ½ c. diet peaches coffee, tea	3 oz. chicken ½ c. FF mix vegetables ½ c. FF cabbage ½ c. FF potatoes 1 2" biscuit - 1 oleo ½ c. diet peaches coffee, tea	3 oz. chicken ½ c. FF mix vegetables ½ c. FF cabbage ½ c. FF potatoes 2 2" biscuits ½ c. diet peaches coffee, tea	3 oz. chicken ½ c. FF mix vegetables ½ c. FF cabbage ½ c. FF potatoes 2 2" biscuits ½ c. diet peaches coffee, tea
SNACK	1 c. skim milk 2 sq. graham crackers	1 c. skim milk 2 sq. graham crackers	1 c. skim milk 2 sq. graham crackers	1 c. skim milk 2 sq. graham crackers	1 c. skim milk 4 sq. graham crackers

At least one menu per day is to be prepared with bran.

DATE Wednesday   WEEK NO. Three   MENU CYCLE Spring/Summer

	REGULAR	SOFT/BLAND	2-3 gram sodium	LOW FAT	LOW RESIDUE
BREAKFAST	Orange juice Egg Cereal Toast Bacon Milk Coffee, tea	Orange juice Egg Cereal (no whole grain) Toast Crisp bacon Milk Coffee, tea/Sanka	Orange juice 1 Egg Cereal Toast Milk Coffee, tea	Orange juice 1 FF Egg FF Cereal Toast Skim milk Coffee, tea	Orange juice Egg Cereal (no whole grain) Toast Crisp bacon Milk Coffee, tea
DINNER	BBQ pork Crowder peas Baked Squash Cornbread Ice cream Milk Coffee, tea	Mild BBQ pork Potatoes Baked Squash Cornbread Ice cream/no choc. Milk Coffee, tea/Sanka	Plain uncured pork Crowder peas Baked Squash Cornbread Ice cream Coffee, tea	Lean BBQ pork FF Crowder peas FF Squash Bread Sherbet Skim milk Coffee, tea	Mild BBQ pork Potatoes Baked Squash Bread Ice cream Coffee, tea
SUPPER	Salmon pattie Green peas Fruited jello square Pear delight - topping Bread Milk Coffee, tea	Baked salmon pattie Green peas Fruit jello square Pear delight - topping Bread Milk Coffee, tea/Sanka	Chicken pieces Green peas Fruited jello square Pear delight - topping Bread Milk Coffee, tea	Baked salmon pattie FF Green peas Fruited jello square Pears - topping Bread Skim milk Coffee, tea	Baked salmon pattie Green peas Fruited jello square Pear delight - topping Bread ½ cup Milk Coffee, tea

At least one menu per day is to be prepared with bran.

DATE __Wednesday__   WEEK NO. __Three__   MENU CYCLE   __Spring/Summer__

	1000 Calories	1200 Calories	1500 Calories	1800 Calories	2000 Calories
B R E A K F A S T	½ c. orange juice 1 FF egg 1 toast 1 bacon coffee, tea	½ c. orange juice 1 FF egg 1 toast 1 bacon 1 c. skim milk coffee, tea	½ c. orange juice 1 FF egg ¾ c. dry cereal 1 bacon 1 c. skim milk coffee, tea	½ c. orange juice 1 FF egg 1 toast ¾ c. dry cereal 2 bacon 1 c. skim milk coffee, tea	½ c. orange juice 2 FF eggs 1 toast ¾ c. dry cereal 2 bacon 1 c. skim milk coffee, tea
D I N N E R	1 oz. pork 1 c. FF squash 1 oleo 2 diet purple plums 1 c. skim milk coffee, tea	2 oz. pork 1 c. FF squash ½ c. FF crowder peas 1 oleo 2 diet purple plums coffee, tea	2 oz. pork 1 c. FF squash ½ c. FF crowder peas 2 diet purple plums ½ c. ice cream coffee, tea	3 oz. pork 1 c. FF squash ½ c. FF crowder peas 2 diet purple plums ½ c. ice cream coffee, tea	3 oz. pork 1 c. FF squash ½ c. FF crowder peas 1 bread 2 diet purple plums ½ c. ice cream coffee, tea
S U P P E R	2 oz. salmon ½ c. FF tomatoes 1 bread 1 tsp. mayonnaise 2 diet pear halves coffee, tea	2 oz. salmon ¼ c. FF green peas ½ c. FF tomatoes 1 bread 1 tesp. mayonnaise 2 diet pear halves coffee, tea	3 oz. salmon ¼ c. FF green peas ½ c. FF tomatoes 2 bread 1 tsp. mayonnaise 2 diet pear halves coffee, tea	3 oz. salmon ¼ c. FF green peas ½ c. FF tomatoes 2 bread 2 tsp. mayonnaise 2 diet pear halves 5 vanilla wafers coffee, tea	3 oz. salmon ¼ c. FF green peas ½ c. FF tomatoes 2 bread 2 tsp. mayonnaise 2 diet pear halves 5 vanilla wafers coffee, tea
S N A C K	1 c. skim milk 2 sq. graham crackers	1 c. skim milk 2 sq. graham crackers	1 c. skim milk 2 sq. graham crackers	1 c. skim milk 2 sq. graham crackers	1 c. skim milk 4 sq. graham crackers

At least one menu per day is to be prepared with bran.

MENU CYCLE   Spring/Summer

WEEK NO.   Three

DATE   Thursday

	REGULAR	SOFT/BLAND	2-3 gram sodium	LOW FAT	LOW RESIDUE
BREAKFAST	Orange juice Egg Cereal Toast Milk Coffee, tea	Orange juice Egg Cereal - no whole grain Toast Milk Coffee, tea/Sanka	Orange juice 1 Egg Cereal Toast Milk Coffee, tea	Orange juice 1 FF Egg FF Cereal Toast Skim milk Coffee, tea	Orange juice Egg Cereal - no whole grain Toast Milk Coffee, tea

DINNER	Crispy fried chicken
	Potato salad
	Glazed Carrots
	Roll
	Banana pudding/tpg
	
	Milk
	Coffee, tea
		Baked chicken
		Potato salad
		  (no onion, pepper)
		Glazed Carrots
		Roll
		Banana pudding/tpg
		
		Milk
		Coffee, tea/Sanka
			Crispy fried chicken
			Potato salad
			  (no pickles)
			Glazed Carrots
			Roll
			Banana pudding/tpg
			
			Coffee, tea
				Baked chicken - no skin
				FF Potatoes
				FF Carrots
				Roll
				Ripe banana
				
				Skim milk
				Coffee, tea
					Baked chicken
					Potato salad
					  (no onion, pepper)
					Glazed Carrots
					Roll
					Ripe banana
					
					Coffee, tea

SUPPER	Hamburger/bun French fries Relishes Fruit in season Milk Coffee, tea	Hamburger/bun Baked french fries Sliced tomatoes Soft fruit in season Milk Coffee, tea/Sanka	Hamburger/bun French fries Relishes - no pickle Fruit in season ½ cup Milk Coffee, tea	Hamburger/bun Baked french fries Relishes Fruit in season Skim milk Coffee, tea	Hamburger/bun Baked French fries Tomato juice Ripe fruit in season Milk Coffee, tea

At least one menu per day is to be prepared with bran.

DATE __Thursday__ WEEK NO. __Three__ MENU CYCLE __Spring/Summer__

	1000 Calories	1200 Calories	1500 Calories	1800 Calories	2000 Calories
BREAKFAST	½ c. orange juice 1 FF egg ½ c. FF cooked cereal 1 oleo coffee, tea	½ c. orange juice 1 FF egg ½ c. FF cooked cereal 1 oleo 1 c. skim milk coffee, tea	½ c. orange juice 1 FF egg ½ c. FF cooked cereal 1 oleo 1 c. skim milk coffee, tea	½ c. orange juice 1 FF egg ½ c. FF cooked cereal 1 toast 2 oleo 1 c. skim milk coffee, tea	½ c. orange juice 2 FF eggs ½ c. FF cooked cereal 1 toast 2 oleo 1 c. skim milk coffee, tea
DINNER	1 oz. baked chicken 1 c. FF carrots ½ small banana 1 oleo 1 c. skim milk coffee, tea	2 oz. baked chicken 1 c. FF carrots ½ c. FF potatoes ½ small banana 1 oleo coffee, tea	2 oz. baked chicken 1 c. FF carrots ½ c. FF potatoes 1 roll ½ small banana 1 oleo coffee, tea	3 oz. baked chicken 1 c. FF carrots ½ c. FF potatoes 1 roll ½ small banana 2 oleo coffee, tea	3 oz. baked chicken 1 c. FF carrots ½ c. FF potatoes 2 rolls ½ small banana 2 oleo coffee, tea
SUPPER	2 oz. hamburger ½ c. FF cabbage 8 baked fries 1 tsp. mayonnaise ½ c. baked cinnamon apples# coffee, tea	2 oz. hamburger sliced tomatoes ½ c. FF cabbage 8 baked fries 1 tsp. mayonnaise ½ c. baked cinnamon apples# coffee, tea	3 oz. hamburger sliced tomatoes ½ c. FF cabbage 16 baked fries 2 tsp. mayonnaise ½ c. baked cinnamon apples# coffee, tea	3 oz. hamburger sliced tomatoes ½ c. FF cabbage 16 baked fries 1 bread 2 tsp. mayonnaise ½ c. baked cinnamon apples# coffee, tea	3 oz. hamburger sliced tomatoes ½ c. FF cabbage 16 baked fries 1 bread 2 tsp. mayonnaise ½ c. baked cinnamon apples# coffee, tea
SNACK	1 c. skim milk 2 sq. graham crackers	1 c. skim milk 2 sq. graham crackers	1 c. skim milk 2 sq. graham crackers	1 c. skim milk 2 sq. graham crackers	1 c. skim milk 4 sq. graham crackers

At least one menu per day is to be prepared with bran.   # see recipe (1 fruit)

DATE ____ Friday ____ WEEK NO. Three ____ MENU CYCLE Spring/Summer

	REGULAR	SOFT/BLAND	2-3 gram sodium	LOW FAT	LOW RESIDUE
BREAKFAST	Orange juice Egg Cereal Toast Milk Coffee, tea	Orange juice Egg Cereal - no whole grain Toast Milk Coffee, tea/Sanka	Orange juice 1 Egg Cereal Toast Milk Coffee, tea	Orange juice 1 FF Egg FF Cereal Toast Skim milk Coffee, tea	Orange juice Egg Cereal - no whole grain Toast Milk Coffee, tea
DINNER	Fried fish Okra/tomatoes Au gratin Potatoes Coleslaw Hush puppy Frosted cake square Milk Coffee, tea	Baked fish Okra/tomatoes Au gratin Potatoes Bread Tinted pear halves Frosted cake square/ no choc. Milk Coffee, tea/Sanka	Baked fish Okra/tomatoes Au gratin Potatoes Coleslaw Hush puppy Frosted cake square Coffee, tea	Baked fish FF Okra/tomatoes FF Potatoes Coleslaw Bread Plain cake square Skim milk Coffee, tea	Baked fish Tomato juice Au gratin Potatoes Bread Tinted pear halves Frosted cake square Coffee, tea
SUPPER	Spaghetti/ meat sauce Tossed salad Salad dressing Toast triangles Peach half on lettuce leaf Brownie Milk Coffee, tea	Spaghetti/meat sauce (no onion, pepper) Shredded lettuce Salad dressing Toast triangles Peach half on lettuce leaf Brownie - no nuts BLAND - plain cookies Milk Coffee, tea/Sanka	Spaghetti/scrambled beef Tossed salad Salad dressing Toast triangles Peach half on lettuce leaf Brownie Milk Coffee, tea	Spaghetti/meat sauce Tossed salad 1 T. French dressing Toast triangles Peach half on lettuce leaf Graham crackers Skim milk Coffee, tea	Spaghetti/meat sauce (no onion, pepper) Shredded lettuce Toast triangles Peach half on lettuce leaf Vanilla wafers Milk Coffee, tea

At least one menu per day is to be prepared with bran.

DATE ___ Friday ___ WEEK NO. ___ Three ___ MENU CYCLE ___ Spring/Summer

	1000 Calories	1200 Calories	1500 Calories	1800 Calories	2000 Calories
BREAKFAST	½ c. orange juice	½ c. orange juice	½ c. orange juice	½ c. orange juice	½ c. orange juice
	1 FF egg	1 FF egg	1 FF egg	1 FF egg	2 FF eggs
	1 toast	1 toast	1 toast	1 toast	1 toast
	1 oleo	1 oleo	1 oleo	½ c. FF cooked cereal	½ c. FF cooked cereal
				2 oleo	2 oleo
	1 c. skim milk	1 c. skim milk	1 c. skim milk	1 c. skim milk	1 c. skim milk
	coffee, tea	coffee, tea	coffee, tea	coffee, tea	coffee, tea
DINNER	1 oz. baked fish	2 oz. baked fish	2 oz. baked fish	3 oz. baked fish	3 oz. baked fish
	½ c. FF okra	½ c. FF okra	½ c. FF okra	½ c. FF okra	½ c. FF okra
	½ c. FF coleslaw	½ c. FF coleslaw	½ c. FF coleslaw	½ c. FF coleslaw	½ c. FF coleslaw
	1 exchange fresh fruit	½ c. FF potatoes	½ c. FF potatoes	½ c. FF potatoes	½ c. FF potatoes
	1 oleo	1 exchange fresh fruit	1 exchange fresh fruit	1 exchange fresh fruit	1 exchange fresh fruit
		1 oleo	1 bread	1 bread	2 bread
			1 oleo	2 oleo	2 oleo
	1 c. skim milk				
	coffee, tea	coffee, tea	coffee, tea	coffee, tea	coffee, tea
SUPPER	2 oz. scrambled beef	2 oz. scrambled beef	3 oz. scrambled beef	3 oz. scrambled beef	3 oz. scrambled beef
	½ c. FF spaghetti	½ c. FF spaghetti	½ c. FF spaghetti	½ c. FF spaghetti	½ c. FF spaghetti
	½ c. FF tomatoes	½ c. FF tomatoes	½ c. FF tomatoes	½ c. FF tomatoes	½ c. FF tomatoes
	1 oleo	tossed salad	tossed salad	tossed salad	tossed salad
	½ c. diet peaches	1 Tbsp. Fr. dressing	1 Tbsp. Fr. dressing	1 Tbsp. Fr. dressing	1 Tbsp. Fr. dressing
		½ c. diet peaches	1 toast - 1 oleo	2 toasts - 1 oleo	2 toasts - 1 oleo
			½ c. diet peaches	½ c. diet peaches	½ c. diet peaches
	coffee, tea	coffee, tea	coffee, tea	coffee, tea	coffee, tea
SNACK	1 c. skim milk	1 c. skim milk	1 c. skim milk	1 c. skim milk	1 c. skim milk
	2 sq. graham crackers	2 sq. graham crackers	2 sq. graham crackers	2 sq. graham crackers	4 sq. graham crackers

At least one menu per day is to be prepared with bran.

DATE ___Saturday___   WEEK NO. ___Three___   MENU CYCLE ___Spring/Summer___

	REGULAR	SOFT/BLAND	2-3 gram sodium	LOW FAT	LOW RESIDUE
B R E A K F A S T	Orange juice Egg Cereal Toast Milk Coffee, tea	Orange juice Egg Cereal (no whole grain) Toast Milk Coffee, tea/Sanka	Orange juice 1 Egg Cereal Toast Milk Coffee, tea	Orange juice 1 FF Egg FF Cereal Toast Skim milk Coffee, tea	Orange juice Egg Cereal (no whole grain) Toast Milk Coffee, tea
D I N N E R	Cheddar steak Hash browns Broccoli Cornbread Fruited vanilla pudding Milk Coffee, tea	Cheddar steak Hash browns Seasoned Greens Cornbread Fruited vanilla pudding Milk Coffee, tea/Sanka	Plain steak Hash browns Broccoli Cornbread Fruited vanilla pudding Coffee, tea	Plain steak FF Potatoes FF Broccoli Roll Fruit mix Skim milk Coffee, tea	Plain steak Hash browns Seasoned Greens Roll Fruit mix Coffee, tea
S U P P E R	Beef barley vegetable soup Egg salad sandwich Fruit/cottage cheese Ice cream Milk Coffee, tea	Beef barley vegetable soup Egg salad sandwich Soft fruit/cottage cheese Ice cream/no choc. Milk Coffee, tea/Sanka	SF Beef barley vegetable soup Chicken sandwich Fruit/cottage cheese Ice cream ½ cup Milk Coffee, tea	FF Beef barley vegetable soup Chicken sandwich Fruit salad Sherbet Skim milk Coffee, tea	Beef barley vegetable soup Egg salad sandwich Soft fruit/cottage cheese Ice cream Coffee, tea

At least one menu per day is to be prepared with bran.

DATE ____ Saturday ____ WEEK NO. ____ Three ____ MENU CYCLE ____ Spring/Summer

	1000 Calories	1200 Calories	1500 Calories	1800 Calories	2000 Calories
BREAKFAST	½ c. orange juice	½ c. orange juice	½ c. orange juice	½ c. orange juice	½ c. orange juice
	1 FF egg	1 FF egg	1 FF egg	1 FF egg	2 FF egg
	½ c. FF cooked cereal	½ c. FF cooked cereal	½ c. FF cooked cereal	½ c. FF cooked cereal	½ c. FF cooked cereal
	1 oleo	1 oleo	1 oleo	1 toast	1 toast
				2 oleo	2 oleo
		1 c. skim milk	1 c. skim milk	1 c. skim milk	1 c. skim milk
	coffee, tea	coffee, tea	coffee, tea	coffee, tea	coffee, tea
DINNER	1 oz. plain steak	2 oz. plain steak	2 oz. plain steak	3 oz. plain steak	3 oz. plain steak
	½ c. FF broccoli	½ c. FF broccoli	½ c. FF broccoli	½ c. FF broccoli	½ c. FF broccoli
	½ c. FF greens	½ c. FF greens	½ c. FF greens	½ c. FF greens	½ c. FF greens
	1 oleo	½ c. FF potatoes	½ c. FF potatoes	½ c. FF potatoes	½ c. FF potatoes
			1 roll	1 roll	2 rolls
		1 oleo	1 oleo	2 oleo	2 oleo
	4 diet apricot halves	4 diet apricot halves	4 diet apricot halves	4 diet apricot halves	4 diet apricot halves
	1 c. skim milk				
	coffee, tea	coffee, tea	coffee, tea	coffee, tea	coffee, tea
SUPPER	1 FF egg	1 FF egg	2 FF eggs	2 FF eggs	2 FF eggs
	½ c. hot tomato juice	½ c. FF mixed vegetables	½ c. FF mixed vegetables	½ c. FF mixed vegetables	½ c. FF mixed vegetables
	1 bread - 1 oleo	½ c. hot tomato juice	½ c. hot tomato juice	½ c. hot tomato juice	½ c. hot tomato juice
	¼ c. cottage cheese	1 bread - 1 oleo	1 bread	2 bread	2 bread
	1 diet pineapple ring	¼ c. cottage cheese	¼ c. cottage cheese	¼ c. cottage cheese	¼ c. cottage cheese
	1 diet pear half	1 diet pineapple ring	1 diet pineapple ring	1 diet pineapple ring	1 diet pineapple ring
		1 diet pear half	1 diet pear half	1 diet pear half	1 diet pear half
			½ c. ice cream	½ c. ice cream	½ c. ice cream
	coffee, tea	coffee, tea	coffee, tea	coffee, tea	coffee, tea
SNACK	1 c. skim milk	1 c. skim milk	1 c. skim milk	1 c. skim milk	1 c. skim milk
	2 sq. graham crackers	2 sq. graham crackers	2 sq. graham crackers	2 sq. graham crackers	4 sq. graham crackers

At least one menu per day is to be prepared with bran.

DATE ____ Sunday ____   WEEK NO. ____ Three ____   MENU CYCLE ____ Spring/Summer

	REGULAR	SOFT/BLAND	2-3 gram sodium	LOW FAT	LOW RESIDUE
BREAKFAST	Orange juice Egg Cereal Toast Bacon Milk Coffee, tea	Orange juice Egg Cereal (no whole grain) Toast Crisp bacon Milk Coffee, tea/Sanka	Orange juice 1 Egg Cereal Toast Milk Coffee, tea	Orange juice 1 FF Egg FF Cereal Toast Skim milk Coffee, tea	Orange juice Egg Cereal (no whole grain) Toast Crisp bacon Milk Coffee, tea
DINNER	Baked ham Sweet potatoes & apples Steamed cabbage Cornbread Lemon pie Milk Coffee, tea	Baked ham Sweet potatoes & apples Green beans Cornbread Lemon pie Milk Coffee, tea/Sanka	Uncured pork Sweet potatoes & apples Steamed cabbage Cornbread Lemon pie Coffee, tea	Lean uncured pork FF Sweet potatoes & apples FF Steamed cabbage Roll Sherbet Skim milk Coffee, tea	Uncured pork Sweet potatoes & apples Green beans Roll Lemon pudding Coffee, tea
SUPPER	Chicken & dumplings Peas & carrots Home-made Biscuit Fruit in season Milk Coffee, tea	Chicken & dumplings Peas & carrots Home-made Biscuit Soft fruit in season Milk Coffee, tea/Sanka	Chicken & dumplings Peas & carrots Home-made Biscuit Fruit in season Milk Coffee, tea	Baked chicken - no skin FF Sliced potatoes FF Peas & carrots Bread Fruit in season Skim milk Coffee, tea	Baked chicken Sliced potatoes Peas & carrots Bread Soft fruit in season ½ cup Milk Coffee, tea

At least one menu per day is to be prepared with bran.

DATE ___Sunday___   WEEK NO. ___Three___   MENU CYCLE   Spring/Summer

	1000 Calories	1200 Calories	1500 Calories	1800 Calories	2000 Calories
BREAKFAST	½ c. orange juice 1 FF egg 1 toast 1 bacon 1 c. skim milk coffee, tea	½ c. orange juice 1 FF egg 1 toast 1 bacon 1 c. skim milk coffee, tea	½ c. orange juice 1 FF egg 1 toast 1 bacon 1 c. skim milk coffee, tea	½ c. orange juice 1 FF egg 1 toasts ½ c. FF cooked cereal 2 bacon 1 c. skim milk coffee, tea	½ c. orange juice 2 FF eggs 1 toast ½ c. FF cooked cereal 2 bacon 1 c. skim milk coffee, tea
DINNER	1 oz. baked ham ½ c. FF cabbage ½ c. FF green beans ½ c. apple fluff* 1 oleo 1 c. skim milk coffee, tea	2 oz. baked ham ½ c. FF cabbage ½ c. FF green beans ¼ c. FF sweet potatoes ½ c. apple fluff* 1 oleo coffee, tea	2 oz. baked ham ½ c. FF green beans ½ c. FF cabbage ½ c. FF sweet potatoes 2" square cornbread ½ c. apple fluff* coffee, tea	3 oz. baked ham ½ c. FF cabbage ½ c. FF green beans ¼ c. FF sweet potatoes 2" sq. cornbread ½ c. apple fluff* 1 oleo coffee, tea	3 oz. baked ham ½ c. FF cabbage ½ c. FF green beans ¼ c. FF sweet potatoes 2" sq. cornbread ½ c. apple fluff* coffee, tea
SUPPER	2 oz. chicken ½ c. FF carrots 1 home-made 2" biscuit 1 exchange fresh fruit coffee, tea	2 oz. chicken ½ c. FF carrots ½ c. baked noodles** 1 oleo 1 exchange fresh fruit coffee, tea	3 oz. chicken ½ c. FF carrots ½ c. baked noodles** 1 home-made 2" biscuit 1 oleo 1 exchange fresh fruit coffee, tea	3 oz. chicken ½ c. FF carrots ½ c. baked noodles** 2 2" home-made biscuits 1 exchange fresh fruit coffee, tea	3 oz. chicken ½ c. FF carrots ½ c. baked noodles** 2 2" home-made biscuits 1 exchange fresh fruit coffee, tea
SNACK	1 c. skim milk 2 sq. graham crackers	1 c. skim milk 2 sq. graham crackers	1 c. skim milk 2 sq. graham crackers	1 c. skim milk 2 sq. graham crackers	1 c. skim milk 4 sq. graham crackers

* see recipe (1 fruit)   ** see recipe (1 bread, 1 vegetable)

BEEF STEW

One serving equals about one cup.

	For 25 Servings	For 50 Servings	For 100 Servings
beef cubes, cut in 1½ inch pieces	6 lb.	12 lb.	24 lb.
shortening	¼ cup	½ cup	1 cup
beef broth	4 cans (10½ oz. each)	8 cans (10½ oz. each)	16 cans (10½ oz. each)
water	3 cups	1½ qt.	3 qt.
chopped onions	2 cups (about 1 lb.)	1 qt. (about 2 lb.)	2 qt. (about 4 lb.)
salt	3 t.	2 T.	4 T.
thyme leaves, crushed	1 t.	2 t.	4 t.
carrots, cut in 1-inch pieces	5 cups (about 2 lb.)	2½ qt. (about 4 lb.)	5 qt. (about 8 lb.)
potatoes, cut in 2-inch cubes	5 cups (about 2 lb.)	2½ qt. (about 4 lb.)	5 qt. (about 8 lb.)
frozen peas	2 pkgs. (10 oz. each) about 3 cups	4 pkgs. (10 oz. each) about 1½ qt.	8 pkgs. (10 oz. each) about 3 qt.
flour	½ to ⅔ cup	1 to 1⅓ cups	2 to 2⅔ cups
Yield:	1½ gal.	3 gal.	6 gal.

For 25 Servings:

1. In large heavy skillets, brown beef in shortening; pour off fat.
2. Divide beef between 2 large shallow roasting pans. (14 x 10 x 2" each).
3. To each pan add 2 cans beef broth, ½ cup water, 1 cup onion, 1½ teaspoons salt and ½ teaspoon thyme. Cover; bake at 350° for 1 hour.
4. Add carrots; stir. Bake covered 1 hour more.
5. Add potatoes; stir. Bake covered 30 minutes more.
6. Add peas; stir. Bake covered 30 minutes more or until done.
7. Blend remaining 2 cups water into flour until smooth. On top of range, in roasting pans, slowly stir half the flour mixture into each pan. Cook, stirring until thickened.

Note: For 50 servings: Prepare two 25-serving recipes. Bake in 4 pans.
For 100 servings: Prepare four 25-serving recipes. Bake in 8 pans.

SWISS STEAK

One steak with about ¼ cup sauce poured over it equals one serving.

	For 25 Servings	For 50 Servings	For 100 Servings
cubed steak	25 (or about 8 lbs.)	50 (or about 16 lbs.)	100 (or about 32 lbs.)
shortening	2 T.	¼ cup	½ cup
tomato soup	4 cans (10¾ oz. each)	8 cans (10¾ oz. each)	16 cans (10¾ oz. each)
water	3 cups	1½ qts.	3 qts.
salt	2 t.	4 t.	8 t.
pepper	¼ t.	½ t.	1 t.
thinly sliced onions	2 cups (about ½ lb.)	1 qt. (about 1 lb.)	2 qts. (about 2 lbs.)
thinly sliced celery	1 cup	2 cups	1 qt.
flour	¼ cup	½ cup	1 cup
Yield:			
	25 steaks 7½ cups sauce	50 steaks 3¾ qts. sauce	100 steaks 7½ qts. sauce

For 25 Servings:
1. In large heavy skillets, brown steaks in shortening; pour off fat.
2. To make sauce, combine soup, 2 cups water, salt, and pepper.
3. In 2 shallow roasting pans (18 x 12 x 2″ each), arrange steaks; top with onions and celery. Divide sauce equally between each pan.
4. Cover; bake at 350° for 1 hour 15 minutes or until done.
5. Remove steaks from pan; keep warm. Gradually blend remaining 1 cup water into flour until smooth. On top of range, in roasting pans, slowly stir half the flour mixture into each pan. Cook, stirring until thickened.

Note: For 50 servings: Prepare two 25-serving recipes. Bake in 4 pans.
For 100 servings: Prepare four 25-serving recipes. Bake in 8 pans.

BAKED CINNAMON APPLES

1 apple equals 1 fruit exchange.

	For 6 Servings	For 12 Servings
small cooking apples	6	12
water	2 cups	4 cups
vanilla	2 t.	4 t.
cinnamon	½ t.	1 t.
sugar substitute	to equal ⅔ cup sugar	to equal 1⅓ cups sugar

1. Wash and core the apples.
2. Remove the peeling from the top ⅓ of each apple.
3. Arrange the apples in baking dish.
4. In saucepan bring water, vanilla, cinnamon and sugar substitute to a boil and pour over apples.
5. Bake at 350° for 1 hour or until easily pierced by fork. Baste frequently.
6. When done remove and let cool in the sauce. They are good hot or cold.

MARINATED GREEN BEAN SALAD

1 serving equals 1 vegetable exchange.

	For 4 Servings	For 8 Servings	For 12 Servings
dry mustard	½ t.	1 t.	1½ t.
red wine vinegar	½ cup	1 cup	1½ cups
water	¼ cup	½ cup	¾ cups
oregano	½ t.	1 t.	1½ t.
sweet basil	½ t.	1 t.	1½ t.
ground black pepper	¼ t.	½ t.	¾ t.
sugar substitute	to equal 1 t. sugar	to equal 2 t. sugar	to equal 1 T. sugar
salt	1 t.	2 t.	1 T.
Worcestershire sauce	½ t.	1 t.	1½ t.
green beans, cooked	2 cups	4 cups	6 cups
finely chopped onion	½ cup	1 cup	1½ cup

1. Mix the dry mustard with 1 T. of the vinegar until completely dissolved.
2. Add all of the other ingredients except beans and onion and mix well.
3. Pour over cooked, drained green beans and marinate for at least 2 hours before serving.
4. Serve cold with finely chopped onion sprinkled over the top.

BAKED NOODLES

1 serving equals 1 bread and 1 vegetable exchange.

	For 1 Serving	For 5 Servings	For 10 Servings
wide noodles, cooked	½ cup	2½ cups	5 cups
tomato juice	½ cup	2½ cups	5 cups
onion, grated	1 t.	5 t.	3 T., 1 t.
salt and pepper	to taste	to taste	to taste
sage	pinch	pinch	⅛ t.

1. Place the cooked noodles in a casserole.
2. Add grated onion, salt, pepper, and sage to tomato juice.
3. Pour the tomato juice over the noodles.
4. Cover and bake in a moderate oven for about ½ hour.

STUFFED EGGS

1 serving equals 1 meat exchange.

	For 1 Serving	For 5 Servings	For 10 Servings
egg, hard cooked	1	5	10
mustard	1 t.	5 t.	3 T., 1 t.
pepper and salt	to taste	to taste	to taste

1. Hard cook the egg. Cut in half and scoop out the yolk.
2. Cream the yolk with a fork, and mix the mustard, salt and pepper in.
3. Return yolk to egg white and sprinkle with paprika. Serve 2 halves.

SPARKLE DESSERT

| 1 envelope | sugar free lemon flavored gelatin dessert |
| 1 envelope | sugar free lime flavored gelatin dessert |

1. Prepare the gelatin using the directions on the envelopes.
2. Pour each flavor separately in small pans and place in refrigerator to gel.
3. As soon as the gelatin is set, take a sharp knife and cut into ½" cubes.
4. Pile the cubes into a large size sherbet glass, alternating the flavors.

SOUR BEETS
Serves 1

1 serving equals one vegetable exchange.

½ cup beets, sliced
2-3 thin slices onion
vinegar to cover
few cloves

1. Mix the ingredients listed and allow to stand for a few hours.
2. Chill and serve as salad or with main dish.

APPLE FLUFF

1 serving equals 1 fruit exchange.

	For 1 Serving	For 5 Servings	For 10 Servings
sugar-free gelation dessert (lemon flavor)	1 envelope	5 envelopes	10 envelopes
hot water	½ cup	2½ cups	5 cups
unsweetened applesauce	½ cup	2½ cups	5 cups

1. Dissolve sugar-free gelatin dessert in hot water.
2. Chill until cold and syrupy.
3. Set the bowl into a large bowl containing cracked ice. Beat until fluffy and thick like whipped cream.
4. Fold in the applesauce.
5. Chill and serve.

CRUSHED PINEAPPLE AND COTTAGE CHEESE SALAD

For 25 servings		For 100 servings
3¾ lb.	cottage cheese	15 lb.
¼ #10 can	crushed pineapple	1 #10 can

1. Mix cottage cheese and pineapple well.
2. Serve on bed of lettuce.

MOCK PECAN PIE

Bake in 350° over for 50-60 minutes. Yields 8 eight-inch pies.

Filling

24 eggs
 4 cups sugar
 8 cups dark corn syrup
 1 t. salt
 3 T. vanilla
 2 cups melted butter
 4 cups oats, uncooked, quick cooking
 4 cups coconut, shredded

Crust

5 cups all purpose flour
2 cups shortening or lard (1 pound)
2 t. salt
1 egg
1 T. vinegar
2 T. brown sugar

Crust

1. Blend together with pastry blender: flour, shortening and salt.
2. In a measuring cup beat egg, vinegar, brown sugar.
3. Fill to 1 cup with water. Add to flour mixture. Mix well. Divide into 8-5½ ounce portions. Roll slightly thicker than regular crust.

Filling

1. Beat eggs.
2. Add sugar, dark corn syrup, salt, vanilla, melted butter.
3. Add oats and coconut.
4. Mix well, pour into the unbaked crust lined pie pans. Bake until top is brown and filling is set.

BANANA SPLIT CAKE

Filling

1 box commercial vanilla pudding
4 bananas
1 large can crushed pineapple, drained
1 large size Cool Whip
roasted chopped pecans

Crust

2 cups crushed graham cracker crumbs
¼ cup sugar
1 stick margarine

Crust

1. Mix together graham cracker crumbs, sugar, margarine.
2. Press into 11 x 14 pan.
3. Bake at 350° until browned.

Filling

1. Prepare pudding according to directions on box.
2. Spread pudding over baked pie crust.
3. Slice bananas over pudding layer.
4. Spread pineapple over bananas.
5. Spread carton of Cool Whip over pineapple.
6. Sprinkle roasted chopped pecans over Cool Whip.
7. Refrigerate 4-6 hrs.

FRUIT COCKTAIL SCALLOP

Serve 4 oz. portions with Miracle Topping, if desired.

For 25 servings		For 100 servings
4 lb.	cake crumbs	16 lb.
2 qt.	stewed fruit cocktail	2 gal.
1 cup	sugar	4 cups
1	lemon(s)	4
4 oz.	margarine	1 lb.

1. Spread ⅔ of cake crumbs in buttered baking dishes (9 x 14 pans).
2. Spread the stewed fruit cocktail over the crumbs.
3. Spread sugar over the fruit.
4. Squeeze lemon over all.
5. Sprinkle rest of cake crumbs over all.
6. Dot margarine over all.
7. Brown at 350°

PEAR DELIGHT

For 25 Servings		For 100 Servings
¼ can	# 10 can pears	1 can
6 T.	cornstarch	1½ cups
6 T.	cold water	1½ cups
4 oz.	margarine	1 lb.
1 cup	sugar	4 cups
3	eggs	12
1 pt.	milk	2 qt.
¾ T.	vanilla	3 T.
3 cups	flour	3 lb.
½ T.	salt	2 T.
1 T.	baking powder	4 T.

1. Drain pears. Fill baking pan.
2. Dissolve cornstarch in cold water. Add to pears and mix well.
3. Cream together margarine and sugar.
4. Beat eggs; add to margarine mixture.
5. Add milk and vanilla to eggs, etc. Mix well.
6. Sift together flour, salt and baking powder. Add to creamed mixture.
7. Spread over fruit.
8. Bake in 375° oven for ½ hour or until crust is browned.

JELLIED APPLESAUCE SALAD

Yields two 12 x 20 pans of salad (14 quarts).

(use 2-1 lb. 8 oz. pkgs.) Gelatin dessert
  powder lemon flavored
  1 gal. Boiling water
  ½ gal. apple juice

½ qt. (approx. 8 lemons) lemon juice
¼ cup boiling water
2 #10 cans applesauce
2 T. cinnamon

1. Thoroughly dissolve gelatin in water. Add apple and lemon juice.
2. Make smooth paste of cinnamon and water. Combine with gelatin mixture. Chill until slightly thickened.
3. Fold in applesauce. Pour 7 qt. into each 12 x 20 steam table pan or pour into individual jello molds. Serve with mayonnaise or fruit salad dressing. Garnish with cherry.

CHICKEN SUPREME

Yields 100 servings with 5½ quarts of sauce.

40 lbs. chicken parts or 100 quarters
2 lbs. or 8 cups flour, A. P.
4 T. salt
4 t. paprika

2 t. pepper
2 cups margarine
6¼ qt. cream of mushroom soup
(use 4-50 oz. cans)
1 qt. water

1. Cut chicken quarters in half, leg and thigh, wing and breast.
2. Dredge chicken pieces in mixture of flour, salt, paprika, and pepper. Arrange in greased 12" x 20" steam table pans (leg on top of thigh, wing on top of breast).
3. Sprinkle melted margarine over chicken.
4. Bake in a hot oven (400°) for 50-60 minutes.
5. Blend soup and water; pour over hot chicken. Return to oven and continue to bake until sauce is bubbling (about 10 minutes).

SUNSHINE GINGERBREAD

Bake in 360° oven for 35 minutes. Yields 3 pans, or 96 servings.

1 lb. margarine
2 lbs. light brown sugar
topping

2 #10 cans peach slices
7½ lbs. gingerbread mix

1. Cream margarine and sugar. Spread in bottom of 3 12 x 20 x 2 pans.
2. Drain peaches. Arrange over sugar and margarine.
3. Prepare gingerbread as directed. Spoon over peaches.
4. Bake
5. Serve inverted with topping.

MOCK SWISS STEAK

Yields 50 servings.

10 pounds raw beef
4 pounds raw potatoes
6 eggs, slightly beaten
1 cup minced parsley
3 T. salt

3 qts. strained tomatoes
2 cups flour
1½ cups drippings
1 T. salt
1 t. paprika

1. Boil potatoes and mash.
2. Mix beef, potatoes, eggs, parsley, and three tablespoons salt.
3. Shape into round flat cakes.
4. Roll in flour.
5. Saute until brown in drippings, remove to casseroles.
6. Add fat to pan to make one and one-half cups; stir in flour and add hot tomatoes, stirring constantly.
7. Add paprika and one tablespoon of salt; add to meat cakes.
8. Cook fifteen or twenty minutes at 350°.

CHEDDAR STEAK

One steak with 1 oz. cheese sauce poured over it equals one serving.

For 25 servings		For 100 servings
25	beef patties or steak	100
6 oz.	margarine, melted	1½ lb.
2 T.	seasoning salt	½ cup
¾ T.	Worcestershire sauce	3 T.
¾ t.	dry mustard	1 T.
½ t.	paprika	2 t.
8 drops	Tabasco sauce	½ t.
¾ t.	salt	1 T.
16 oz.	tomato juice (46 oz. can)	1½ cans
1 lb.	cheese	4 lbs.

1. Brush margarine on steaks.
2. Broil 2 minutes.
3. Sprinkle on salt.
4. Mix to a smooth paste: Worcestershire sauce, dry mustard, paprika, Tabasco sauce and salt.
5. Bring tomato juice to boil.
6. Add to paste.
7. Grate cheese. Melt in the sauce.

SPARKLING FRUIT SAUCE

Yields 24 one-half cup servings.

1 #10 can cling peach slices or fruit cocktail
1 cup sugar
½ cup cornstarch

1 t. salt
2 cups orange juice
¼ cup butter

1. Drain fruit, saving syrup (1 qt.) for sauce.
2. Combine sugar, cornstarch, salt in large saucepan.
3. Blend in orange juice and fruit syrup.
4. Cook, stirring constantly until thickened and clear.
5. Remove from heat.
6. Stir in butter and fold in drained fruit.
7. Serve over cake.

CAPE COD SALAD OR DESSERT

Yields 96 one-half cup servings.

1 # 10 can jellied cranberry
   sauce
5 qt. water

3 lb. strawberry jello
1 #10 can fruit cocktail
4½ lb. bananas, sliced

1. Heat cranberry sauce and water, stirring until sauce is dissolved.
2. Dissolve gelatin in hot mixture. Chill until slightly thickened.
3. Drain fruit cocktail; save syrup for other uses.
4. Fold bananas and cocktail into gelatin.
5. Pour into three 20 x 12 x 2 inch pans, allowing 1 gallon per pan.
6. Chill until firm.
7. Cut into squares.

Appendix B
Portion Control Data

Source: Hobart Food Equipment
Foodservice Bulletin 641

PORTION CONTROL DATA

The use of standardized recipes is an important factor in portion control. A recipe, however, can be depended upon to give the stated number of portions only if the servings are of a uniform size. The most dependable method to use when measuring portions is to serve the food with ladles, scoops, and spoons of standard size.

LADLES

Ladles may be used in serving soups, creamed dishes, stews, sauces, gravies, and other similar products.

The following sizes of ladles are most frequently used for serving:

1/4 cup (2 ounces)
1/2 cup (4 ounces)
3/4 cup (6 ounces)
1 cup (8 ounces)

SERVING SPOONS

A serving spoon (solid or perforated) may be used instead of a scoop. Since these spoons are not identified by number, it is necessary to measure or weigh food in the spoons used to obtain the approximate serving size desired.

SCOOPS

The number of the scoop indicates the number of scoopfuls it takes to make one quart. The table below shows the level measures of each scoop in cups or tablespoons.

Scoop Number	Level Measure
6	2/3 cup
8	1/2 cup
10	2/5 cup
12	1/3 cup
16	1/4 cup
20	3 1/5 tablespoons
24	2 2/3 tablespoons
30	2 1/5 tablespoons
40	1 3/5 tablespoons

Scoops may be used for portioning such items as drop cookies, muffins, meat patties, and some vegetables, salads, and sandwich fillings.

FRACTIONAL EQUIVALENTS FOR USE IN CONVERTING RECIPES

The following chart is designed to help you change fractional parts of pounds, gallons, cups, etc., to accurate weights or measures. For example, reading from left to right, the table shows that 7/8 of one pound is 14 ounces, 1/3 of a gallon is 1 quart plus $1\frac{1}{3}$ cups; 1/16 of a cup is 1 tablespoon; etc.

	1 TABLESPOON	1 CUP	1 PINT	1 QUART	1 GALLON	1 POUND
1	3 tsp	16 Tbsp	2 cups	2 pints	4 quarts	16 ounces
7/8	$2\frac{1}{2}$ tsp	1 cup less 2 Tbsp	$1\frac{3}{4}$ cups	$3\frac{1}{2}$ cups	3 quarts plus 1 pint	14 ounces
3/4	$2\frac{1}{4}$ tsp	12 Tbsp	$1\frac{1}{2}$ cups	3 cups	3 quarts	12 ounces
2/3	2 tsp	10 Tbsp plus 2 tsp	$1\frac{1}{3}$ cups	$2\frac{2}{3}$ cups	2 quarts plus $2\frac{2}{3}$ cups	$10\frac{2}{3}$ ounces
5/8	2 tsp (scant)	10 Tbsp	$1\frac{1}{4}$ cups	$2\frac{1}{2}$ cups	2 quarts plus 1 pint	10 ounces
1/2	$1\frac{1}{2}$ tsp	8 Tbsp	1 cup	2 cups	2 quarts	8 ounces
3/8	$1\frac{1}{8}$ tsp	6 Tbsp	$\frac{3}{4}$ cup	$1\frac{1}{2}$ cups	1 quart plus 1 pint	6 ounces
1/3	1 tsp	5 Tbsp plus 1 tsp	$\frac{2}{3}$ cup	$1\frac{1}{3}$ cups	1 quart plus $1\frac{1}{3}$ cups	$5\frac{1}{3}$ ounces
1/4	$\frac{3}{4}$ tsp	4 Tbsp	$\frac{1}{2}$ cup	1 cup	1 quart	4 ounces
1/8	$\frac{1}{2}$ tsp (scant)	2 Tbsp	$\frac{1}{4}$ cup	$\frac{1}{2}$ cup	1 pint	2 ounces
1/16	$\frac{1}{4}$ tsp (scant)	1 Tbsp	2 Tbsp	4 Tbsp	1 cup	1 ounce

PORTION CONTROL DATA

CONVERSION CHART I

CONTAINER PORTIONS

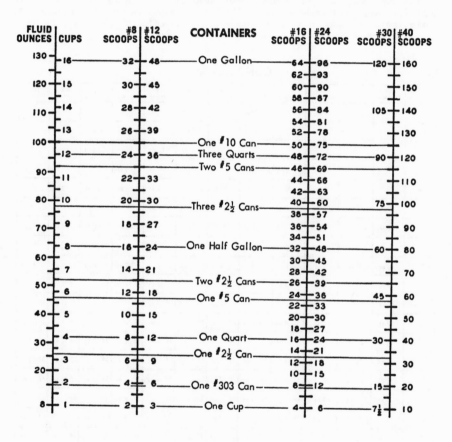

PORTION CONTROL DATA

CONVERSION CHART 2

These two conversion charts, the OUNCE CHART below, and the POUND CHART on the back of this sheet, have been designed to permit easy adjustment of basic recipes for the number of portions actually needed.

EXAMPLE: A basic 100-portion recipe calls for 7 ounces of a particular ingredient. When adjusting to 25 portions, find the column headed "100 Portions" and move down to the space marked "7". Then move across this space, horizontally to the left, to the column headed "25" Portions. The figure "1¾" then appears as the number of ounces of the ingredient needed.

OUNCE CHART

25 Portions	50 Portions	75 Portions	100 Portions	200 Portions	300 Portions	400 Portions	500 Portions	600 Portions	700 Portions	800 Portions	900 Portions	1000 Portions
–	–	1/8 oz	1/8 oz	1/4 oz	3/8 oz	1/2 oz	5/8 oz	3/4 oz	7/8 oz	1 oz	1 1/8 oz	1 1/4 oz
–	–	1/6 oz	1/6 oz	1/3 oz	1/2 oz	2/3 oz	5/6 oz	1 oz	1 1/6 oz	1 1/3 oz	1 1/2 oz	1 2/3 oz
–	–	1/5 oz	1/5 oz	2/5 oz	3/5 oz	4/5 oz	1 oz	1 1/5 oz	1 2/5 oz	1 3/5 oz	1 4/5 oz	2 oz
–	–	1/4 oz	1/4 oz	1/2 oz	3/4 oz	1 oz	1 1/4 oz	1 1/2 oz	1 3/4 oz	2 oz	2 1/4 oz	2 1/2 oz
–	–	1/3 oz	1/3 oz	2/3 oz	1 oz	1 1/3 oz	1 2/3 oz	2 oz	2 1/3 oz	2 2/3 oz	3 oz	3 1/3 oz
–	1/4 oz	3/8 oz	1/2 oz	1 oz	1 1/2 oz	2 oz	2 1/2 oz	3 oz	3 1/2 oz	4 oz	4 1/2 oz	5 oz
–	1/3 oz	1/2 oz	2/3 oz	1 1/3 oz	2 oz	2 2/3 oz	3 1/3 oz	4 oz	4 2/3 oz	5 1/3 oz	6 oz	6 2/3 oz
–	3/8 oz	5/8 oz	3/4 oz	1 1/2 oz	2 1/4 oz	3 oz	3 3/4 oz	4 1/2 oz	5 1/4 oz	6 oz	6 3/4 oz	7 1/2 oz
1/4 oz	1/2 oz	3/4 oz	1 oz	2 oz	3 oz	4 oz	5 oz	6 oz	7 oz	8 oz	9 oz	10 oz
1/2 oz	1 oz	1 1/2 oz	2 oz	4 oz	6 oz	8 oz	10 oz	12 oz	14 oz	1#	1# 2 oz	1# 4 oz
3/4 oz	1 1/2 oz	2 1/4 oz	3 oz	6 oz	9 oz	12 oz	15 oz	1# 2 oz	1# 5 oz	1# 8 oz	1# 11 oz	1# 14 oz
1 oz	2 oz	3 oz	4 oz	8 oz	12 oz	1#	1# 4 oz	1# 8 oz	1# 12 oz	2#	2# 4 oz	2# 8 oz
1 1/4 oz	2 1/2 oz	3 3/4 oz	5 oz	10 oz	15 oz	1# 4 oz	1# 9 oz	1# 14 oz	2# 3 oz	2# 8 oz	2# 13 oz	3# 2 oz
1 1/2 oz	3 oz	4 1/2 oz	6 oz	12 oz	1# 2 oz	1# 8 oz	1# 14 oz	2# 4 oz	2# 10 oz	3#	3# 6 oz	3# 12 oz
1 3/4 oz	3 1/2 oz	5 1/4 oz	7 oz	14 oz	1# 5 oz	1# 12 oz	2# 3 oz	2# 10 oz	3# 1 oz	3# 8 oz	3# 15 oz	4# 6 oz
2 oz	4 oz	6 oz	8 oz	1#	1# 8 oz	2#	2# 8 oz	3#	3# 8 oz	4#	4# 8 oz	5#
2 1/4 oz	4 1/2 oz	6 3/4 oz	9 oz	1# 2 oz	1# 11 oz	2# 4 oz	2# 13 oz	3# 6 oz	3# 15 oz	4# 8 oz	5# 1 oz	5# 10 oz
2 1/2 oz	5 oz	7 1/2 oz	10 oz	1# 4 oz	1# 14 oz	2# 8 oz	3# 2 oz	3# 12 oz	4# 6 oz	5#	5# 10 oz	6# 4 oz
2 3/4 oz	5 1/2 oz	8 1/4 oz	11 oz	1# 6 oz	2# 1 oz	2# 12 oz	3# 7 oz	4# 2 oz	4# 13 oz	5# 8 oz	6# 3 oz	6# 14 oz
3 oz	6 oz	9 oz	12 oz	1# 8 oz	2# 4 oz	3#	3# 12 oz	4# 8 oz	5# 4 oz	6#	6# 12 oz	7# 8 oz
3 1/4 oz	6 1/2 oz	9 3/4 oz	13 oz	1# 10 oz	2# 7 oz	3# 4 oz	4# 1 oz	4# 14 oz	5# 11 oz	6# 8 oz	7# 5 oz	8# 2 oz
3 1/2 oz	7 oz	10 1/2 oz	14 oz	1# 12 oz	2# 10 oz	3# 8 oz	4# 6 oz	5# 4 oz	6# 2 oz	7#	7# 14 oz	8# 12 oz
3 3/4 oz	7 1/2 oz	11 1/4 oz	15 oz	1# 14 oz	2# 13 oz	3# 12 oz	4# 11 oz	5# 10 oz	6# 9 oz	7# 8 oz	8# 7 oz	9# 6 oz

PORTION CONTROL DATA

CONVERSION CHART 3

· POUND CHART

25 Portions	50 Portions	75 Portions	100 Portions	200 Portions	300 Portions	400 Portions	500 Portions	600 Portions	700 Portions	800 Portions	900 Portions	1000 Portions
4oz	8oz	12oz	1#	2#	3#	4#	5#	6#	7#	8#	9#	10#
5oz	10oz	15oz	1# 4oz	2# 8oz	3#12oz	5#	6# 4oz	7# 8oz	8#12oz	10#	11# 4oz	12# 8oz
6oz	12oz	1# 2oz	1# 8oz	3#	4# 8oz	6#	7# 8oz	9#	10# 8oz	12#	13# 8oz	15#
7oz	14oz	1# 5oz	1#12oz	3# 8oz	5# 4oz	7#	8#12oz	10# 8oz	12# 4oz	14#	15#12oz	17# 8oz
8oz	1#	1# 8oz	2#	4#	6#	8#	10#	12#	14#	16#	18#	20#
9oz	1# 2oz	1#11oz	2# 4oz	4# 8oz	6#12oz	9#	11# 4oz	13# 8oz	15#12oz	18#	20# 4oz	22# 8oz
10oz	1# 4oz	1#14oz	2# 8oz	5#	7# 8oz	10#	12# 8oz	15#	17# 8oz	20#	22# 8oz	25#
11oz	1# 6oz	2# 1oz	2#12oz	5# 8oz	8# 4oz	11#	13#12oz	16# 8oz	19# 4oz	22#	24#12oz	27# 8oz
12oz	1# 8oz	2# 4oz	3#	6#	9#	12#	15#	18#	21#	24#	27#	3G#
13oz	1#10oz	2# 7oz	3# 4oz	6# 8oz	9#12oz	13#	16# 4oz	19# 8oz	22#12oz	26#	29# 4oz	32# 8oz
14oz	1#12oz	2#10oz	3# 8oz	7#	10# 8oz	14#	17# 8oz	21#	24# 8oz	28#	31# 8oz	35#
15oz	1#14oz	2#13oz	3#12oz	7# 8oz	11# 4oz	15#	18#12oz	22# 8oz	26# 4oz	30#	33#12oz	37# 8oz
1#	2#	3#	4#	8#	12#	16#	20#	24#	28#	32#	36#	40#
1# 1oz	2# 2oz	3# 3oz	4# 4oz	8# 8oz	12#12oz	17#	21# 4oz	25# 8oz	29#12oz	34#	38# 4oz	42# 8oz
1# 2oz	2# 4oz	3# 6oz	4# 8oz	9#	13# 8oz	18#	22# 8oz	27#	31# 8oz	36#	40# 8oz	45#
1# 3oz	2# 6oz	3# 9oz	4#12oz	9# 8oz	14# 4oz	19#	23#12oz	28# 8oz	33# 4oz	38#	42#12oz	47# 8oz
1# 4oz	2# 8oz	3#12oz	5#	10#	15#	20#	25#	30#	35#	40#	45#	50#
1# 5oz	2#10oz	3#15oz	5# 4oz	10# 8oz	15#12oz	21#	26# 4oz	31# 8oz	36#12oz	42#	47# 4oz	52# 8oz
1# 6oz	2#12oz	4# 2oz	5# 8oz	11#	16# 8oz	22#	27# 8oz	33#	38# 8oz	44#	49# 8oz	55#
1# 7oz	2#14oz	4# 5oz	5#12oz	11# 8oz	17# 4oz	23#	28#12oz	34# 8oz	40# 4oz	46#	51#12oz	57# 8oz
1# 8oz	3#	4# 8oz	6#	12#	18#	24#	30#	36#	42#	48#	54#	60#
1#12oz	3# 8oz	5# 4oz	7#	14#	21#	28#	35#	42#	49#	56#	63#	70#
2#	4#	6#	8#	16#	24#	32#	40#	48#	56#	64#	72#	80#
2# 4oz	4# 8oz	6#12oz	9#	18#	27#	36#	45#	54#	63#	72#	81#	90#
2# 8oz	5#	7# 8oz	10#	20#	30#	40#	50#	60#	70#	80#	90#	100#
2#12oz	5# 8oz	8# 4oz	11#	22#	33#	44#	55#	66#	77#	88#	99#	110#
3#	6#	9#	12#	24#	36#	48#	60#	72#	84#	96#	108#	120#
3#12oz	7# 8oz	11# 4oz	15#	30#	45#	60#	75#	90#	105#	120#	135#	150#
4# 4oz	8# 8oz	12#12oz	17#	34#	51#	68#	85#	102#	119#	136#	153#	170#
4# 8oz	9#	13# 8oz	18#	36#	54#	72#	90#	108#	126#	144#	162#	180#
5#	10#	15#	20#	40#	60#	80#	100#	120#	140#	160#	180#	200#
5#12oz	11# 8oz	17# 4oz	23#	46#	69#	92#	115#	138#	161#	184#	207#	230#
6# 4oz	12# 8oz	18#12oz	25#	50#	75#	100#	125#	150#	175#	200#	225#	250#

NOTE: The material in these charts was developed by the New York Department of Mental Health, and furnished through the courtesy of Mrs. Katherine Flack, Director of Nutrition Service.

PORTION CONTROL DATA

CONVERSION CHART 4

AVOIRDUPOIS TO METRIC SYSTEM
(LINEAR MEASUREMENTS)

INCHES	FEET	YARDS	MILLIMETERS	CENTIMETERS	DECIMETERS	METERS	KILOMETERS
1	0.0833	0.0277	25.4	2.54	.254	.0254	.00254
2	0.1666	0.0555	50.8	5.08	.508	.0508	.00508
3	0.2500	0.0833	76.2	7.62	.762	.0762	.00762
3.937	0.3280	0.1093	100.0	10.00	1.000	.1000	.01000
4	0.3333	0.1111	101.6	10.16	1.016	.1016	.01016
5	0.4166	0.1388	127.0	12.70	1.270	.1270	.01270
6	0.5000	0.1666	152.4	15.24	1.524	.1524	.01524
7	0.5833	0.1944	177.8	17.78	1.778	.1778	.01778
7.874	0.6561	0.2187	200.0	20.00	2.000	.2000	.02000
8	0.6666	0.2222	203.2	20.32	2.032	.2032	.02032
9	0.7500	0.2500	228.6	22.86	2.286	.2286	.02286
10	0.8333	0.2777	254.0	25.40	2.540	.2540	.02540
11	0.9166	0.3055	279.4	27.94	2.794	.2794	.02794
11.811	0.9842	0.3280	300.0	30.00	3.000	.3000	.03000
12	1.0000	0.3333	304.8	30.48	3.048	.3048	.03048
15	1.2500	0.4166	381.0	38.10	3.810	.3810	.03810
15.748	1.3123	0.4374	400.0	40.00	4.000	.4000	.04000
18	1.5000	0.5000	457.2	45.72	4.572	.4572	.04572
19.685	1.6404	0.5468	500.0	50.00	5.000	.5000	.05000
21	1.7500	0.5833	533.4	53.34	5.334	.5334	.05334
23.620	1.9683	0.6561	600.0	60.00	6.000	.6000	.06000
24	2.0000	0.6666	609.6	60.96	6.096	.6096	.06096
27	2.2500	0.7500	685.8	68.58	6.858	.6858	.06858
27.559	2.2965	0.7655	700.0	70.00	7.000	.7000	.07000
30	2.5000	0.8333	762.0	76.20	7.620	.7620	.07620
31.496	2.6246	0.8748	800.0	80.00	8.000	.8000	.08000
33	2.7500	0.9166	838.2	83.82	8.382	.8382	.08382
35.433	2.9527	0.9842	900.0	90.00	9.000	.9000	.09000
36	3.0000	1.0000	914.4	91.44	9.144	.9144	.09144
39	3.2500	1.0833	990.6	99.06	9.906	.9906	.09906
39.370	3.2808	1.0936	1000.0	100.00	10.000	1.0000	.10000
42	3.5000	1.1666	1066.8	106.68	10.668	1.0668	.10668
43.307	3.6089	1.2029	1100.0	110.00	11.000	1.1000	.11000
45	3.7500	1.2500	1143.0	114.30	11.430	1.1430	.11430
47.244	3.9370	1.3123	1200.0	120.00	12.000	1.2000	.12000
48	4.0000	1.3333	1219.2	121.92	12.192	1.2192	.12192
51.181	4.2650	1.4216	1300.0	130.00	13.000	1.3000	.13000
54	4.5000	1.5000	1371.6	137.16	13.716	1.3716	.13716
55.118	4.5931	1.5310	1400.0	140.00	14.000	1.4000	.14000
59.055	4.9212	1.6404	1500.0	150.00	15.000	1.5000	.15000
60	5.0000	1.6666	1524.0	152.40	15.240	1.5240	.15240
62.992	5.2493	1.7497	1600.0	160.00	16.000	1.6000	.16000
66	5.5000	1.8333	1676.4	167.64	16.764	1.6764	.16764
66.929	5.5774	1.8591	1700.0	170.00	17.000	1.7000	.17000
70.866	5.9055	1.9685	1800.0	180.00	18.000	1.8000	.18000
72	6.0000	2.0000	1828.8	182.88	18.288	1.8288	.18288
74.803	6.2335	2.0778	1900.0	190.00	19.000	1.9000	.19000
78.740	6.5616	2.1872	2000.0	200.00	20.000	2.0000	.20000
84	7.0000	2.3333	2133.6	213.36	21.336	2.1336	.21336
90	7.5000	2.5000	2286.0	228.60	22.860	2.2860	.22860
96	8.0000	2.6667	2438.4	243.84	24.384	2.4384	.24384
98.425	8.2020	2.7340	2500.0	250.00	25.000	2.5000	.25000
108	9.0000	3.0000	2743.2	274.32	27.432	2.7432	.27432
118.110	9.8425	3.2808	3000.0	300.00	30.000	3.0000	.30000
137.795	11.4829	3.8276	3500.0	350.00	35.000	3.5000	.35000
144	12.0000	4.0000	3657.6	365.76	36.576	3.6576	.36576
157.480	13.1233	4.3744	4000.0	400.00	40.000	4.0000	.40000
177.165	14.7637	4.9212	4500.0	450.00	45.000	4.5000	.45000
180	15.0000	5.0000	4572.0	457.20	45.720	4.5720	.45720
196.85	16.4041	5.4680	5000.0	500.00	50.000	5.0000	.50000
360	30.0000	10.0000	9144.0	914.40	91.440	9.1440	.91440

PORTION CONTROL DATA
CONVERSION CHART 5

AVOIRDUPOIS TO METRIC SYSTEM
(VOLUME MEASUREMENTS)

FLUID OUNCES	CUPS	QUARTS	GALLONS	LITERS	MILLILITERS
2	0.250	0.063	0.016	0.059	59.1
4	0.500	0.125	0.031	0.118	118.2
6	0.750	0.188	0.047	0.177	177.4
8	1.000	0.250	0.063	0.237	236.5
8.448	1.056	0.264	0.066	0.250	250.0
10	1.250	0.313	0.078	0.296	295.7
11.264	1.408	0.352	0.088	0.333	333.3
12	1.500	0.375	0.094	0.355	354.8
14	1.750	0.438	0.109	0.414	414.0
16	2.000	0.500	0.125	0.473	473.1
16.896	2.112	0.528	0.132	0.500	500.0
18	2.250	0.563	0.141	0.532	532.2
20	2.500	0.625	0.156	0.591	591.4
22	2.750	0.688	0.172	0.651	650.5
22.544	2.818	0.705	0.176	0.667	666.7
24	3.000	0.750	0.188	0.710	709.7
25.357	3.170	0.793	0.198	0.750	750.0
32	4.000	1.000	0.250	0.946	946.3
33.814	4.227	1.057	0.264	1.000	1,000.0
40	5.000	1.250	0.313	1.183	1,182.8
42.269	5.284	1.321	0.330	1.250	1,250.0
48	6.000	1.500	0.375	1.419	1,419.4
50.723	6.340	1.585	0.396	1.500	1,500.0
56	7.000	1.750	0.438	1.656	1,656.0
59.178	7.397	1.848	0.462	1.750	1,750.0
64	8.000	2.000	0.500	1.893	1,892.6
67.629	8.454	2.113	0.528	2.000	2,000.0
72	9.000	2.250	0.563	2.129	2,129.1
80	10.000	2.500	0.625	2.366	2,365.7
84.538	10.567	2.642	0.660	2.500	2,500.0
88	11.000	2.750	0.688	2.602	2,602.3
96	12.000	3.000	0.750	2.839	2,838.9
101.446	12.681	3.170	0.793	3.000	3,000.0
118.355	14.794	3.699	0.925	3.500	3,500.0
128	16.000	4.000	1.000	3.785	3,785.2
135.261	16.908	4.227	1.057	4.000	4,000.0
169.079	21.135	5.284	1.321	5.000	5,000.0
192	24.000	6.000	1.500	5.678	5,677.8
202.893	25.362	6.340	1.585	6.000	6,000.0
256	32.000	8.000	2.000	7.570	7,570.4
320	40.000	10.000	2.500	9.463	9,463.0
384	48.000	12.000	3.000	11.356	11,355.6
448	56.000	14.000	3.500	13.248	13,248.2
512	64.000	16.000	4.000	15.141	15,140.8

PORTION CONTROL DATA

CONVERSION CHART 6

AVOIRDUPOIS TO METRIC SYSTEM
(WEIGHT MEASUREMENTS)

OUNCES	GRAMS	OZ. DECIMAL OF POUND	GM. DECIMAL OF KILOGRAM	OZ. FRACTION OF POUND
1/8	3.54	.007813	.00354	1/128
1/4	7.09	.015625	.00709	1/64
1/3	9.45	.020833	.00945	1/48
1/2	14.17	.031250	.01417	1/32
5/8	17.71	.039063	.01771	1/26
3/4	21.26	.046875	.02126	3/64
2/3	18.90	.041666	.01890	1/24
1	28.35	.062500	.02835	1/16
2	56.70	.125000	.05670	1/8
3	85.05	.187500	.08505	3/16
4	113.40	.250000	.11340	1/4
5	141.75	.312500	.14175	5/16
6	170.10	.375000	.17010	3/8
7	198.45	.437500	.19845	7/16
8	226.80	.500000	.22680	1/2
9	255.14	.562500	.25514	9/16
10	283.49	.625000	.28349	5/8
11	311.84	.687500	.31184	11/16
12	340.19	.750000	.34019	3/4
13	368.54	.812500	.36854	13/16
14	396.89	.875000	.39689	7/8
15	425.24	.937500	.42524	15/16
16	453.59	1.000000	.45359	1
20	566.99	1.250000	.56699	1 1/4
24	680.39	1.500000	.68039	1 1/2
28	793.78	1.750000	.79378	1 3/4
32	907.18	2.000000	.90718	2
35.273	1000.00	2.204600	1.00000	2 1/5
36	1020.58	2.250000	1.02058	2 1/4
40	1133.98	2.500000	1.13398	2 1/2
44	1247.37	2.750000	1.24737	2 3/4
48	1360.77	3.000000	1.36077	3
52	1474.17	3.250000	1.47417	3 1/4
56	1587.57	3.500000	1.58757	3 1/2
60	1700.97	3.750000	1.70097	3 3/4
64	1814.37	4.000000	1.81437	4
70.546	2000.00	4.409000	2.00000	4 2/5
80	2267.96	5.000000	2.26796	5
96	2721.55	6.000000	2.72155	6
105.819	3000.00	6.613800	3.00000	6 9/16
112	3175.14	7.000000	3.17514	7
128	3628.73	8.000000	3.62873	8
141.09	4000.00	8.818000	4.00000	8 3/5
160	4535.90	10.000000	4.53590	10

PORTION CONTROL DATA

CONVERSION CHART 7

METRIC EQUIVALENTS

Linear Measure

1 centimeter = 0.3937 in.
1 decimeter = 3.937 in. = 0.328 feet
1 meter = 39.37 in. = 1.0936 yards
1 dekameter = 1.9884 rods
1 kilometer = 0.62137 mile

1 in. = 2.54 centimeters
1 ft. = 3.048 decimeters
1 yard = 0.9144 meter
1 rod = 0.5029 dekameter
1 mile = 1.6093 kilometers

Square Measure

1 sq. centimeter = 0.1550 sq. in.
1 sq. decimeter = 0.1076 sq. ft.
1 sq. meter = 1.196 sq. yd.
1 acre = 3.954 sq. rods
1 hektar = 2.47 acres
1 sq. kilometer = 0.386 sq. m.

1 sq. inch = 6.452 sq. centimeters
1 sq. foot = 9.2903 sq. decimeters
1 sq. yd. = 0.8361 sq. meter
1 sq. rod = 0.2529 acre
1 acre = 0.4047 hektar
1 sq. m. = 259 sq. kilometers

Measure of Volume

1 cu. centimeter = 0.061 cu. in.
1 cu. decimeter = 0.353 cu. ft.
1 cu. meter = 1.308 cu. yd.
1 stere = 0.2759 cord
1 liter = 0.908 dry
1 liter = 1.0567 q. liq.
1 dekaliter = 2.6417 gal.
1 dekaliter = .135 peck
1 hektoliter = 2.8375 bu.

1 cu. in. = 16.39 cu. centimeters
1 cu. ft. = 28.317 cu. decimeters
1 cu. yd. = 0.7646 cu. meter
1 cord = 3.642 steres
1 qt. dry = 1.101 liters
1 qt. liquid = 0.9463 liter
1 gal. = 0.3785 dekaliter
1 peck = 0.881 dekaliter
1 bu. = 0.3524 hektoliter

Weights

1 gram = .03547 ounce
1 kilogram = 2.2046 lbs.
1 metric ton = 1.1023 English ton

1 ounce = 28.35 grams
1 lb. = 0.4536 kilogram
1 English ton = 0.9072 metric ton
1 kilogram = 1,000 grams

Approximate Metric Equivalents

1 decimeter = 4 inches
1 meter = 1.1 yards
1 kilometer = 5/8 mile
1 hektar = 2 1/2 acres
1 stere or cu. meter = 1/4 of a cord

1 metric ton = 2.200 lbs.
1 liter = 1.06 qt. liquid
1 liter = 0.9 qt. dry
1 hektoliter = 2 5/8 bushel
1 kilogram = 2 1/5 lbs.

PORTION CONTROL DATA

CONVERSION CHART 8

TABLE OF STANDARD WEIGHTS AND MEASURES

Avoirdupois Weight

16 drams = 1 ounce	112 pounds = Long 100 wt. (cwt.)
16 ounces = 1 pound	4 quarters = 1 hundred wt.
25 pounds = 1 quarter	2,000 lbs. = 1 short ton = 20 short hundred wt.
100 pounds = Short 100 wt. (cwt.)	2,240 lbs. = 1 long ton = 20 long hundred wt.

Dry Measures

2 pints = 1 quart	4 pecks = 1 bushel
8 quarts = 1 peck	36 bushels = 1 chaldron

Liquid Measures

3 teaspoons = 1 tablespoon	2 pints = 1 quart
16 tablespoons = 1 cup	4 quarts = 1 gallon
2 cups = 1 pint	31½ gallons = 1 barrel
4 gills = 1 pint	2 barrels = 1 hogshed

Long Measure

12 inches = 1 foot	40 rods = 1 furlong
3 feet = 1 yard	8 furlongs = 1 statute mile
5½ sq. yds. = 1 sq. rod	3 miles = 1 league

Square Measure

144 sq. ins. = 1 sq. foot	40 sq. rods = 1 rood
9 sq. feet = 1 sq. yard	40 roods = 1 acre
3¼ sq. yds. = 1 sq. rod	640 acres = 1 sq. mile

Cubic Measure

1,728 cubic in. = 1 cu. ft.	2,150.42 cu. inches = 1 standard bushel
27 cubic ft. = 1 cu. yard	1.24 cu. ft. = 1 bushel
128 cu. ft. = 1 cord (wood)	1 cu. ft. = about four-fifths of a bushel
40 cu. ft. = 1 ton (shipping)	

PORTION CONTROL DATA

CONVERSION CHART 9

The middle column refers to the given temperature whether in degrees Celsius or Fahrenheit. If the reading is in degrees Celsius read the Fahrenheit equivalent in the left hand column. If the reading is in degrees Fahrenheit, read the Celsius equivalent in the right hand column.

CONVERSION FORMULAS

Temperature $°F = (9/5 \times °C) + 32.$
Temperature $°C = 5/9 \ (°F - 32).$

-40 to 33			34 to 75			76 to 212		
F◄—C or F—►C			F◄—C or F—►C			F◄—C or F—►C		
-40.0	-40	-40.00	93.2	34	1.11	168.8	76	24.44
-22.0	-30	-34.44	95.0	35	1.67	170.6	77	25.00
-11.2	-24	-31.11	96.8	36	2.22	172.4	78	25.56
- 7.6	-22	-30.00	98.6	37	2.78	174.2	79	26.11
- 4.0	-20	-28.89	100.4	38	3.33	176.0	80	26.67
- 0.4	-18	-27.78	102.2	39	3.89	177.8	81	27.22
14.0	-10	-23.33	104.0	40	4.44	179.6	82	27.78
24.8	- 4	-20.00	105.8	41	5.00	181.4	83	28.33
32.0	0	-17.78	107.6	42	5.56	183.2	84	28.89
33.8	1	-17.22	109.4	43	6.11	185.0	85	29.44
35.6	2	-16.67	111.2	44	6.67	186.8	86	30.00
37.4	3	-16.11	113.0	45	7.22	188.6	87	30.56
39.2	4	-15.56	114.8	46	7.78	190.4	88	31.11
41.0	5	-15.00	116.5	47	8.33	192.2	89	31.76
42.8	6	-14.44	118.4	48	8.89	194.0	90	32.22
44.6	7	-13.89	120.2	49	9.44	195.8	91	32.78
46.4	8	-13.33	122.0	50	10.00	197.6	92	33.33
48.2	9	-12.78	123.8	51	10.56	199.4	93	33.89
50.0	10	-12.22	125.6	52	11.11	201.2	94	34.44
51.8	11	-11.67	127.4	53	11.67	203.0	95	35.00
53.6	12	-11.11	129.2	54	12.22	204.8	96	35.56
55.4	13	-10.56	131.0	55	12.78	206.6	97	36.11
57.2	14	-10.00	132.8	56	13.33	208.4	98	36.67
59.0	15	- 9.44	134.6	57	13.89	210.2	99	37.22
60.8	16	- 8.89	136.4	58	14.44	212.0	100	37.78
62.6	17	- 8.33	138.2	59	15.00	215.6	102	38.89
64.4	18	- 7.78	140.0	60	15.56	221.0	105	40.56
66.2	19	- 7.22	141.8	61	16.11	224.6	107	41.67
68.0	20	- 6.67	143.6	62	16.67	230.0	110	43.33
69.8	21	- 6.11	145.4	63	17.22	235.4	113	45.00
71.6	22	- 5.56	147.2	64	17.78	240.8	116	46.67
73.4	23	- 5.00	149.0	65	18.33	246.2	119	48.33
75.2	24	- 4.44	150.8	66	18.89	251.6	122	50.00
77.0	25	- 3.89	152.6	67	19.44	284.0	140	60.00
78.8	26	- 3.33	154.4	68	20.00	300.2	149	65.00
80.6	27	- 2.78	156.2	69	20.56	316.4	158	70.00
82.4	28	- 2.22	158.0	70	21.11	332.6	167	75.00
84.2	29	- 1.67	159.8	71	21.67	348.8	176	80.00
86.0	30	- 1.11	161.6	72	22.22	365.0	185	85.00
87.8	31	- 0.56	163.4	73	22.78	381.2	194	90.00
89.6	32	0.00	165.2	74	23.33	397.4	203	95.00
91.4	33	0.56	167.0	75	23.89	413.6	212	100.00

PORTION CONTROL DATA

CONVERSION CHART 10

OUNCE AND CUP EQUIVALENTS

FOOD ITEM	Ounces Per Cup Approx.	Cups Per Pound Approx.	COST PER POUND	FOOD ITEM	Ounces Per Cup Approx.	Cups Per Pound Approx.	COST PER POUND
Almonds, Blanched, Whole	5 1/2	3		Egg Solids, Whole, Packed	4	4	
Apples, Fresh, Diced	3 1/3	4 3/4		Egg Solids, Whites, Spray Dry, Sifted	3	5	
Apricots, Dried	5 1/3	3		Egg Solids, Pan Dried, Powdered	4 2/3	3 1/2	
Baking Powder, Phosphate	7	2 1/4		Egg Solids, Yolks, Sifted	3	5 2/3	
Baking Powder, S A S Phosphate	6 1/2	2 1/2		Egg Solids, Yolks, Packed	3 1/2	4 3/4	
Baking Powder, Tartrate	6 1/2	2 1/2		Egg, Fresh, Hard Cooked, Diced	6	2 2/3	
Baking Soda	6 3/4	2 1/3		Figs, Cut Fine	6	2 2/3	
Bananas, Fresh, Sliced	7 1/4	2 1/4		Filberts, Whole	4 3/4	3 1/3	
Bananas, Fresh, Dried	3 1/2	4 1/2		Flour, Corn	4	4	
Barley, Pearl, Dry	8	2		Flour, Gluten	5	3 1/4	
Beans, Dried, Black	6 1/2	2 1/2		Flour, Graham	5	3 1/4	
Beans, Dried, Kidney	6 1/2	2 1/2		Flour, Rice	4 1/2	3 1/2	
Beans, Dried, Lima	6 1/2	2 1/2		Flour, Rye	3	5 2/3	
Beans, Dried, Navy	6 3/4	2 1/3		Flour, Soy, Full Fat	2	7 1/2	
Bran, Dry	2	8		Flour, Soy, Low Fat	3	5 1/2	
Brazil Nuts, Whole	11 1/2	1 1/3		Flour, Whole Wheat	7	2 1/4	
Bread Crumbs, Dry	4	4		Flour, White, All Purpose	4	4	
Bread Cubes, Fresh	1	16		Flour, White, Bread	4	4	
Brown Sugar, Packed	7	2 1/4		Flour, White, Cake	3 1/3	4 3/4	
Butter	8	2		Flour, White, Pastry	3 1/2	4 1/2	
Catsup	8	2		Flour, White, Self-Rising	4	4	
Cheese, Cheddar, Chopped	4	4		Gelatin, Granulated	5 1/3	3	
Cheese, Cottage	8	2		Gelatin, Flavored	7	2 1/3	
Cheese, Cream	8	2		Ginger, Crystalized, Diced	6	2 2/3	
Cherries, Whole, Candied	7	2 1/4		Grapenuts	4	4	
Chocolate, Grated	4	4		Hominy, Grits	5 1/2	3	
Chocolate, Melted	9	1 3/4		Hominy, Whole	6 1/2	2 1/2	
Citron, Dried, Sliced	6 1/2	2 1/2		Honey	12	1 1/3	
Cocoa	4	4		Hydrogenated Fat	6 2/3	2 1/2	
Coconut, Long Thread	2 1/4	7		Lard	8	2	
Coconut, Moist, Canned	3	5 1/3		Lentils	7	2 1/4	
Coffee, Dry	3	5 1/3		Macaroni, 1" Piece, Dry	4	4	
Coffee, Instant	2	8		Macaroni, Shell, Dry	4	4	
Corn Flour	4	4		Maple Syrup	11	1 1/2	
Corn Meal, White or Yellow	5	3		Margarine	8	2	
Corn Syrup	11 1/2	1 1/3		Marshmallows	4	4	
Corn Starch	4 1/2	3 1/2		Milk, Whole	8 2/3	2	
Crackers, Graham, Crumbs (Fine)	5	3 1/4		Milk, Buttermilk	8 2/3	2	
Crackers, Soda, Crumbs (Fine)	2 1/2	6 1/2		Milk, Condensed	10 3/4	1 1/2	
Cranberries, Raw	3 1/3	4 3/4		Milk, Evaporated	9	1 3/4	
Cream, 40%	8 1/3	2		Milk, Skimmed	8 2/3	2	
Cream, 20%	8 1/2	2		Milk, Whole, Dry	3 3/4	4 1/4	
Cream of Tartar	5 1/3	3		Milk, Non-fat, Dry, Powder	4	4	
Currants	5	3 1/4		Milk, Non-fat, Dry, Crystal	2 3/4	5 2/3	
Dates, Pitted, Cut	6 1/3	2 1/4		Mincemeat	8	2	
Eggs, Fresh or Frozen, Whole	8 2/3	2		Molasses, Cane	11 1/2	1 1/3	
Eggs, Fresh or Frozen, White	8 2/3	2		Noodles, 1" Piece, Dry	2 2/3	6	
Eggs, Fresh or Frozen, Yolks	8 2/3	2		Nut Meats, Chopped	4	4	
Egg Solids, Whole, Sifted	3	5		Oats, Rolled (Quick)	3	5 2/3	

—continued—

PORTION CONTROL DATA

CONVERSION CHART 10 (Cont.)

FOOD ITEM	Ounces Per Cup Approx.	Cups Per Pound Approx.	COST PER POUND	FOOD ITEM	Ounces Per Cup Approx.	Cups Per Pound Approx.	COST PER POUND
Oils, All	8	2		Salt, Free Running	10 1/4	1 1/2	
Onions, Dried	3 1/2	4 1/2		Salt, Cooking	8	2	
Peanuts	5	3 1/4		Sorghum	11 2/3	1 1/3	
Peanut Butter	8	2		Soybeans	7 1/2	2 1/4	
Peas, Split	7	2 1/4		Soy Flour, Full Fat	2	7 1/2	
Pecan Halves	3 3/4	4 1/4		Soy Flour, Low Fat	3	5 1/2	
Pimiento	7	2 1/4		Soy Grits	5	3 1/3	
Potato Starch, Sifted	5	3 1/4		Spaghetti, 2" Pieces	3 1/3	4 3/4	
Prunes, Pitted, Dried, Raw	7	2 1/4		Suet, Chopped	4 1/4	3 3/4	
Prunes, Cooked, Drained	8	2		Sugar, Cane or Beet Confectioners	4 1/2	3 1/2	
Raisins, Seeded, Whole	5	3 1/4		" " " " Granulated	7	2 1/4	
Raisins, Seeded, Chopped	6 1/2	2 1/2		" " " " Superfine	7	2 1/4	
Raisins, Seedless, Whole	5 3/4	2 3/4		Tapioca, Quick Cooking	5 1/2	3	
Raisins, Seedless, Chopped	8	2		Tea	2 1/2	6 1/3	
Rice Flour, Sifted	4 1/2	3 1/2		Vermicelli, 2" Pieces	3	5 2/3	
Rice, White, Long Grain	6 1/2	2 1/2		Walnuts, English, Half	3 1/2	4 1/2	
Rice, White, Medium Grain	6 3/4	2 1/3		Wheat Germ	2 1/2	6 2/3	
Rice, White, Short Grain	7	2 1/4		Whole Wheat Flour	7	2 1/4	
Rice, Wild	5 1/2	3		Yeast, Dry	4 3/4	3 1/3	
Rye Flour	3	5 2/3					

CONVERSION CHART 11

WEIGHT & VOLUME OF COMMONLY SERVED FOODS

FOOD	WEIGHT	MEASURE (Approx)
Baking powder	1 oz.	2 Tbsp.
Baking soda	1 oz.	2-1/3 Tbsp.
Bread, loaf	1 lb.	18 slices
sandwich	2 lbs.	36-40 slices
crumbs, dry	1 lb.	1 qt.
Butter, lard, margarine	1 lb.	2 cups
Flour, all purpose	1 lb.	4 cups
white, bread, sifted	1 lb.	4 cups
cake, sifted	1 lb.	4-3/4 cups
Honey	1 lb.	1-1/3 cups
Lemon juice	1 lb.	2 cups (8-10 lemons)
Lettuce, average head	9 oz.	1
Macaroni, dry	1 lb.	4 cups
1 lb. cooked	3 lbs.	2-1/4 qts.
Oats, rolled, A.P. (quick)	1 lb.	6 cups
Oil, vegetable	1 lb.	2→2-1/8 cups
Onions, A.P.	1 lb.	4-5 medium
chopped	1 lb.	2-3 cups
Pepper, ground	1 oz.	4 Tbsp.
Potatoes, white, A.P.	1 lb.	3 medium
Rice, dry	1 lb.	2 cups
1 lb. cooked	4→4-½ lbs.	2 qts.
Salad dressing, mayonnaise	1 lb.	2 cups
Shortening, hydrogenated	1 lb.	2-1/4 cups
Spaghetti, dry	1 lb.	5 cups
1 lb. cooked	4 lbs.	2-1/2 qts.
Sugar, brown, solid pack	1 lb.	2 cups
granulated	1 lb.	2 cups
powered, XXXX, sifted	1 lb.	3 cups
Vanilla extract	1 oz.	2 Tbsp.
Vinegar	1 lb.	2 cups
Walnuts, E.P.	1 lb.	4 cups

PORTION CONTROL DATA
CONVERSION CHART 12
INGREDIENT SUBSTITUTION CHART

Ingredient	Substitute
1 gal. liquid whole milk	2 qts. evaporated milk & 2 qts. water
	1 lb. dry whole milk & 7-1/2 pts. water
	1 gal. reconstituted nonfat dry milk & 6-1/2 oz. butter or margarine
1 gal. liquid skim milk	3/4 lb. nonfat dry milk & 7-3/4 pts. water
1 lb. liquid whole milk	2 oz. dry whole milk & 14 oz. water
1 lb. sweetened condensed whole milk	4-1/2 oz. dry whole milk & 6-1/2 oz. sugar & 5 oz. water
1 qt. buttermilk or sour milk	4 Tbsp. vinegar or lemon juice & enough whole milk to make 1 qt. (let stand 5 minutes)
	7 tsp. cream of tartar & 1 qt. whole milk.
1 tsp. baking powder	1/4 tsp. baking soda & 1/2 cup fully soured milk or soured buttermilk
	1/4 tsp. baking soda & 1/4-1/2 cup molasses
	1/4 tsp. baking soda & 5/8 tsp. cream of tartar
	1/4 tsp. baking soda & 1/2 Tbsp. vinegar or lemon juice used with whole milk to make 1/2 cup.
1 Tbsp. active dry yeast	1 pkg. active dry yeast
	1 cake yeast, compressed (1/2 oz.)
1 lb. flour, all purpose	1/2 lb. cornstarch, potato starch, rice starch or arrowroot starch.
1 oz. chocolate	3 Tbsp. cocoa & 1 Tbsp. fat
1 cup butter	1 cup margarine
	7/8-1 cup hydrogenated shortening & 1/2 tsp. salt
1 cup coffee cream (20%)	3 Tbsp. butter & 7/8 cup milk
1 cup heavy cream (40%)	1/3 cup butter & 3/4 cup milk
1 lb. whole eggs	2 cups, 9-11 whole eggs, fresh or frozen
	2 cups, 19-22 egg yolks, fresh or frozen
	1-1/2 cups (5 oz.) sifted dry whole egg powder & 1/2 cup of water
1 lb. egg yolks	2 cups (19-22 egg yolks, fresh or frozen)
	2-3/4 cups sifted dry egg yolk powder & 7/8 cup water
1 lb. egg whites	2 cups (17-20 egg whites, fresh or frozen)
	3/4 cup & 1 Tbsp. sifted dry egg white powder & 2-1/3 cups water

PORTION CONTROL DATA

CONVERSION CHART 13

RATIOS OF BASIC FOODS

Flavorings:
1/4-1/2 tsp. salt to 1 cup flour. (The larger amount if salt-free fat is used or if the recipe has much sugar.)

Leavening agents:
2 tsp. quick-acting baking powder to 1 cup flour
1 tsp. slow-acting baking powder to 1 cup flour
1 egg (without baking powder) to 1/2 cup flour. (When egg white is used as a leavening agent and much fat is present, the effect of egg white is greatly decreased.)
1 egg yolk (without baking powder) to 1/8 cup flour
1/2 tsp. soda to 1 cup sour milk (clabbered)
1/2 tsp. soda to 1 cup molasses (approximate)
1/4 tsp. soda plus sour milk (1 tsp. quick-acting baking powder plus sweet milk)
1/2 tsp. quick-acting baking powder plus 1 egg

Flour as a thickening agent:

1 cup flour to 1 cup liquid.	Thin batters, as popovers
1 cup flour to 2/3 cup liquid.	Pour batters as griddle cakes
1 cup flour to 1/2 cup liquid.	Drop batter, as muffins, cakes
1 cup flour to 1/3 cup liquid.	Soft doughs, as biscuits, doughnuts
1 cup flour to 1/4 cup liquid.	Stiff dough, as bread, starchy pudding
1 tbsp. flour to 1 cup liquid.	Sauce for soups, gravies
2 tbsp. flour to 1 cup liquid.	Sauce for creamed meats and vegetables
3 tbsp. flour to 1 cup liquid.	Binding sauce for scalloped dishes, souffles, and croquettes.

Other thickening agents:

1 tbs. gelatin to 2 cup liquids	unmolded gelatin dishes
1 1/2 tbs. gelatin to 2 cup liquid	molded gelatin
1 tbs. minute tapioca to 1 cup liquid	pudding
1/3 cup whole cereal to 1 cup liquid	breakfast cereals, rice
1/5 cup ground cereal to 1 cup liquid	breakfast cereal
2 tbs. cornstarch to 1 cup liquid	cornstarch pudding
1 egg to 1 cup liquid	baked and stirred custards
1 egg yolk to 1/2 cup liquid	baked and stirred custards

PORTION CONTROL DATA

PORTION COST CHART I

SCOOPS - # 10 CAN, FIGURED AT 12 CUPS (3 QUARTS)

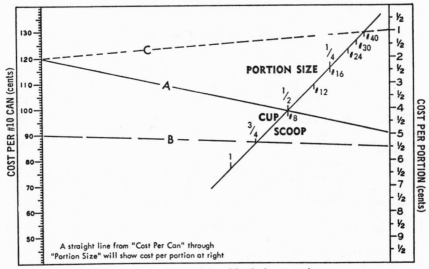

A straight line from "Cost Per Can" through "Portion Size" will show cost per portion at right

Above is an example of a work saver chart which is useful in food cost control.

This chart, called a nomograph, is valuable to the food service operator because it reduces the time spent on portion data and reduces mathematical errors.

It is made up of three scales:

1. Cost per unit of purchase.
2. Portion size.
3. Cost per portion.

How To Use:

To use Portion Cost Charts, factors on two of the three scales must be known. Place a straight-edge through the two known factors. The third factor is located at the point where the straight-edge crosses the third scale.

Examples, using the above chart:

EXAMPLE No. 1 (Line A)
To determine the portion cost of an item served in ½-cup portions, and which cost $1.20 per #10 can:
Place a straight-edge through the "120" on the left hand scale and "½-cup" on the center scale. The point where it crosses the right hand scale is "5". This shows a portion cost of 5¢ per serving.

EXAMPLE No. 2 (Line B)
To determine the portion size of an item that costs 90¢ for a #10 can and which is budgeted at 5½¢ a portion:
Place the straight-edge through "90" on the left hand scale and "5½" on the right hand scale. The point where it crosses the center scale is "¾". This means that ¾-cup can be served to fit the budget allowance of 5½¢ per serving.

EXAMPLE No. 3 (Line C)
To decide which relish to use if the budget allows 1¢ for a #40 scoop:
Place the straight-edge through "#40" on the center scale and "1" on the right hand scale. It will cross the left hand scale at "120", which means that an appropriate relish that costs about #1.20 for a #10 can may be used.

PORTION CONTROL DATA

PORTION COST CHART 2

PORTIONS / # 303 & # 2½ CANS

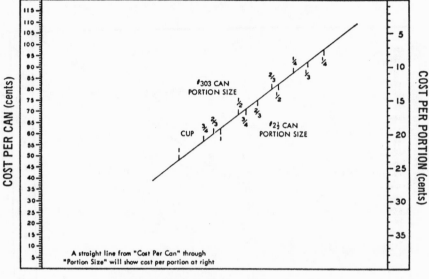

PORTION COST CHART 3

PORTIONS / #5 CAN

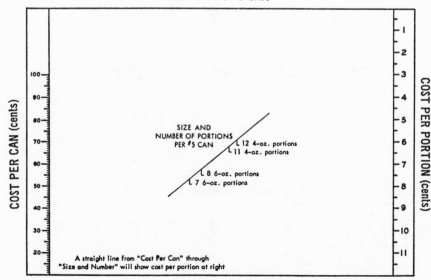

PORTION CONTROL DATA

PORTION COST CHART 4

POUNDS AND OUNCES

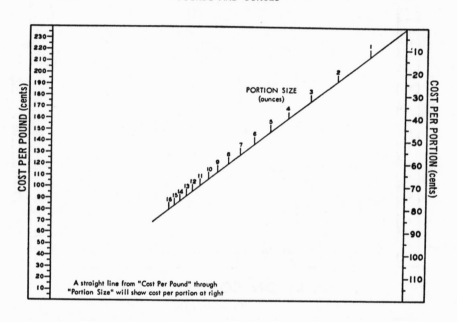

A straight line from "Cost Per Pound" through "Portion Size" will show cost per portion at right

PORTION COST CHART 5

FROZEN VEGETABLES

APPROXIMATE NUMBER OF SERVINGS PER PACKAGE

Ounces per Serving	2-lb. Size	2½-lb. Size	5-lb. Size
2	16	20	40
2½	13	16	32
3	10	13	26
3½	9	11	23
4	8	10	20
4½	7	9	18
5	6	8	16

APPROXIMATE COST PER SERVING

Cost per lb.	2½ oz.	3 oz.	3½ oz.	4 oz.	4½ oz.	5 oz.
14c	2.2c	2.6c	3.1c	3.5c	3.9c	4.4c
16c	2.5c	3.0c	3.5c	4.0c	4.5c	5.0c
18c	2.8c	3.4c	3.9c	4.5c	5.1c	5.6c
20c	3.1c	3.8c	4.4c	5.0c	5.6c	6.3c
22c	3.4c	4.1c	4.8c	5.5c	6.2c	6.9c
24c	3.8c	4.5c	5.3c	6.0c	6.8c	7.5c
26c	4.1c	4.9c	5.7c	6.5c	7.3c	8.1c
28c	4.4c	5.3c	6.1c	7.0c	7.9c	8.8c

Cost per lb.	2½ oz.	3 oz.	3½ oz.	4 oz.	4½ oz.	5 oz.
30c	4.7c	5.6c	6.6c	7.5c	8.4c	9.4c
32c	5.0c	6.0c	7.0c	8.0c	9.0c	10.0c
34c	5.3c	6.4c	7.4c	8.5c	9.6c	10.6c
36c	5.6c	6.8c	7.9c	9.0c	10.1c	11.3c
38c	5.9c	7.1c	8.3c	9.5c	10.7c	11.9c
40c	6.3c	7.5c	8.8c	10.0c	11.3c	12.5c
42c	6.6c	7.9c	9.2c	10.5c	11.8c	13.1c
44c	6.9c	8.3c	9.6c	11.0c	12.4c	13.8c

PORTION CONTROL DATA
PORTION COST CHART 6
OUNCES AND TABLESPOONS

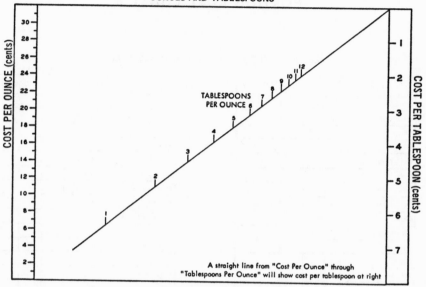

COST PER OUNCE (cents)

COST PER TABLESPOON (cents)

TABLESPOONS
PER OUNCE

A straight line from "Cost Per Ounce" through
"Tablespoons Per Ounce" will show cost per tablespoon at right

PORTION COST CHART 7
COST OF CUPS PER POUND

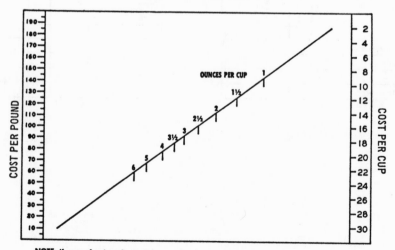

COST PER POUND

COST PER CUP

OUNCES PER CUP

NOTE: If a cup of an ingredient weighs more than 6 ounces, divide the number of ounces into two parts. Determine the cost of each part. Add these together to find the cost of one cup.

PORTION CONTROL DATA

PORTION COST CHART 8

TABLESPOONS PER OUNCE OF COMMONLY USED FOODS

ITEM	Tbsp Per Oz.	Cost Per Oz.	DATE	Cost Per Oz.	DATE
Allspice, Ground	5				
Allspice, Whole	10				
Baking Powder	3				
Basil	8				
Cassia Buds	6				
Celery Salt	4				
Celery Seed	6				
Chili Powder	4				
Cinnamon, Ground	6				
Cloves, Ground	5				
Cloves, Whole	6				
Cocoa	4				
Coconut, Grated	6				
Coffee	5				
Coriander	10				
Cornmeal	3				
Cornstarch	3				
Cream of Tartar	3				
Curry Powder	8				
Flour, All Purpose	4				
Garlic Salt	3				
Ginger, Ground	8				
Honey	1				
Mace	6				
Margarine	2				

ITEM	Tbsp. Per Oz.	Cost Per Oz.	DATE	Cost Per Oz.	DATE
Marjoram	10				
Milk, Dry	4				
Mustard, Dry	5				
Mustard, Prepared	4				
Nutmeg, Ground	6				
Onion Juice	2				
Onion Salt	3				
Paprika	6				
Pepper, Ground Black	5				
Pepper, Red	7				
Pepper, White	6				
Pickling Spice	8				
Poppy Seeds	6				
Poultry Seasoning	10				
Sage, Ground	8				
Salt	2				
Shortening	2				
Soda, Baking	3				
Thyme	12				
Vanilla Extract	2				

TRAY CAPACITY CHART

ITEM			SPACE BETWEEN SLIDES (INCHES)	TRAY CAPACITY 14"x18"	TRAY CAPACITY 18"x26"
PAPER PORTION CUPS		1/2 oz.	1	88	187
		3/4 oz.	2	88	187
	1	oz.	2	63	150
	2	oz.	2	42	84
	2 1/2 oz.		2	35	77
	4	oz.	2	24	54
	6	oz.	2	12	28
	8	oz.	3	12	28
	10	oz.	3	12	24
MILK CARTON, 1/2 pint	2 7/8" square		4	20	40
MILK CARTON, 1/2 pint	2 1/4" square		4	35	70
MILK CARTON, 1/3 quart	2 1/4" square		5	35	70
JUICE GLASS	5	oz.	4	35	84
WATER GLASS	10	oz.	5	20	40
GLASSWARE	2 7/8" Sherbet		3	20	40
	3 7/16" Sherbet		3	12	28
	4 11/16" Fruit Nappie		–	6	15
	3 9/16" Supreme Insert		3	12	28
	5 3/4" Supreme Insert		3	5	8
DISHES	5 1/2" Bread and Butter		–	6	12
	6 3/8" Salad		–	5	11
	7 3/8" Dessert		–	4	8
	4 9/16" Fruit Nappie		–	12	24
	4 5/8" Fruit Nappie		–	8	21
	3" Custard Cup		3	20	40
	3 3/4" Bouillon Cup		3	12	28
	5" Soup		–	5	15
	5 7/8" Salad Bowl		–	5	11
	5 11/16" Salad Bowl		–	5	11
FOOD ITEMS	#12 Scoop in 4 5/8" Nappie		3-4	8	21
	#8 Scoop on 7 3/8" Plate		3	4	8
	Gelatine Salad on 6 3/8" Plate		3	5	11
	Pie Wedge on 6 3/8" Plate		2	5	11
	Cake Wedge on 6 3/8" Plate		3-4	5	11
	1/6 Cantaloupe on 7 3/8" Plate		3-4	4	8

PAN CAPACITY CHART

PAN	DEPTH OF PAN (INCHES)	Space Between SLIDES (INCHES)	APPROXIMATE PAN CAPACITY		
			USABLE CAPACITY QUARTS	1/2 CUP SERVINGS 4 FL. OZ.	1 CUP SERVINGS 8 FL. OZ.
Full Size (12" X 20") 12 3/4" W X 20 3/4" L	2 1/2	3	7	56	28
	4	5	13	104	52
	6	7	18 1/2	148	74
1/2 Size 12 3/4" W X 10 3/8" L	2 1/2	4	3 1/2	28	14
	4	6	6 1/2	52	26
	6	8	9	72	36
1/4 Size 6 3/8" W X 10 3/8" L	2 1/2	4	1 2/3	13	6 1/2
	4	6	2 2/3	21	10 1/2
	6	8	4	32	16
2/3 Size 12 3/4" W X 13 3/4" L	2 1/2	4	5	40	20
	4	6	8	64	32
	6	8	12	96	48
1/3 Size 6 7/8" W X 12 3/4" L	2 1/2	4	2 1/2	20	10
	4	6	4	16	16
	6	8	6	24	24
1/6 Size 6 3/8" W X 6 7/8" L	2 1/2	4	1	8	4
	4	6	1 2/3	13	6 1/2
	6	8	2 2/3	21	10 1/2
Sheet Pan 18" W X 26" L	2 1/4	3	15	120	60
	3 1/2	4	23	184	92
Cheese Cake Pan 18" W X 26" L	3	4	21	168	84

PAPER PORTION CONTAINER CAPACITY CHART

SIZE PORTION (Oz.)	HEIGHT OF CUP (inches)	SPACE BETWEEN SLIDES (inches)	NUMBER OF PORTIONS IN*						
			#2 Can	#2½ Can	1 Quart	5-lb. Can	#10 Can	1 Gallon	10-lb. Can
½	7/8" --- 1"	1"	36	52	64	160	224	256	320
¾	1 1/8"	2"	24	34	43	106	148	171	212
1	1 1/4"	2"	18	26	32	80	112	128	160
1¼	1 1/4"	2"	14	20	26	64	90	102	128
2	1 1/4" --- 1 3/8"	2"	9	13	16	40	56	64	80
2½	1 7/16"	2"	7	10	13	32	45	51	64
3¼	1 1/2"	2"	5	8	10	24	34	39	50
4	1 5/8"	2"	5	6	8	20	28	32	40
5½	1 3/4"	2"	3	5	6	15	20	22	29
6	1 7/8"	2"	3	4	5	13	19	21	27
8	2 3/4"	3"	2	3	4	10	14	16	20
10	2 1/2"	3"	2	3	3	8	11	13	16

*From Paper Cup and Container Institute

Cost Per Fuel of Energy Saving Vent Hood (New Installations)

GAS

One cubic foot of gas yields 1,000 BTU at the point of delivery. System efficiency is approximately 65%; therefore, the effective number of available BTU at the point of use is:

$$1,000 \text{ BTU} \times .65 = 650 \text{ BTU}$$

Assumed cost of gas = $2.50/1,000 cu. ft.

$$\frac{265,888,896 \text{ BTU (winter loss)}}{650 \text{ BTU/cu. ft.}} = \begin{array}{l} 409,060 \text{ cu. ft.} \\ \text{of gas lost/winter} \end{array}$$

409,060 cu. ft. x $2.50/1,000 cu. ft. = $1,023.00 lost/winter

However, the energy saving hood retains 80% of this loss:

Dollar Value of Winter Fuel Loss

100% Exhaust Hood	Energy Saving Hood	Savings Differential/Winter
$1,023.00	$205.00	$818.00

Installed Cost*

100% Exhaust Hood	Energy Saving Hood	Initial Cost Differential
$.60/cfm.	$1.00/cfm.	$.40/cfm

Savings Per Winter of Energy Saving Hood

$$\frac{\$818.00 \text{ (savings/winter)}}{4000 \text{ cfm}} = \$.20/\text{cfm. savings/winter}$$
(40 sq. ft. x 100 cfm)

$$\text{Payback} = \frac{\$.40/\text{cfm Cost}}{\$.20/\text{cfm/winter savings}} = 2 \text{ Winters}$$

*Based on average installed costs including ductwork.

OIL

One gallon of oil yields 140,000 BTU at point of delivery. System efficiency is approximately 65%. Therefore, the effective number of available BTU at the point of use is:

$$140,000 \text{ BTU} \times .65 = 91,000 \text{ BTU}$$

$$\text{Assumed cost of oil} = \$.40/\text{gallon}$$

$$100\% \text{ exhaust hood}$$

$$\frac{265,888,896 \text{ BTU (winter loss)}}{91,000 \text{ BTU/gal}} = \begin{array}{l} 2,922 \text{ gallons} \\ \text{of oil lost/winter} \end{array}$$

$$2,922 \text{ gallons} \times \$.40/\text{gallon} = \$1,168.00 \text{ lost/winter}$$

Dollar Value of Winter Fuel Loss

100% Exhaust Hood	Energy Saving Hood	Savings Differential/Winter
$1,168.00	$234.00	$934.00

Installed Cost

100% Exhaust Hood	Energy Saving Hood	Initial Cost Differential/Winter
$.60/cfm	$1.00/cfm	$.40/cfm

Savings Per Winter of Energy Saving Hood

$$\frac{\$934.00 \text{ (savings/winter)}}{4000 \text{ cfm}} = \$.23/\text{cfm savings/winter}$$
$$(40 \text{ sq. ft.} \times 100 \text{ cfm})$$

$$\text{Payback} = \frac{\$.40/\text{cfm cost}}{\$.23/\text{cfm/winter savings}} = 2 \text{ Winters}$$

ELECTRICITY

One KWH yields 3,413 BTU at point of delivery. System efficiency is approximately 85%. Therefore, the effective number of BTU at the point of use is:

$$3,413 \text{ x } .85 = 2,900 \text{ BTU}$$

Assumed cost of KWH = \$.04/KWH

100% Exhaust Hood

$$\frac{265,888,896 \text{ BTU}}{2,900 \text{ BTU}} = 91,685 \text{ KWH (winter loss)}$$

$$91,685 \text{ x } \$.04 = \$3,667.00 \text{ lost/winter}$$

Dollar Value of Winter Fuel Loss

100% Exhaust Hood	Energy Saving Hood	Savings Differential/Winter
\$3,667.00	\$734.00	\$2,933.00

Installed Cost

100% Exhaust Hood	Energy Saving Hood	Initial Cost Differential
\$.60/cfm	\$1.00/cfm	\$.40/cfm

Savings Per Winter of Energy Saving Hood

$$\frac{\$2,933.00}{4,000 \text{ cfm}} = \$.73/\text{cfm savings/winter}$$
(40 sq. ft. x 100 cfm)

$$\text{Payback} = \frac{\$.40/\text{cfm}}{\$.73/\text{cfm}} = \text{approximately 1/2 winter}$$

ELECTRIC EQUIPMENT ENERGY OPERATING
INFORMATION
APPROXIMATE ELECTRIC ENERGY AND TIME REQUIRED
TO PREHEAT AND MAINTAIN VARIOUS TYPES
AND SIZES OF COMMERCIAL ELECTRIC EQUIPMENT

OVENS

Type Oven	Size	kW Input	Time to Preheat (Minutes) 450F	Watts to maintain; at degrees F				
				300F	350F	400F	450F	550F
All-Purpose	1 Pan	6	20	487	594	702	810	
All-Purpose	2 Pan	6.2	36	531	649	767	885	
Bake	2 Pan	6.2	30	510	623	737	850	
Bake	4 Pan	7.5	90	660	807	953	1100	
Bake	6 Pan	11	120	1020	1247	1473	1700	
Pizza	6 Pizzas	7.2	45	410	507	599	691	875
Convection	STD	11	9-10(350F)		1800			
Convection	Deep	17.7	6(350F)		2100			

RANGES

	kW Input	Time to Preheat (Minutes)	Watts to Maintain
Hot Plate @ Unit	5.3	12 (400F)	690 (350F)
French Plate @ Unit	2.1	30 (960F)	
High Speed @ Unit	2.6	2 (350F)	

FRYERS

Pounds of Fat Capacity	Nameplate kW	Minutes to Preheat (350F)	Watts to Maintain Including Fat
15	5.5	6	485
28	12	5	770
45 b	18	6	1050
50	22	6	836

GRIDDLE

Griddle Size in Width (inches)	Nameplate kW	Minutes to Preheat		Watts to Maintain 400F
		350F	400F	
18[c]	3	7	12	500
24[c]	6	10	12	980
24[c]	8.2	7	12½	1205
30[c]	6.5	7	12	925
36	16.5	7	12	2080
48	22.4	7	12	2800
72	32.4	7	12	4200

STEAM EQUIPMENT

Width	Nameplate kW	Watts/hr to Maintain
25"	8	500

BROILERS

Nameplate kW	Minutes to Preheat	Watts/hr to Maintain
	Char-Broilers	
4.6	10	–
5.4	8	–
6.6	9	2640@600F
9.9	9(600F)	–
10.8	8	–
12	11(650F)	–
16.5	9(600F)	–
	Overfired Broilers	
12	5-10	810
12.6	6	810
14	6	810
16	7	–

[a]The data are representative and will vary according to manufacturer. For specific information consult individual manufacturer's catalog.

[b]High speed fryer with insulated fat container.

[c]Only 16 inches to 20 inches deep.

Courtesy of Georgia Power Company

ENERGY MANAGEMENT ANALYSIS

ELECTRIC FOOD SERVICE FACILITIES

This Energy Analysis Form was designed for analyzing present energy management practices in an existing food service kitchen and for recording recommended procedures. It may also be used as a guide for developing a similar form tailored to fit a particular size and type of operation. The suggestions should not be a restatement of the questions but should be explicit, such as: "turn on Number 1 and 2 fryers at 11:00 A.M.; Turn on fryers 3, 4 and 5 at 11:45 A.M.; Turn Numbers 1, 2 and 5 fryers off at 2:00 P.M.; Turn on Number 3 exhaust fan when you arrive; Turn on fans Number 1, 2 and 4 as and when needed for removing cooking vapors."

When fully completed, the Analysis Form may also be helpful in training new personnel and retraining present personnel to help attain maximum efficiency in using electric energy without reducing food quality and production efficiency.

ENERGY ANALYSIS - COOKING EQUIPMENT

Major Type Of Cooking Equipment	Number	Major Type of Cooking Equipment	Number
Ranges	_____	Fryers	_____
Deck Ovens	_____	Griddles	_____
Convection Ovens	_____	Broilers	_____
Microwave Ovens	_____	Other	_____

Operating Procedures

	Yes	No
Is only the equipment that will be used preheated?	☐	☐

Suggestions: _____

	Yes	No

Is the equipment being preheated just before it is going to be used?   ☐ ☐

Suggestions: _____

Is temperature reduced or equipment turned off during slack periods of the day?   ☐ ☐

Suggestions _____

Is full production capacity of equipment used every time that it is possible to do so?   ☐ ☐

When practical, are ovens fully loaded for each baking cycle?   ☐ ☐

Is another load put on right after one has been removed?   ☐ ☐

Suggestions: _____

Is the correct size of equipment being used for cooking operation?   ☐ ☐

Suggestions: _____

Is equipment used properly?   ☐ ☐

Are pots and pans with flat bottoms used on range hot plate and hearths of deck ovens?   ☐ ☐

Do pots used on french plates cover the entire surface of the plate?   ☐ ☐

Are fryer baskets sometimes overfilled?   ☐ ☐

Are standard sized pans used in ovens to prevent waste of space?   ☐ ☐

	Yes	No
Is care taken to space pans equal distance from walls (sides, front and back) of convection ovens to eliminate cripped runs?	☐	☐
Is a timer used in baking operations to prevent opening of oven doors unnecessarily to check on products?	☐	☐
Is the deck oven damper closed except when baking very moist products?	☐	☐
Are convection ovens used to cook large quantities of hamburgers or to finish large quantities of steaks that have been marked on a broiler?	☐	☐
Are microwave ovens being misapplied for large quantity primary cooking functions?	☐	☐

Suggestions: _____

Maintenance of Equipment

	Yes	No
Are indicator lights functioning on all equipment?	☐	☐
Are indexes and numbers on control knobs clearly visible?	☐	☐
Are themostat bulbs and capillary tubes properly fastened in place on fryers and deck ovens?	☐	☐
Do oven doors close properly?	☐	☐
Are there light and dark spots on griddling surfaces, indicating a burned/out or loose element?	☐	☐
Are thermostats checked periodically?	☐	☐

Suggestions: _____

	Yes	No

Cleaning of Equipment

Is equipment kept clean? ☐ ☐

Is spillage cleaned up as it happens throughout the day? ☐ ☐

Is there a build-up of burned-on food on hearths of deck ovens, griddling surfaces and grates of broilers? ☐ ☐

Are heating elements kept clean on fryers? ☐ ☐

Is the breather space on deck ovens clear of crumbs or other food particles? ☐ ☐

Are contact surfaces on ovens and oven doors clean so that doors will close properly? ☐ ☐

Suggestions: _____

_____

Is cleaning scheduled to prevent wasting energy? ☐ ☐

Are griddles cleaned at end of cooking cycle and before they cool enough to require reheating for easier cleaning? ☐ ☐

Are heating elements on fryers burned off too frequently? ☐ ☐

Are heating elements burned off as soon as cooking oil has dripped off to save some energy on reheating from room temperature? ☐ ☐

Is frying fat strained at the end of the day before it congeals and must be reheated? ☐ ☐

Are broiler grids brushed off while they are still hot? ☐ ☐

Are drip pans cleaned before cooking oil cools enough to congeal? ☐ ☐

Suggestions: _____

_____

_____

ENERGY ANALYSIS - HOT FOOD HOLDING AND TRANSPORTING

Operation of Equipment

	Yes	No
Is the equipment sized right for the job required and not expected to do more than it is designed to do?	☐	☐
Is the equipment located in an area where it is not affected by low temperatures?	☐	☐
Is the equipment being preheated before loading with food products?	☐	☐
Is the equipment being used at full capacity?	☐	☐

Suggestions: _____

_____

_____

Maintenance of Equipment

	Yes	No
Are timers or timing devices and thermostat readings periodically checked with actual performance temperatures?	☐	☐
Are units properly cleaned and loose parts reassembled regularly?	☐	☐
Are door seals checked periodically for a potential loss of heat?	☐	☐

Suggestions: _____

_____

_____

ENERGY ANALYSIS - REFRIGERATION EQUIPMENT

Refrigerators	Number	Freezers	Number
Reach-In	_____	Reach-In	_____
Roll-In	_____	Roll-In	_____
Walk-In	_____	Walk-In	_____

	Yes	No
Do door gaskets fit snuggly?	☐	☐

Suggestions: _____

_____

Is refrigerated and frozen food placed into
refrigerator and freezer immediately upon arrival
from supplier?

Suggestions: _____

_____

Are doors on refrigeration equipment opened frequently or held open for long periods of time?	☐	☐
Is all food to be used for each meal preparation removed from refrigerated storage at the same time when practical?	☐	☐
Is as much food as is practical loaded quickly into the refrigeration equipment?	☐	☐

Suggestions: _____

_____

_____

Are evaporator coils kept free of excessive frost?	☐	☐

Suggestions: _____

_____

	Yes	No
Are condenser coils kept free of lint, dust, or other obstructions?	☐	☐

Suggestions: _____

_____

	Yes	No
Is refrigeration equipment located in a cool environment or shielded from heat radiating equipment?	☐	☐
Can air circulate freely around refrigeration equipment, particularly condensers and condenser motors?	☐	☐

Suggestions: _____

_____

	Yes	No
Is equipment maintained in good repair?	☐	☐
Are drive belts in good condition and properly adjusted?	☐	☐
Are suspension springs in good condition?	☐	☐
Are units fully charged with refrigerant?	☐	☐

Suggestions: _____

_____

_____

ENERGY ANALYSIS - WAREWASHING EQUIPMENT

Operating Procedures

	Yes	No
Is machine turned on just before needed?	☐	☐

Suggestions: _____

_____

Yes   No

Is machine fully loaded on each cycle?   ☐   ☐

Suggestion: _____

_____

Are loads cycled one right after another?   ☐   ☐

Suggestions: _____

_____

Cleaning Equipment

Is machine flushed after each meal period?   ☐   ☐

Suggestions: _____

_____

Is machine washed thoroughly after each day's operation?   ☐   ☐

Suggestions: _____

_____

Is the removal of mineral deposits performed on a regular
basis?   ☐   ☐

Suggestions: _____

_____

Maintenance of Equipment

Is the machine oiled or lubricated according to
predetermined schedule?   ☐   ☐

Suggestions: _____

_____

Is preventive maintenance performed periodically?   ☐   ☐

Suggestions: _____

_____

ENERGY ANALYSIS – WATER HEATING

	Yes	No
Is the storage tank sized properly?	☐	☐

Suggestions: _____

Are the primary water heater and booster water heater located close to the point of most frequent use? ☐ ☐

Suggestions: _____

Is the temperature as low as possible? (Caution! 180° is required if used for sanitizing dishes.) ☐ ☐

Suggestions: _____

Are hot water pipes insulated? ☐ ☐

Suggestions: _____

Are faucets leaking? ☐ ☐

Suggestions: _____

ENERGY ANALYSIS – VENTILATING EQUIPMENT

Number of Exhaust Fans_____Single Speed_____Two Speed_____

Method of Extracting Grease: Filters ☐ Extractors ☐

	Yes	No

Are only the number of exhaust fans required
to remove the cooking vapors and smoke and cool
kitchen being operated at any one time?   ☐   ☐

Suggestions: _____

_____

Are two-speed fans operated at the lower speed
required to capture cooking vapors or smoke and
cool the kitchen?   ☐   ☐

Suggestions: _____

_____

Are fans turned off when they are not needed?   ☐   ☐

Suggestions: _____

_____

Are filters and extractors kept clean?   ☐   ☐

Suggestions: _____

_____

General Comments: _____

_____

_____

_____

_____

_____

_____

_____

_____

_____

Courtesy of Georgia Power Company

CONVERSION TABLE

TABLE OF WEIGHTS AND MEASURES

For convenience, the cubic centimeter is considered equivalent to 1 gram (1 cc. = 1 gm.). One ounce equals 28.35 gms. For easy computing purposes, however, 30 gms. or 30 cc. is considered equivalent to 1 oz. The following equivalents are based on water weights.

1 tsp.	=	5 gm. 5 cc.	2 cups (approximately)	=	16 oz. 1 lb. 1 pint 480 gm.
3 tsp.	=	1 Tbsp.			
1 Tbsp.	=	15 gm. 15 cc. ½ fluid oz.	4 cups	=	1 quart 2 pints 960 cc.
2 Tbsp.	=	1 fluid oz. ⅛ cup 30 cc. 30 gm.	1 pint	=	480 cc. 16 oz. 2 cups
4 Tbsp.	=	2 oz. ¼ cup	1 quart	=	960 cc. 32 oz.
8 Tbsp.	=	4 oz. ½ cup	4 quarts 1 liter	= =	1 gallon 1 kilogram 1000 cc. 2.2 lbs.
16 Tbsp.	=	8 oz. 1 cup ½ lb. 240 gm.	1 oz., liquid	=	30 gm. 2 Tbsp. 30 cc.
1 cup	=	½ pint 8 oz. 240 cc. ½ lb.	1 lb.	=	480 gm. 0.45 kilogram

To change ounces to grams, multiply ounces by 30 (exact figure 28.35).
To change pounds to kilograms multiply pounds by 0.45 or divide by 2.2.
To change inches to centimeters multiply inches by 2.54.

MILLIEQUIVALENT (mEq) CONVERSION TABLE

For Determining mEq Values of	Divide Milligrams by mEq Weight*
Sodium	23
Potassium	39
Magnesium	12.16
Phosphorus	15.5
Calcium	20
Chlorides	35.5

TABLE OF WEIGHTS AND MEASURES

3 tsp. = 1 tbsp.
1 tbsp. = 15 gm. = 15 ml. = 15 cc. = ½ oz.
30 gm. (actual 28.35 gm.) = 30 cc. = 1 oz. = 2 tbsp.
1 gm. = 1 cc. = 1 ml.
1 tsp. = 5 cc. = 5 ml. = 5 gm.
16 tbsp. = 240 cc. = 240 ml. = 240 gm. = 8 oz. = 1 cup
2 cups = 480 cc. = 480 ml. = 480 gm. (1 lb.) = 16 oz. = 1 pint
2 pints = 960 cc. = 960 ml. =960 gm. = 32 oz. = 1 quart
1 inch = 2.54 centimeters
1 liter = 1.0567 quarts
1 kilocalorie = 4.180 joules
1 milliequivalent = one thousandth of an equivalent
1 microgram (mcg.) = one thousandth of a milligram
1 milligram (mg.) = one thousandth of a gram
1 gram (gm.) = one thousandth of a kilogram
4 quarts = 1 gallon   4 pecks = 1 bushel
1 pound = 453.6 gm.   2.2 pounds = 1 kilogram (kg.)

To convert milligrams to milliequivalents divide the milligrams by the atomic weight: multiply the results by the valence.

$$\text{mEq} = \frac{\text{milligrams per units}}{\text{atomic weight of the ion}} \times \text{valence} \qquad \text{Example:} \quad \frac{1000 \text{ mg. Na}}{23} \times 1 = 43.4 \text{ mEq}$$

Element	Atomic Weight	Valence
Sodium (Na)	23	1
Potassium (K)	39	1
Chlorine (Cl)	35.4	1
Phosphorus (P)	31	2
Calcium (Ca)	40	2
Magnesium (Mg)	24	2

1000 mg. Na = 43.4 mEq
2000 mg. Na = 87 mEq
1000 mg. K = 25.6 mEq
2000 mg. K = 51 mEq

To convert ounces to grams multiply by 30
To convert grams to ounces divide by 30
To convert pounds to kilograms divide by 2.2
To convert kilograms to pounds multiply by 2.2
To convert inches to centimeters multiply by 2.54
To convert a specified weight of NaCl to Na multiply by 0.393
To convert a specified weight of Na to NaCl multiply by 2.54

CONVERTING IS EASY[2]

	To Change	to	Multiply by
W			
E	Ounces	Grams	30*
I	Pounds	Kilograms	0.45
G	Grams	Ounces	0.035
H	Kilograms	Pounds	2.2
T			
	Teaspoons	Milliliters	5
	Tablespoons	Milliliters	15
V	Fluid Ounces	Milliliters	30
O	Cups	Liters	0.24
L	Pints	Liters	0.47
U	Quarts	Liters	0.95
M	Gallons	Liters	3.8
E	Milliliters	Fluid Ounces	0.03
	Liters	Pints	2.1
	Liters	Quarts	1.06
	Liters	Gallons	0.26
L	Inches	Centimeters	2.5
E	Feet	Centimeters	30
N	Yards	Meters	0.9
G	Millimeters	Inches	0.04
T	Centimeters	Inches	0.4
H	Meters	Feet	3.3
	Meters	Yards	1.1

---

* The precise figure is 28.25. However, some dietitians find it more convenient to use 30.

[2] American Diabetes Association, Inc., and The American Dietetic Association: Exchange Lists for Meal Planning. 1976, p. 24.

Index

About the Author

Judy Ford Stokes is a Registered Dietitian and President of Judy Ford Stokes & Associates, Inc., a firm of Registered Dietary Consultants whose clients include the United States Penitentiary in Atlanta and more than 100 hospitals and nursing homes with more than 9000 beds, serving in excess of ten million meals a year. Her dietary consulting firm was the first in the nation, and it is one of the largest employers of Registered Dietitians in the south.

Mrs. Stokes is the Editor of *Atlanta Cooks for Company* that has sold more than 150,000 copies and has been designated by the city of Atlanta as its official cookbook.

A nationally known speaker, Mrs. Stokes conducts food management seminars on the economics and the operation of institutional food service. She serves on several boards of directors and has received many awards for her professional expertise.